HAROLD ICKES

of the New Deal

HAROLD L. ICKES
1874–1952

HAROLD
ICKES
OF THE NEW DEAL

·HIS PRIVATE LIFE·
AND PUBLIC CAREER

Graham White and John Maze

HARVARD UNIVERSITY PRESS
Cambridge, Massachusetts, and London, England
1985

Copyright © 1985 by the President and Fellows of Harvard College
All rights reserved
Printed in the United States of America
10 9 8 7 6 5 4 3 2 1

This book is printed on acid-free paper, and its binding
materials have been chosen for strength and durability.

Library of Congress Cataloging in Publication Data

White, Graham J.
   Harold Ickes of the New Deal.

   Bibliography: p.
   Includes index.
   1.   Ickes, Harold L. (Harold LeClair), 1874–1952.
2.   Statesmen—United States—Biography.   3.   New Deal,
1933–1939.   4.   United States—Politics and government—
1933–1945.   I.   Maze, J. R.   II.   Title.
E748.I28W54   1985   973.917′092′4 [B]   84-19150
ISBN 0-674-37285-9 (alk. paper)

Preface

WHILE GRAHAM WHITE was researching his book *FDR and the Press* (1979) in the Library of Congress, he found himself confronted more and more with the figure of Harold Ickes, one of Roosevelt's front-line soldiers in the war with the Press. White was well aware of Ickes' public career as Secretary of the Interior and of his near-legendary status among American liberals, not only as executant of the New Deal but as an outspoken defender of minority rights and civil liberties. Yet, as he became more familiar with Ickes' autobiographical writings—*The Autobiography of a Curmudgeon, The Secret Diary,* the *Saturday Evening Post* articles "My Twelve Years with FDR"—he began to discover a personality that did not jibe with the public image. Ickes seemed to lack insight into his own motives, to be sometimes obtuse in understanding others, to become obsessed with certain goals to a degree that approached the irrational.

White, a historian, turned to John Maze, his colleague in psychology, for possible insights; together they wrote an article giving some interpretations of this unusual character. Then in 1980 White found in the Ickes papers in the Library of Congress, first, a letter revealing that Ickes had been thrown out of the marital house by a wife whom he bitterly accused of victimizing him ever since they had married, then a batch of letters to the same wife, from France, during World War I, declaring undying and passionate devotion! What kind of turbulent private life lay behind this? Before long a veritable gold mine of information came to light. Ickes had left millions of words of unpublished autobiography—a political memoir and a personal memoir running side by side but rarely synchronized. The private, personal material had lain virtually unexplored since Ickes' death. Such a mass of primary data has rarely been equalled, not just for size but for frankness and immediacy. We explored it with equal fascination, our two disciplines enhancing each other's findings. This book is the result.

We wish to thank Richard Bosworth and Stephen Salsbury for their forthright and exceedingly helpful comments on our manuscript, Stephen Judd and Shane White, who have been excellent research assistants, and Ann Louise McLaughlin of Harvard University Press for her perceptive suggestions as to textual amendments.

G.J.W.
J.R.M.

Contents

HAROLD ICKES
of the New Deal

Chronology

1874	Harold L. Ickes born March 15 in Altoona, Pennsylvania.
1890	Moves to Chicago after death of his mother.
1893	Enters the University of Chicago.
1897–1912	Becomes involved in numerous Chicago campaigns for political reform and social justice.
1903	Takes up his residence in the home of James and Anna Thompson.
1907	Obtains law degree from the University of Chicago.
1911	Marries Anna Wilmarth Thompson.
1912	Helps organize Progressive Party campaign in Illinois. Son, Raymond, born.
1918	Goes to France as YMCA supplies officer.
1920–1932	Continues work in Chicago for both political and social reform.
1933	Appointed Secretary of Interior and Public Works Administrator. Affair with X begins.
1935	Wife, Anna, killed in an automobile accident.
1936	Resigns over PWA; resignation refused.
1938	Marries Jane Dahlman.
1939	Son, Harold Jr., born.
1940	Resigns over Forestry; resignation refused.
1941	Appointed Petroleum Coordinator. Daughter, Elizabeth, born.
1946	Resigns over Pauley appointment; resignation accepted.
1952	Death, February 3.

Prologue

FEW COULD could have been unaware, as he rose to address them, that Franklin Delano Roosevelt's crusty, pugnacious Secretary of the Interior had done more for America's minority groups than anyone in the New Deal, and all must have anticipated that on this as on other occasions he would speak his mind. At his official request they had come to the shrine of the Great Emancipator to hear the black woman Marian Anderson sing, and to rebuke, by their coming, those who had closed the doors of the capital's musical venues against her. Now, as Harold Ickes prepared to introduce the famous singer, the vast crowd of 75,000 fell silent and listened expectantly. "In our own time," he began, in a reference to the Lincoln Memorial and the Washington Monument at either end of the reflecting pool, "too many pay mere lip service to these twin planets in our democratic heaven." If the admonition was indirect, the significance of his words could not be mistaken. "In this great auditorium under the sky," they heard him say, "all of us are free . . . [God] made no distinction of race, or creed, or color."[1] In such uncompromising terms Harold Ickes sought to express the feelings of the crowd and to affirm his own lifelong commitment to the principles of equality and justice for all.

That was in 1939. Thirteen years later he was dead, and the people had gathered to honor him.

Under God's heaven and before Lincoln's shrine, intoned the minister, recalling the words that Ickes had used on that earlier occasion, all men were brothers. Those who had assembled again at the Memorial had done so to celebrate the image of a man of integrity, a fearless leader who had torn down the barriers of prejudice and championed unpopular causes. The invocation over, Marian Anderson sang songs by Bach and Schubert; then, as the music died, Secretary of the Interior Oscar L. Chapman stepped forward to deliver the main address. He, too, took the crowd back to that Easter Sunday thirteen years before, to the event that had so vividly dramatized Harold Ickes' leadership. On that great occasion Marian Anderson's thrilling voice had symbolized America's basic belief in equality. It would do so again today. Ickes, he went on to say, had served longer than any Secretary of the Interior, had made a demoralized department a by-word for honesty and efficiency, had to a remarkable degree applied his own high ethical and moral principles to the conduct of public affairs. He had relentlessly opposed totalitarianism and fought to conserve the resources of the nation. Americans should be thankful for his singular public career.[2]

The brief, formal tributes paid to Harold Ickes that day hardly bear comparison with the flood of praise that had poured in to Ickes' widow from all over the nation after his death two months before. Many saluted his honesty and courage, his fierce determination to fight for what was right. As long as Ickes had been in Washington, declared another writer, he had been confident that everything was all right, or that, if it were not, the people would pretty soon know of it. Employees or former employees were particularly effusive. From Ickes, one wrote, he had learned righteousness in public life, hatred of tyranny, and a concern for human dignity. Every tribute paid to the late Secretary was true, said another, but there was something else besides: Harold Ickes had been a fine man to work for, an experience which the writer would not have traded for any other. Representatives of minorities—blacks, Japanese Americans, Indians, and Jews—acknowledged their debt to him. Walter White of the NAACP, recalling Ickes' decision to abolish discrimination in the Department of the Interior, acknowledged the greatness of his soul. Mike Masaoka of the Japanese American Citizens' League paid tribute to his courageous defense of that persecuted group during the war. The Continental Confederation of Adopted Indians mourned the passing of the best friend that American Indians had ever had; their ranks had been grievously thinned by the death of this mighty chieftain. Jewish refugees from Hitler's Europe told how Ickes' name had been a symbol of hope and courage, assuring them in their desperation that human decency had not died. Rex Tugwell, the former New Dealer, felt as though the most energetic member of the nation's board of trustees had been removed. And Justice William O. Douglas, plainly shattered by the death, told Ickes' widow that her husband had been his ideal and that he had loved him as a brother.[3]

Some, who knew him well, spoke of Harold Ickes' warmth and humanity and essential kindness; to others, he was simply the foremost American of his generation, or the best Secretary of the Interior who had ever lived. One, who expressed the thoughts of many, likened Ickes' death to a great oak crashing down amidst a forest of tiny trees.[4]

Similar expressions of feeling had been provoked by Ickes' decision to resign in 1946. As always with him, the issue involved had been one of high principle. Harry S Truman had nominated as Under Secretary of the Navy Edwin W. Pauley, a man Ickes regarded as a tool of predatory oil interests, who had actually, Ickes claimed, offered to raise several hundred thousand dollars for the Democratic Party if Ickes could persuade the federal government not to press its claim to the submerged oil lands off California. This information emerged at Pauley's confirmation hearings, to which Ickes had been summoned as a witness, and when the President, in an attempt to defend Pauley, subsequently told reporters that Ickes may have been mistaken, his Secretary of the Interior sent in a withering letter of resignation. He did not, he said bluntly, deal carelessly with the truth—and that certainly was a part of his image.[5] Neither would he remain in an administration in which he was required to perjure himself for the good of the party.[6] When Harold Ickes finally dropped from the firmament of government, it was not to fade gradually from sight but to burn out brilliantly in a blaze of righteous glory.

The resignation was a personal triumph for Ickes, who was swamped with a flood of adulatory mail. His name would endure as one of the great public servants. It was amazing that he could, for thirteen years, have administered his department and expended millions of PWA dollars without the integrity of one of his subordinates once being questioned; he deserved to be the next President of the United States; he had done more to advance American democracy than all the politicians who had ever lived. The columnist Drew

Pearson, scourge of the powerful and the corrupt, wrote an uncharacteristically warm tribute, which rather pointedly, given the circumstances of Ickes' resignation, referred to him as a "rat killer." Drawn together by their unquenchable sense of moral outrage, he and the Old Curmudgeon had been friends. Not a few feared for the morality of government or wondered, now that one of the last standard-bearers of the New Deal had fallen, how liberalism could any longer endure.[7]

This last concern was understandable, for time and again during his long period in office Harold Ickes had led the forces of liberalism into battle. He had been the first to desegregate a great federal government department, the first publicly to attack the isolationist Charles Lindbergh. In the teeth of cabinet opposition, and prior to official hostilities, he had blocked the sale of helium to Nazi Germany. Well before the United States entered the global conflict, Ickes had mortified the State Department by his savage attacks on Adolph Hitler, who he dubbed "Esau, the Hairy Ape."[8] He had been quick to challenge the illiberal procedures of the Dies Committee, and later boldly denounced Joseph McCarthy (he called McCarthyism "a putrescent and scabious object"), at a time when few had discerned the real nature of the Senator's crusade, and fewer still had been moved to condemn it.[9] When would such a liberal appear again in American public life? What unique confluence of forces had formed him? With such questions in mind, several of those who wrote to him on his resignation urged Harold Ickes to publish a full account of his life. The people were waiting for his story, one averred; for the benefit of all, it should be told.[10]

In fact, few men can have left a more complete record of their public and private lives than did Harold Ickes. There is, to begin with, the famous *Secret Diary*, that richly detailed account of his career in government from 1933 to 1946. As he went about his various activities during that long period, Ickes could often be observed scribbling down notes on small pieces of paper, which he then stuffed into his pockets. These jottings recorded his immediate and largely uninhibited impressions of the people whom he encountered and the feuds and policy decisions in which he was involved. He referred to them as he periodically dictated his reflections on the events of his time to his private secretary. After she had produced a first draft of the diary, he would correct it and, when the final version had been typed, would lock it away in a place to which only he had access. His secretary's shorthand notes, together with the original draft, were then, summer and winter, methodically burned in his fireplace.[11]

After Ickes' death the diary was discovered in his farmhouse near Olney, Maryland. It had grown to prodigious length. The text contained some 6,000,000 words and an extensive index had been appended. For Harry Hopkins, who, more than any of Ickes' contemporaries, aroused his jealousy and ire, there were eighty-three closely typed index cards.[12] The *Secret Diary*, sections of which were published in 1953 and 1954, became the basis for a lengthy political autobiography, on which Ickes labored for several years but which lay unfinished among his papers at his death. This autobiography was intended as a continuation of a long narrative entitled "On My Interest in Politics and Public Affairs," which covered his career as a Chicago Progressive. He may even have intended to combine the two memoirs.

The *Secret Diary* is the most vivid and intimate account of the inner history of the Roosevelt administration. It allows us to observe, from Ickes' highly distinctive perspective, the messy processes of official decisionmaking; the rancorous controversies that disturbed the affairs of state; the personal charm and manipulative skills of a president who deftly kept his unruly team together; and, through all these things, the subtle and shifting relationship between idealism and ambition, principle and power. And always, there is Harold Ickes himself, for so long a leading player on the stage of the New Deal, sometimes strutting and fretting, sometimes descending to petty jealousies and personal abuse, but all the while grappling with momentous problems and striving tenaciously, at times even obsessively, toward his goals.

Ickes produced two other works of importance. The *Autobiography of a Curmudgeon*, an account of his background and career published in 1943, is a curious and irritating book, which is as misleading as a record of his life as it is invaluable as a revelation of his inhibitions. The second is a full and amazingly frank memoir of his personal life, which Ickes dictated to May Conley, his long-time private secretary, at various times during the 1930s and early 1940s.[13] This remarkable narrative is unlike anything else that Ickes wrote. There is in it neither the sustained facetiousness of the *Auto-*

biography nor the small-mindedness and rancor that often invade the pages of the *Secret Diary*. Absent, too, are the belligerence and aggressive confidence in his personal rectitude that mark his political writings. It is as though the public mask has been lowered and Harold Ickes has sought to present himself to his future readers without levity or apparent dissimulation—"Honest Harold" being truly honest at last. It is the story not of the inveterate reformer, the uncompromising public moralist and relentless foe of corruption, but of a man striving to understand his own shortcomings, made desolate by a tempestuous and profoundly unhappy first marriage, who contemplated suicide and stoically endured a numbing series of personal tragedies. This personal memoir is also an indispensable key to many of the paradoxes which made up the man.

Why Ickes left such an unusually frank account of his private life is an intriguing question. Given his first wife's death in an automobile accident in 1935, and her son's suicide precisely one year later, it is clear that the story need never have come out. One must suspect a good deal of narcissism in anyone who writes at such length about himself. Probably he realized, and correctly, that no proper evaluation of him could be made without it; that his public and private lives would somehow have to be integrated if his career were ever to be assessed adequately, even though he could see no way in which such a fusion could be effected. Ickes himself appears to have seen them as separate. He wrote extensively on each, but the two accounts run parallel, without ever meeting. Each story is told in its own terms, apparently owing nothing to the other. The same incident, occurring in both, will be explained in different ways. Thus, Ickes' determination to go to Europe during the First World War to "get into the fight" is accounted for in his political memoirs in conventionally patriotic terms. But in the personal memoirs he speaks only of his frantic need to escape from his wife, an escape that might be made permanent by his hoped-for death in France. One can understand his reticence about revealing, in a work which he probably intended for publication, intimate details of his disastrously unhappy private life. But there is more to it than this. He can see no relation between these private experiences and his career as an urban reformer and later as an administrator. And if at times he appears to concede that such a relation must exist—as when, for instance, in preparing to discuss the impact of his father's infidelities on his parents' marriage, he declares that the relationship between his mother, his father, and himself must profoundly have affected the formation of his own character—he clearly does not know what it is.[14]

Yet it cannot have been the case that the one did not significantly influence the other, that the effects of experiences in Ickes' formative years and later private life did not spill over into his public activities. The question, then, must be not whether the two can be brought together, but how their relationship may be shown.

Even a cursory examination of Ickes' personal memoirs, and of, for example, his wartime letters to his wife, must convince the reader that the answer to such a question will not be simple. The nature of a story that includes descriptions of sadistic attacks by his elder brother, a plan by the young Harold to shoot his father, nightlong and sometimes physically violent rows with his wife, thoughts of suicide, and a declared readiness, when he had finally been appointed Secretary of the Interior, to sacrifice his career for the latest and most fulfilling of his sexual relationships outside marriage makes it unlikely that the segments of his private and public life will fall neatly and obviously into place. To look for a moment at the other side of the puzzle is to realize, too, that certain problems relating to Ickes' public career will not be solved by postulating easy and obvious relationships between his private experiences and his public behavior. By any standards that public career was remarkable. For thirteen turbulent years Ickes was an uncommonly effective public official and a widely acknowledged leader of liberal reform. His responsibilities were immense, his energy and resilience amazing. In certain critically important fields, notably energy policy, he was far ahead of his time. Given the appropriate circumstances, he was a matchless fighter for the just cause, who utilized a formidable talent for invective and an inexhaustible supply of moral fervor to flay the representatives of prejudice and self-interest and castigate opponents of the New Deal. But problems remain. To begin with, there was in Ickes a seeming inability to regulate his rage or temper his criticisms, so that his responses to situations were at times geared less to the nature of the issues than to the needs of his driving personality. Often the moral outrage dammed up within him seemed to be released indiscriminately, without being related to the gravity of the supposed offense. When he fought for oppressed minorities, principle and practice were in some sort of balance; when he fought to remove the Forest Service from the Department of Agriculture and add it to his own department, they were not. With any number of important questions requiring his attention, he spent his energies intriguing over Forestry, wasting his time in a futile attempt to re-write the history of a twenty-five-year-old dispute in a way that would strengthen his case. Similarly, when McCarran or McCarthy moved across his sights he could be magnificent; but when he em-ployed the same fervor in insignificant matters he could be absurd. Harold Ickes could, with equal passion and conviction, oppose the sale of helium to Germany and sternly lecture a poor Chicago shoe-maker who had overcharged his son by a trivial amount.[15]

Ickes could never tolerate any questioning of his integrity. He reacted vehemently to even the most muted suggestion of impropri-ety, often writing his accusers at great length and with a ferocity that shocked them. The roots of his combativeness lay deep within his personality. Harry Truman's remark that Ickes was never happy unless he was unhappy may have been uncharitable, but it did point up one of the important motifs of his political life: the need always to be fighting, to be involved in some stirring moral campaign.[16]

There are intriguing questions. One of the reviewers of the *Secret Diary*, Jonathan Daniels, having pointed out that some of the mate-rial in it would fascinate the psychologist as well as the historian, wondered why a man who was one of the more powerful executants of the New Deal should have harbored the feeling that he was being denied the chance to participate in momentous events. Or why, in his diary, Ickes had given as much weight to personal matters, such as the contrasting attitudes of his two wives toward childbirth, as he had to his ambitions to be Secretary of War or Vice-President.[17] But had Daniels scrutinized the whole of Ickes' writings and examined his entire career, he might have posed further questions. Why had Ickes' driving political ambition always stopped short of an attempt to win elective political office in his own right? Why, before he en-tered the federal government, had he attached himself to a suc-cession of dynamic political candidates, whose defeat often seemed predictable? What lay behind Ickes' unusually aggressive attitude toward political life, and behind what amounted to his passion for honesty and parsimony in the expenditure of vast and urgently needed public funds? Or, during the New Deal period, how can one account for his repeated threats to resign or for the fact that the idea of transferring the Forest Service to his own department became an obsession, which poisoned his relations with colleagues and consumed the time of the President? And, in regard to many of these matters, is not the gap between likely explanation and outcome too large, and the implausibility of Ickes' own attempts to rationalize what he is doing too obvious, to avoid the impression that reasonableness had been set aside and deeper, more personal imperatives were taking over?

Harold Ickes has bequeathed to students of his life a major methodological problem: how to integrate his public and private lives. He has written voluminously on the former, a practice that, among prominent political figures, is not unique. But he has also left an unusually uninhibited and comprehensive account of his private life, the significance of which, if it is to be used constructively to throw light on his public career, must be revealed.

We have used insights drawn from psychological theory to build an interpretive bridge between Ickes' private and public lives. We have sought to identify not only certain conscious ideals and ambitions that inspired him and drove him to feverish political activity, but also those psychological imperatives that, always present within his complex personality, surfaced unexpectedly from time to time decisively to influence his actions. The subtle interplay between, on the one hand, the conscious and unconscious factors originating in his private life, and, on the other, the objective political context within which he sought to achieve his goals is the focal point of this study of Harold Ickes' remarkable career.

Altoona Boyhood

HAROLD LeCLAIRE ICKES spent the first sixteen years of his life in Altoona, a city situated in Blair County, Pennsylvania, on the eastern slopes of the Allegheny Mountains. The Pennsylvania Railroad founded the town in 1849 as a base for the westward expansion of its main track across the mountains, and constructed there over the years the largest workshops in the United States. The city developed rapidly, so that by 1890, when, after the death of his mother, Harold Ickes left to live in Chicago, its population had risen to 31,000.[1]

The people were mainly of Scotch-Irish extraction, with a significant German minority. They were industrious and highly skilled and they prospered as the young city expanded. They were also strongly religious, as the large number of Methodist, Presbyterian, and Baptist churches in the community attests. Church records show that when Martha McCune Ickes, Harold's mother, was received into membership of the Second Presbyterian Church on 21 January 1876, its congregation was almost 1,000. Yet it was only one of six Presbyterian churches then in the city.[2]

Martha Ickes' forebears were Scotch-Irish Presbyterians. They were described by Harold, obviously proud of his ancestry, as being part of that determined band of pioneers who had conquered the forests of Pennsylvania and made their homes in the beautiful valleys and foothills of the Alleghenies.[3] After the American Revolution the family had settled in Blair County, and there, in due course, Ickes' mother had been born. The original McEwen (later McCune) to settle there was a farmer, who had also served as a judge for some thirty-six years. A wealthy man, with extensive landholdings, he passed on his property to his son, Harold's grandfather, who unfortunately allowed much of the inheritance to slip through his fingers. Harold's grandfather McCune had been a prominent and widely liked man, physically imposing and unconventional, as Harold recalled him. A committed Republican with a passionate interest in politics, the leading party man of the township (Hollidaysburg, near Altoona) in his day, he served several terms in the state legislature. Despite his carelessness in financial matters, he was still relatively well off when Harold was a boy, with leisure to go about keeping up his political and other connections. Ickes claims that his grandfather was more partial to him than to the other grandchildren, and the boy loved to go about with him in his highly individual old buggy while he inspected his timberlands in the mountains, visited his farms, or called on acquaintances. Harold may well have obtained from this venerable and attractive figure some of his feeling that the political life was a very desirable one, though the interest in politics probably came even more strongly from his mother, also a passionate Republican, who often heatedly discussed political matters with visiting relatives. He recalls her crying at the news that Blaine had been defeated by Cleveland in 1884. His grandmother McCune he remembered affectionately as a sweet and placid old lady, though he could never recall hearing her speak. She and her husband were strict Presbyterians, but neither seemed as rigid and unbending in this regard as was his own mother.

In his personal memoirs Ickes writes enthusiastically of visits to his grandfather McCune's farm, near Hollidaysburg on the banks of the Juniata River, and which he describes in idyllic terms. Returning years later, he found the beauty of the place destroyed. The railroad had built new tracks along the river for its cars, and the once lovely area now looked like a freight yard. That theme recurs in Ickes' account of his early life: the country surrounding Altoona was beautiful, but the city was at the mercy of the railroad company, which dominated its economic life and dirtied its environment. Smoke and gases from the Pennsy's shops and locomotives, he remembered, corroded the paint on the closely packed houses and gave the city a permanently shabby appearance.

Harold's father's family had come to Pennsylvania, possibly from Saxony or present-day Belgium, in 1730, originally establishing itself near Philadelphia. Later generations moved west, until eventually Harold's grandfather settled near Altoona, where he prospered and acquired much property. For some years before his death he lived in a large building in Altoona called the "Green Corner," in one section of which Harold's father, Jesse, and his wife and young family first made their home. Harold remembered his grandfather Ickes only as a big, generous man, who gave pennies to the children. Of his paternal grandmother he could recall little. Grandfather Ickes set Jesse up in a tobacconist store in another section of the Green Corner, but the venture did not prosper. It was nevertheless assumed that Jesse, as the only surviving son, would inherit considerable property, but when the old man died no will could be found, and his apparently ample possessions, when sold and divided up, yielded little. Although Jesse Ickes obtained employment as a clerk for a building contractor, the work was ill-paid and precarious, and the family never recovered financially. Ickes' personal memoirs make it clear that his resentment at the deprivations suffered for so many years was sharpened by the knowledge that, on both sides of his family, fortunes and reputation had been allowed to slip away.

Harold Ickes was born 15 March 1874. He was the second child, thirteen months younger than his brother John. His mother was twenty-two when he was born; before she died in 1890, at the age of thirty-eight, she would bear five more children: Julia; Merrill, who drowned in the Juniata River in 1892; Felix, who died of typhoid in 1901; Mary; and Ada, who died in infancy. After his father's death Jesse Ickes rented accommodations for some years, moving his growing family from place to place before finally building a simple frame house. By Harold's account, he showed little more than a perfunctory interest in the welfare of his wife and children and was never able to provide adequately for their needs. The staple breakfast in the Ickes home was bread and molasses. Under the circumstances, it was Martha Ickes who assumed responsibility for the upbringing of the children, disciplining them, having them educated, and seeking to impress upon them her strong Calvinist convictions. In his personal memoirs Ickes emphasized his mother's scrupulousness in keeping the children in school, whatever the weather or no matter how hard they might try to feign illness. She was even more determined that they should not neglect religious observances. All the children went regularly to Sunday school and to the church service that followed. Household chores usually kept Martha Ickes from church on Sunday mornings, but she compensated for this lapse, as her son put it, by attending evening service and the prayer meetings which were held on Wednesday evenings. To these extra services, when he was old enough, she took Harold, in order to have his company on the way home.

The image Ickes presents of his father in his memoirs is ambivalent, but for the most part he saw him as a weak, self-indulgent man, who was not sufficiently caring toward his children. He was rarely seen in the home except for the evening meal. On most nights he attended meetings of the remarkable number of lodges and similar associations of which he was a member. (Jesse's business card lists the names of seven such organizations, including the Haymakers' Association, the Chickalacamoose Tribe and the Princes of Bagdad, of which he was member number 364½).[4] He was also, his son recalls, an incompetent member of the local volunteer fire brigade. According to Ickes, his father's main ambition was to earn sufficient money, in as little time as was necessary, to insure a comfortable existence, and then to spend the rest of his time enjoying himself. Though probably fond of his children, he paid little attention to them. Martha Ickes was devoutly religious, but her husband appeared in church only for funerals, for which he dressed, to his son's embarrassment, in the regalia of some secret society.

In sharp contrast, Ickes remembers his mother as being conscientious, self-sacrificing, and hardworking. He admired tremendously the way she, who received little money from a husband who denied his family for the sake of his own pleasures, succeeded somehow in making ends meet. It was only because of her genius that the children were fed and properly clothed; nobody else, Ickes later wrote, could have done what she had done.

It is clear from Ickes' account of his childhood that to earn his mother's love and respect required a great deal of hard work, conformity, and good behavior. It is also plain that from a very early age these demands found a ready acquiescence in Harold—a quite unusual recognition of them as being justified, and the fulfilling of them as an act of virtue rather than a grudging obligation. He writes: "The house was immaculately kept . . . As we children grew older we, of course, helped with the house work and I think it will not be denied that the major burden in this respect fell upon my shoulders. I wasn't so rebellious as John and Julia. In fact I wasn't rebellious at all. When I had finished my apportioned chores I helped out with those of the others if they were being recalcitrant, as was often the case."

Ickes' youthful domestic tasks and interests included a large proportion of conventionally feminine ones. Not only did he get up early to build the fire in the kitchen stove, cut kindling, and carry coal and ashes, but he also tells us that when he was young he dusted while his mother swept and that as he grew older he did the sweeping too. The washing was done in a local laundry, but he and his mother did the ironing at home. In referring, in his published autobiography, to such activities, Ickes wrote: "I shudder to think how I was raised to dust and sweep and wash dishes and knead dough and baste the beef and turn (and burn) the toast and flip flapjacks, and of the hours that I spent with my flowers and my chickens!"[5] But of course it is an intentionally transparent disclaimer when he says that he "shuddered" to think this. He was obviously proud of his application and skill in these matters, and it is instructive to find that as an adult he boasted of his current gardening prowess, that he went to considerable trouble to take out the first-ever patent on a flower that he had developed, that he reported in housewifely detail and pride, and without any irony at all, a menu that he had served Franklin Roosevelt, which included "my own special ice cream, black raspberry," and that he successfully encouraged his young second wife to undertake the raising of chickens on the farm which he later bought.[6]

Not only did Harold regard his mother as an active and efficient manager of the house, and a person to be emulated in this, but he also perceived her as a member of an oppressed class, with her relationship to his father typifying the discrepancy in rights between women and men and the generally disadvantageous position which women occupied in society. In his personal memoirs he implies that his father married his mother almost casually, as one might pick up a minor bit of property. He had wed early, without any real sense of responsibility either to his young wife or to society at large. Life had been without hardship for him until that time, and he simply married this young girl and brought her into the home of his father and stepmother, vaguely imagining that his needs would somehow be provided for. A further source of resentment existed, alongside the perpetual grievance that the father controlled what money there was, doling out an insufficient amount to his wife; this additional imposition Ickes plainly felt very keenly, because he was unable to mention it during the first narrative of his early life, yet found himself eventually forced to return to it. This was his father's infidelity. But this part of the discussion must be postponed until we see something of the deeper layers of Harold's attitude toward his mother.

Mixed with his deep attachment to her he felt a good deal of resentment. This appears clearly enough in the comparisons which he repeatedly draws between his mother's rigid Presbyterianism and the more pliable attitudes of other relatives. Though Ickes blames his mother's family for her intolerance, he writes of her parents in a way which makes the attribution of responsibility unconvincing. Grandfather McCune took his religion as a matter of course and was liberal in his general outlook. Grandmother McCune was diminutive, gentle, and uncomplaining. There is also an obvious contrast between the freshness and vivacity of his descriptions of his visits to his relatives' farms or walks in the surrounding hills and his negative view of home life, which, under his mother's exacting regime, was drab, joyless, and oppressive. He loved to stay with his great-aunt and great-uncle Elizabeth and Alex Knox and their son Sam at nearby Newry, where Sam and his father ran several farms. Typically, Ickes remarks on the fact that Aunt Elizabeth's attitude to religion was generally relaxed, even though her brother and son were Presbyterian ministers. What he loved at Newry were the outdoor activities—driving the cows to pasture, riding the horses whenever he chose, going with his cousin to visit Sam's timber interests in the mountains, or taking the horse and buggy off by himself on day trips. He reveled in the freedom of this existence, the lack of irksome restraints, and the companionship of people who enjoyed life and were warmhearted and hospitable.

Aside from such pleasurable visits and the impressive amount of reading which he was able to do (and of which he was enormously proud), Ickes enjoyed mainly rambling in the nearby hills, treading the mossy beds of mountain streams, stopping now and then to eat berries and nuts, picking the beautiful wild flowers—dogwood, trailing arbutus, and rhododendron—that grew profusely in that lovely place. At home he made a little flower garden and rockery which he stocked with ferns and wild flowers collected on his trips to the mountains.

In sharp contrast to all this is the description in his personal memoirs of the extreme restrictions placed by his mother on her children's behavior on Sundays. The memory of those days still horrified him, as he recalled them half a century later. The children could not play, or sing anything other than hymns, or read anything other than religious books approved by their mother. They could not whistle or walk in the sunshine, on pain of damnation. In another place he notes that, as there were no dogs or cats in the home, his father was the only person for whom life on Sundays was at all tolerable. Under such circumstances the children would become fractious and before the day was out fights would begin, with the mother trying to separate the combatants. Though Harold goes on to protest once more the mutual devotion between himself and his mother, he declares:

> Yet as I look back over the years I do not wonder that my father preferred to spend his evenings and his Sundays away from home. If (this) mother (whom I adored) [the words in parenthesis were inserted as an afterthought] had been just a bit of a "good fellow"; if she had had a lighter touch; if father had been met with an occasional smile and cheery word; if his manners and morals had not always been held up as a horrible example; if he had not always had to be reminded of duties unperformed, or to be performed, . . . there would have been a more tranquil family life all around and we children would have gone out into the world with a happier outlook on life. Yet I cannot blame her. She could not overcome the effects of her early training.

This apparently judicious and even-handed paragraph (that is actually very critical of his mother, despite Ickes' disclaimer that he "cannot blame her") is undoubtedly colored by later accretions of feeling provoked by his own hectoring, moralistic first wife, Anna. Having written it, he is then able to reveal the one bit of human weakness breaching his mother's puritanism. She liked to play cards. She had been taught to play "California Jack" by her husband who, Harold notes portentously, was as familiar with card games as he was with other pleasant diversions, and, when Harold was capable of understanding the game, she had with considerable misgiving taught it to him. But they played the game secretively, without any open enjoyment, since both felt a great sense of guilt. Even if one does not apply to this the Freudian view of card-playing as an onanistic equivalent, the feeling Harold evidently had that he was being elevated to some secret and forbidden intimacy in his father's place is plain enough.

The rest of the oedipal drama, incorporating the victimization of the mother, begins to unfold when Harold goes on to relate that his parents' marriage was unhappy and that from the outset his sympathies were all with his mother. But though he was antagonistic toward his father, blaming him for the domestic strife that marred their lives, he would later, he writes, revise this judgment. His own marital experiences would convince him that in such a conflict blame normally attached to both sides.

Despite the earlier reference to his father's pleasant diversions, Ickes does not return to the relations between his parents and make explicit his father's infidelities until a hundred pages later in his personal memoirs. Having progressed in his narrative to the passing of his law examination in 1907, he declares that he must retrace his steps in order to fill in some details essential to his story, realizing that the relation between his father, mother, and himself had much to do with the formation of his own character. He now reveals that from an early age he had realized that his father sometimes drank too much and was a notorious philanderer. Yet, though Jesse Ickes was repeatedly unfaithful to Harold's mother, she regularly bore his children until her death. His parents should have divorced, he felt, but social convention ruled that out. It was customary, Ickes notes, for couples to remain married and continue to have sexual relations, even though the husband's infidelity was known. Wives had to tolerate such situations with as much composure as possible. Here again is the suggestion not only that his mother was being exploited as an individual but that she was also a member of an exploited class. Many women, because they were women, were forced to bear similar humiliation.

As Harold grew older, his mother began to confide in him. He, after all, was her favorite, more in her company than the other children and far more responsible than they. But he later came to feel that to be made the recipient of such confidences placed too great a burden on him. Certainly these verbal intimacies, bringing to the forefront of his consciousness the disturbed sexual relationship between his parents, must have increased his attraction to his mother and his resentment against and competitiveness with his father.

Ickes goes on to tell of a dramatic incident which, he thought, had happened when he was fourteen or fifteen years of age. As he was preparing for bed one evening, his mother broke down and confessed that she was afraid her husband would attack her. Jesse Ickes had been drinking excessively, and these were always dreadful times for Harold's mother. The account continues: "I felt that it was my duty to defend her. I made her promise to call me if she needed help. As I have said, the four boys of us slept in an enormous room that took up practically the entire third storey of the house. John and I slept together in one big four-poster bed and Merrill and Felix in another." It is not immediately clear why Ickes digresses to include this detail of sleeping arrangements. He does not bring out any significance that it may have had. A relevant consideration, as we shall see, is that John, his bed partner and elder brother, was still at this period exerting authority over and physically intimidating him. Harold proceeds to relate how he took a pistol from its hiding place in the house and slept with it under his pillow, intending, if it proved necessary to protect his mother, to shoot his father. But, he quickly adds, he would never have had the nerve to go through with the deed, and in any case his father could easily have overpowered him since he was but a young lad, had never fired a pistol, and knew nothing of how they worked. In the event, Jesse Ickes did not behave violently toward his wife, and Harold's sleep was not disturbed.

It is possible to see in his narration of this event the underlying dynamic of the sophisticated moral judgement that Ickes had made a few paragraphs earlier: that it was unfair of a mother to place such heavy responsibility on a boy whose mind was not yet formed. That is, it was all very well to maintain the fantasy, conscious or unconscious, of killing his father and assuming his place with his mother, but when that fantasy threatened to be translated into the realm of required actions in the real world, that was a different matter. By confiding in him on this occasion and in effect requiring him to protect her against the assult of a husband, she had exposed Harold to actual physical danger and to symbolic castration. Hence his protest that she ought not to have burdened him with her fears. His doubt about the force and reliability of his own male powers is revealed in his description of himself at the age of fourteen or fifteen as a small boy who knew nothing about pistols.

The suggestion that Ickes had experienced castration anxiety with the accompanying anxious repudiation of femininity gains credence from his inclusion in the narrative of this event the apparently irrelevant detail that he was at the time sharing a bed with John. Though his brother was only thirteen months older than Harold, he was much better developed and physically more aggressive at this time, and he was accustomed to arrogate to himself the role and privileges of a disciplinarian—was in this way a surrogate father-figure. In the vacuum of responsibility left by their habitually absent father, John ordered Harold about and regularly beat him up. He also resembled the father in that he was perceived by Harold as victimizing his virtuous mother. There was an obvious need in this large family for the children to help with the chores, a burden, Harold believed, that was far too great for her, but John resented this requirement and especially resented Harold because he was willing to do not only his own tasks but those of his rebellious brothers and sisters. John's temper was so violent and his abuse of his mother so extreme that she was often forced to excuse him from his allotted tasks.

John, then, like his father, was seen by Harold as one of a class of oppressive and exploiting males. The younger boy, allying himself with his mother and helping to carry the burden of domestic labor, must often have felt that he would be seen by other males as feminine and passive, feelings which typically cause an upsurge of castration anxiety and so muster strenuous but unconfident attempts to repudiate the feminine role. In Harold's relation to John this masculine protest finally achieved its aim, though more by good luck than by good management. One evening, shortly after the pistol incident, Martha Ickes went out, leaving John and Harold reading in the dining room. A violent altercation followed, and John began to beat Harold up. Harold, retaliating wildly as best he could, accidently kicked John in the testicles, which left him writhing on the floor in pain and Harold feeling a degree of satisfaction that for once he had successfully repelled his brother's attack. Returning to find John howling in agony, their mother, having learned what had happened, rebuked Harold, though not, he felt, without some sympathetic feeling that justice had finally been done. Harold claims that the experience taught John a lesson and that from that time on he was practically immune from his elder brother's attacks.

The victory over John was consolidated a couple of years later.

After Harold and his sister Mary had gone to live in Chicago, John seized control over the youngest boy, Felix, then aged ten. He attempted minutely to supervise Felix's behavior and, Harold learned, would punish the young boy by depriving him of meals, confiscating his clothing, thrashing his naked body, and locking him in the attic for hours at a time. So notorious did John's behavior become that neighbors were on the point of reporting the situation to the police. When Harold discovered the state of affairs, he confronted John, warning him against further acts of brutality. John moved to attack, but Harold stated calmly that, now that he was John's physical equal, he would welcome the opportunity of administering the beating that his elder brother had so long deserved. John not only failed to accept the challenge but, according to Harold, from that time he ceased chastising Felix.

Other incidents in his childhood on which Ickes, looking back over a distance of half a century, placed great emphasis concerned disputes with his mother over the application of religious principles to life. He tells of a visit to his cousins the Knoxes at nearby Newry, and of hearing there a sermon from a visiting minister who was staying with them. Later that Sabbath Harold heard the minister whistle. This was astonishing to a young boy who had been taught that to whistle on Sunday was sinful. Ickes pondered the matter deeply, finally concluding that if this man could whistle on Sunday without jeopardizing his soul, so could he. He decided to challenge his mother on this point. The following Sunday, without first explaining his action, he began to whistle loudly in her presence. When she rebuked him, he cited the authority of the minister. For once she had no effective answer, and Harold had won the right to whistle whenever he pleased.

On another occasion he successfully questioned his mother's authority over the issue of which books he could read on Sundays. Most books in the Ickes home were of a theological nature, quite acceptable for Sunday reading but without much appeal. The children were not allowed to read public library books on that day. Harold found, however, that he was permitted to bring home books from the Sunday-school library for Sunday reading, and some of these, he notes, were very much more to his taste. When his mother first discovered him reading such a book she began to interrogate him about its contents, but when he showed her the Sunday-school library bookplate, she was satisfied. The result was that Harold was permitted to read anything he pleased from that source. Ickes claims to have seen in this incident an illustration of the fact that in religious matters form is often more important than substance.

Ickes' comments on his parents and the manner in which he related incidents from his childhood provide possible clues to his later attitudes and behavior. His tremendous admiration for his mother, who in a remarkable fashion could eke out the pittance which her husband allowed her and keep the household running, is plain. From early in his life she exemplified for Ickes those virtues which would become universally acknowledged in his own administration of Public Works during the New Deal—virtues that might be described as scrupulously thrifty but growth-oriented housekeeping for the nation.

There was every reason why Harold's mother should have been the parent with whom he mainly identified. She was in the foreground of his life every day, was materially important, and both gave and withheld love in a much higher degree than did Harold's father. His admiration for their immaculately kept house, his willingness to do his brothers' and sisters' allotted tasks as well as his own, indicate that he had taken over as his own the ideals of service, cleanliness, and good housekeeping that his mother exemplified. In addition, there was a more global and unconscious identification with the maternal image. In large measure Ickes experienced his mother's interests, position, and perhaps fate in life as if they were his own. To link his high valuation of proper household management with his approach to his administrative role as Secretary of the Interior is not to depend only on a fanciful leap of the imagination from childhood occupations to the mature, real-world affairs of a committed administrator. Throughout the intervening forty-odd years Ickes showed overt evidence of the continuing strength of his maternal identification not only in such externals as his serious concern with cooking, and his obsessive, minute supervision of the building of the matrimonial home at Hubbard Woods, but more importantly, at a deeper level, in his unpaid legal representation of the interests of women industrial workers, in his defense of minority rights, and in the moral masochism that prevented his escaping from the almost endless misery of his first marriage—a misery and dependency which drove him to compensate outside the home by the most energetic exercise of power as a political kingmaker. The link with minority rights is that, although his mother was the active and efficient manager of the house, Harold also perceived her, quite accurately, as representing an exploited group.

The importance to Ickes of the incidents in which he successfully opposed his bullying brother is suggested by the length and vividness of his description of those happenings (and, in relation to the kicking incident, by his admission that he had cherished the memory of what he had done for more than fifty years). In the second of these confrontations, Harold had progressed from defending himself against unjust bullying to defending a still weaker victim (Felix) against the same aggressor. This double victory, with its assertion of moral supremacy, must have been a powerful encouragement to him to continue such crusades. For the rest of his life he was moved to a passion of indignation whenever he discovered a case of bullying and would intervene in the most spontaneous and forceful, not to say aggressive, way to protect the victim and expose the persecutor. This would be so not only in the case of individuals, but of persecuted minorities as well, in relation to which he would employ the metaphor of bullying again and again. These courageous acts are not of course to be explained merely as symbolic repetitions of the disabling kick to the brutal brother; nevertheless, in some of them there was an emotional intensity, an enraged repugnance, in his condemnations that revealed something more than a reasoned assessment of right and wrong. In brief, what we shall argue is that this was an overcompensatory masculine protest, which had gained special prominence in Ickes' case because of the actual physical humiliations imposed on him by a father-surrogate, his elder brother John, reinforcing the normal, unconscious castration-anxiety focused on his actual father. All this came close to a traumatic intensity in boyhood because of the perceived call on him to protect his victimized mother from these too-powerful males.

It is obvious, too, from Ickes' comments on his formative years, that the demand for impartial justice, for equality before the law, became clearly formulated in his mind at an unusually early age. This was exemplified in the manner in which he won the "right" to whistle on Sundays. What is legitimate for one is legitimate for another; if the minister could whistle, so could he. This exemplifies Reformed Church thinking: each of us stands on an equal footing with God, and the ministry is not a privileged class of intercessors. It seems from his account of this episode that Ickes was confident that his mother would recognize the justice of the case; yet he did not discuss the merits of the case with her in advance, but went ahead with his apparent infringement of the law. The effect of the exchange was to use the law as an instrument to manipulate his mother, treating her as an object.

Similar themes appear in Ickes' confrontation with his mother over Sunday reading. But in this instance he had begun to see that a law, in this case certain rules of the church, might be intrinsically unreasonable. This was an important early step in the formation of a principled, liberal conscience, insofar as that involves the recognition that particular enacted laws may be unjust and discriminatory and may in good conscience be overridden in the name of an abstract conception of universal justice. In the liberal view such an abstract conception derives from the conviction that all men are "born equal," or that there are intrinsic rights inalienable from any human individual.[7]

This is not to say that Ickes had as yet arrived at a fully developed conception of the universality of such a principle, or indeed that he ever did so. An escape clause permanently appended to moral principles for Ickes was the belief, confidently held, in his own personal rectitude. His main goal in these two incidents with his mother was to secure *for himself* freedom from specific irksome restrictions rather than to persuade his mother of their unreasonableness. This he did in both cases by appealing over her head to church authority. His mother's admission of the "justice" of his case must have added a new piquancy to their relationship. It is a considerable feat for a young lad to challenge such a mother, so Christian, so virtuous, so unflagging in her family dedication, on a point of principle. That he could do so is a mark in favor of her mode of discipline, suggesting that it incorporated some attempt to give reasons for her rules rather than imposing them as blank fiats.[8] The fact that she conceded the force of his arguments, thus admitting herself as a rulegiver to be subject to the same rules, is a further instance of the same attitude. Yet is was not in the nature of a palace revolution. She undoubtedly remained in command, though perhaps on a more human scale as one with whom rule-governed negotiations were possible. What was prompted by such encounters was a thoroughly secular conception of law, as something which would be manipulated to secure whatever was identified as one's right.

Whenever Ickes was in difficulty or faced with obstruction (real or imaginary), he was always able to see himself as a virtuous, oppressed minority of one. This is far from being an uncommon defense mechanism, but not many people are able to maintain it so impregnably or pursue its implications so vigorously as could Harold Ickes. This attitude was an important part of his makeup as a public official, and it can once again be seen as originating in his identification with his mother, whom he saw as oppressed, overworked, betrayed, and exploited both economically and sexually. Yet even in his relationship with her he was sometimes able to displace her from the position of the oppressed and occupy it in solitary martyrdom, representing his mother now as the oppressor of himself—as in the matter of Sunday observance. The passage quoted above in which he accused her of too condemnatory and moralistic an attitude toward his father, of not being enough of "a good fellow," could equally have described his view of her behavior toward himself. Throughout most of his life Ickes was too ready to see women with whom he had any close family ties as being nagging, domineering, and moralistic. This applied in the highest possible degree to the first Mrs. Harold Ickes, Anna. It would take many years and a crucial revolution in his personal relationships to ameliorate this stereotype of woman as persecutor.

Although Ickes' conception of virtue was fluid and egocentric, it never became consciously cynical. His one overriding ethical principle in public life was that big business interests should be prevented from using the mechanisms of government to exploit the mass of the people, and this he pursued unwaveringly. Outside that, his ethical views tended to be summed up in nonspecific labels such as "integrity" and "liberalism," which were sometimes used to license policies that others might have seen as thoroughly self-interested. This appeared most strikingly in Ickes' private life but also in his public life; his attempts, for example, to seize administrative control of a wide range of agencies and bureaus were classed by him as being solely in the public interest, while fellow Cabinet members saw them as outright self-aggrandizement. The justification of his actions lay simply in whether he felt them to be in accord with his own conscience, of the intuitive rectitude of which he was never really in doubt.

The primitive foundation of this conception of ethics must have been laid early in life; presumably it derived from his mother's fundamentalist Presbyterianism, a part of Ickes' mental and emotional life from its very beginning. Ickes may have abandoned his religion as a young man, but he never abandoned the conviction that he could tell the essence of righteousness. This conviction must have been reinforced in the episodes of the whistling and the Sunday-school books. He had made his mother admit that his case was more just than hers. She certainly remained a fountain of virtuous motives, but he could compete with her as to the proper understanding of the nature of justice. He was confident, too, that he was morally superior to his father, a poor provider and a loose-living man who was unfaithful and even threatening toward Ickes' admirable but vulnerable mother.

In these ways some useful preliminary light may be thrown on what would become the dominant motifs of Harold Ickes' political and public life: his passion, as an administrator, for honesty and parsimony in the expenditure of vast public funds; his extreme sensitivity to suggestions of impropriety or incompetence, or to real or imagined incursions onto his domain; his intense concern for the rights of persecuted minorities; and, at all times, his unwavering belief in his own moral rectitude. The resentment he felt against the powerful company that dominated the life of his city and damaged its environment would soon be generalized and strengthened as he joined the efforts of Chicago urban reformers to control the great utilities threatening that city. His love of nature and the wilderness, which he equated with freedom from spiritual and emotional restraint, would reappear in his struggles as Secretary of the Interior to resist the greedy exploiter and to preserve and extend the nation's wilderness areas.

When Martha Ickes died of pneumonia in 1890, Harold and Mary were taken by their Aunt Ada Wheeler to live with her family in Chicago. Harold's father, Julia, John, Merrill, and, for a time, Felix remained in the family home, but when Julia married, Jesse went to live with her and her husband. Harold left Altoona without regret; with his mother dead, there was little to hold him.

Anna and Chicago Reform

ADA AND Felix Wheeler, who had agreed to care for Harold and his sister Mary, lived in Englewood on Chicago's South Side. They were not well-to-do, and to help make ends meet Harold was required to assist in the family drugstore. He opened the store at 6:30 each morning and, after returning from school, served in it until 10 o'clock at night. The work was irksome and the long hours made studying difficult. Because Jesse Ickes was unable to send his son any money, Harold was forced into a humiliating dependence on another uncle, Sam McCune, for basic items of clothing. Sensitive to his situation, he kept a careful record of every cent that this relative grudgingly outlaid on his behalf and eventually repaid him in full.

Overcoming her husband's objections, Ada Wheeler had insisted that Harold be allowed to complete his education, and he had duly entered Englewood High School. He did so well that the school administration allowed him to do the final two years' work in one. Unpromising circumstances did not diminish his moral confidence. Even in high school he showed a consciousness that he merited an executive position. In his crowded final year one of the Latin teachers was taken ill, and as no substitute was available the principal asked Ickes to take over the class. He did so with obvious relish, enjoying for a time the experience of instructing his contemporaries in Cicero. When some students became insubordinate, Ickes quickly demanded that the ringleader leave the room. The culprit hesitated, but Ickes insisted and threatened to send the next offender to the principal. After that he had no further trouble.

Even though Ickes was combining his junior and senior years, he was elected senior class president, which, he says, taught him to face opposition boldly and overcome it and greatly boosted his self-confidence. He closely studied parliamentary law, with the result that he was always able to remain in control of class meetings. On one occasion he outmaneuvered an opposing faction by dramatically resigning (a maneuver he was often to try later on). Confusion followed until, overwhelmingly, the class refused to recognize his resignation. From that time his authority was unchallenged.[1]

Ickes graduated near the top of his class, despite having to spend time working in the drugstore. The entry alongside his name in the school's yearbook for 1893 states that he expected to study law.[2] The principal considered him an outstanding scholar who had made an impressive record as a student.[3] Inspired by a young teacher, Miss Agnes Rogers, for whom he formed a strong attachment and to whom he was genuinely grateful for the remainder of his life, he decided to go to college. There was no prospect of financial assistance either from his father or from the Wheelers, but by various shifts, part-time work, obtaining some of his tuition on credit to be repaid after graduation, and so on he was able to enter the University of Chicago in November 1893, in the middle of the first quarter.

Writing many years later in his personal memoirs, Ickes claimed that no one had assisted him as he fought his way through college, that, indeed, he had had to struggle against almost universal opposition. What he achieved was solely the product of his own efforts. Although it is true that he worked his way through the university under decidedly rigorous conditions, that he had to live extremely frugally and was in fact in a state of penury throughout, it is untrue that he faced concerted opposition or that he had no support. Ickes himself admitted that someone, probably Miss Rogers, told Professor Boyer of his plight. Boyer then introduced him to W. R. Harper, President of Chicago University, who was sympathetic and offered to find enough work for Ickes within the university to meet at least the cost of his tuition. Ickes still had to find some way to secure food and lodging, so he applied for a position as a teacher in the public night school. Unbeknown to him, he writes, someone was working on his behalf. The daughter of the night-school supervisor had known Ickes by sight at high school, and she nagged and harassed her reluctant father until eventually he gave him the job. His friend Henry Adkinson's Aunt Sylvia provided lodging for most of the first two years in a cottage that she owned in 57th Street near the night school (where he taught English to Scandinavian immigrants for two hours a week while there were any students). The cottage was flimsy and freezing, but it was free. Each summer he went back to Altoona and lived with his father for nothing. In his final year he had to study through the summer quarter to make up his courses. He tried to obtain financial assistance from various cousins, but failed. At long last, however, his father yielded to sustained pressure from Harold and began sending him ten dollars a month for his senior year, and in this way he managed to graduate.

Without disputing the rigor of his conditions or the determination that he showed in his studies, we can say nevertheless that Ickes shows a rather exaggerated need to protest his self-sustaining independence, to an extent which rather falsifies the facts. This tendency, which appears in later years also, probably can be traced to his need to deny feminine dependency.

As an undergraduate he demonstrated the persistence, energy, and organizing ability that he had admired so much in his mother and that would mark his political and civil service career. He conceived and brought into being the University of Chicago Intercollegiate Tennis Association and organized its first two annual tournaments, in 1896 and 1897. For two years he managed the Tennis Association, and he boasted that he was the only student in the University's history to have held such a position. He edited the student newspaper, was a member of the track team (in walking), and organizer and first president of the Chicago chapter of Phi Delta Theta—all of this in his final quarter.[4]

Only in his social and romantic relations with the women undergraduates was Ickes at first unsuccessful. But there was one girl in history class whom he found himself studying and wondering about. She was Anna Wilmarth, who would eventually become his wife, but the development of this relationship was extraordinarily circuitous and stressful, and its consummation profoundly demoralizing. He was initially attracted by her relatively exalted social position.

> When people spoke of her it was somewhat with baited [*sic*] breath. She was said to be the richest girl in college and she probably was . . . Romantic tales were told of her and her wealth and social standing

which had the effect of setting her somewhat in a class by herself. Certainly it was clear, even to my inexperienced eye, that she dressed more richly and in better taste than any other girl on the campus. ... Miss Wilmarth lived in Beecher Hall, but she spent her weekends at the Auditorium Hotel reputedly in sumptuous quarters with her mother, who was said to own all of the ground on which the Auditorium Hotel and the Congress Hotel stood. I wished that I might be introduced to Miss Wilmarth, but I never suggested it to anyone, nor did anyone to me. I realized that she travelled in an orbit so different and so far removed from mine that we might never meet.

Then one day as I was mounting the first floor flight of stairs leading from the main floor of Cobb Hall I looked up and saw Miss Wilmarth descending in the middle of the stairway ... just as I was about to pass her, of course without any sign of recognition, she bowed and spoke my name. With a swish of her skirts she was gone.[5]

He wrote that last sentence after twenty-five years of embittered marriage, a mutual misery that nevertheless could be terminated only by Anna's death. Its self-deceptive romanticism—"with a swish of her skirts she was gone"—will crop up again, astonishingly, in his letters to her from France during the Great War, where he had gone in desperation to get away from her and, he claims, half-hoping that he would be killed. He must have gone on clinging to an unrealizable illusion of romantic love brought with him from his boyhood, characteristic enough of a social milieu which profoundly alienated the sexes from each other.

Sentimental attachment was only part of the story. Ickes was class-conscious throughout his life and strongly motivated to fight his way upward in the social hierarchy, perhaps in reaction against his father's ne'er-do-well complacency. Most of the people who appear however briefly in the pages of his personal memoirs are identified by family background, level of education, positions achieved by themselves and their connections, and, as like as not, by the jobs which the mature Ickes, from his achieved eminence, kindly arranged for their offspring.

He recounts with a fascinated intensity the story of this doom-laden romance with Anna Wilmarth, and it illuminates the background against which his developing career was played out. After this first sign of recognition, Ickes began to meet Anna at the informal college dances, and eventually mustered up the courage to invite her to one. To his great surprise she accepted. Then one day in the summer of 1896 she asked him to spend a weekend with her and her mother at their country home, an estate called Glen Arden, on Lake Geneva in Wisconsin. Ickes says that, to the largely middle-class students at the university, this country estate seemed a magnificent place. Only a few had been invited there, so that when Anna approached him he was delighted.

There were three other guests: two young women and James Westfall Thompson, a graduate student in history at Chicago. Anna seemed to show Harold some particular marks of favor; she brought him from the station in her dogcart, while the others were put in the carriage with the family coachman. He enjoyed the weekend in the company of these agreeable and charming people, whose impressive social backgrounds and evident economic security freed them from snobbishness or affectation.

Miss Wilmarth told him that instead of returning to college the following year she was going to Europe with her mother. Ickes asked whether he might write to her and was told that he might; he also asked for and was given a photograph. They met two or three more times before Anna went to Europe, and while she was there they corresponded quite regularly. Ickes even began to hope that she might wait for him until he could graduate and get a job. Then came a great shock. Thompson, his fellow weekend guest, asked him to dinner at the Quadrangle Club and there told him that he was soon to leave for London where he and Anna would be married. Anna had wanted him to know. Though stunned, Ickes was able to conceal his feelings and, looking back, felt proud of his ability to take such a blow without flinching. The wedding of James and Anna in London, in June 1897, coincided with his graduation from college.[6]

Years later, when the relationship between Ickes and Anna was becoming more intimate, she explained that she really had cared for him all along. But her relationship with her mother had grown intolerable, and marriage seemed the only means of escape; Ickes was still a penniless undergraduate, while Thompson had obtained his second degree and a teaching position at the university.

A growing involvement in politics helped Ickes overcome any distress over Anna's marriage. In his political memoirs he states that he had been interested in politics and public affairs all his life.[7] His grandfather McCune's political career and the family speculation that he might have become governor of his state had he not wearied of the political game probably accounted for some of this interest, as did his mother's intense political partisanship. Even Ickes' father had on one occasion run for membership of the Select Council of Altoona and, despite the strongly Democratic character of his ward, had only narrowly been defeated. Proudly Ickes recalled that he, though only a very young boy, had assisted his father in this campaign, the first illustration, he says, of his "uncanny ability to pick losers!"[8] (As we shall see, by his "uncanny ability to pick losers" he really meant his courage in joining forces with meritorious candidates who were struggling against the stream—that is to say, against the forces of "evil"—and by skill and dedication bringing them closer to victory than anyone would have dreamed possible.)

Harold Ickes had come to Chicago a committed Republican, but he soon began to look more critically at public issues and party alignments. The eager political conversation in the house of his friend Henry Adkinson challenged him, as did the reformist views of the *Chicago Record*, which he began to read. He still thought of himself as a Republican and, while studying at the University of Chicago held office in collegiate and intercollegiate Republican clubs, but he took pride in his increasingly independent political stances as against docile acceptance of his parents' views.

He felt drawn to strong political leaders, an indication, as was his bellicosity, of secret self-doubts and the unconscious feminine attachment that such dynamic figures inspired. In 1896 he heard Theodore Roosevelt speak at the Universtiy of Chicago and was so impressed by this ebullient and dynamic figure that, he later wrote, from that day on he became his avid supporter.[9] John Harlan evoked a similar response. Harlan, the youngest son of Justice Marshall Harlan of the United State Supreme Court, had by 1897 become the aggressive champion of the Chicago reformers. As a member of the City Council, and backed by the newly formed Municipal Voters' League, he headed a campaign to prevent traction magnate Charles T. Yerkes from extending his franchises over the north- and west-side transport systems. In 1897 Harlan stood as an independent candidate for mayor.

Ickes heard Harlan speak some months before he announced his candidacy and was captivated by his eloquence and sincerity. "Then and there," he later wrote, "convinced of his political integrity and high courage, I fell hard for him." Harlan, he decided, "not only had the moral courage to say what he thought, but the physical courage to back it up if necessary" (he boxed regularly to keep himself in perfect physical condition). If interrupted during a speech, he would "advance truculently to the footlights, [and] invite the obstructor to the platform, there to fight it out."[10] At the urging of Professor William Hill of the University of Chicago's Department of Political Economy, Ickes agreed to organize support for Harlan within the university. Later, when the *Record* published a call for volunteers, he temporarily discontinued his studies and went to work for the Harlan organization.

This was his first real venture into practical politics and it thrilled him. Toward the end of the campaign, with public excitement rising, Harlan boldly decided to hold lunch-hour meetings in the city center. Great crowds thronged to hear him strike out at his opponents. At his final meeting he held his vast audience spellbound by the sheer power of his words, and as the meeting concluded, Ickes witnessed a sight that enthralled him. The great audience began to applaud, then spontaneously rose to its feet and stood waving wildly and cheering John Harlan for several minutes.[11] Reform politics, Harold Ickes had found, was greatly to his taste. Here in the city the moral world of his childhood was once more clearly expressed, with Ickes again on the side of the upright, though without much of the ambivalence which his mother's restrictions on his boyish desires had produced. With a strong leader in control, Ickes' powers were fully released: under such circumstances politics would always be for him a pleasure before which all others faded.

Meanwhile, after graduating and relaxing in Altoona for the summer, Ickes had a living to make. Back in Chicago, he was living on credit in the fraternity house when he ran into Thompson in the street. After returning from Europe, James and Anna Thompson resided in the Del Prado Hotel, and Thompson urged Ickes so strongly to call that he did so within a day or two. In a minor way Thompson helped Ickes obtain his first job, as a space writer on the *Chicago Record*, where he received $5 per column for anything he wrote that the paper published. He earned 75 cents the first week. For a while he had to rely on small loans from Stacy Mosser, a college acquaintance, and other old friends, but he soon made enough to supply his needs. Through industry and luck he brought in some good stories and was offered a job on the regular staff. But just at the same time he applied for and received a more attractive position as university correspondent with the *Chicago Tribune*.

Although he was successful, getting a good deal of copy into print, within a few months he returned to the *Record*, as assistant sports editor. Ickes regarded this as a dead-end assignment, and soon transferred to the political department. His new beat took him to the offices of leading city officals—mayor, sheriff, county treasurer— where, with other newsmen, he "chewed the political fat." It also took him into the malodorous sludge of Chicago politics. As he would later depict it, the city was controlled by "wolves and jackals," who gathered tribute from contractors and the controllers of vice, manipulated ballots, and delivered votes to the major parties in return for the installation of a mayor and police chief prepared to wink at their nefarious activities. Carter Harrison, victor over Harlan in 1897, allowed such men "to roam unmolested in the highways and byways . . . to pick up anything that wasn't nailed down."[12]

Ickes took to this work with relish. He seemed to have a real flair for it, an unusual ability to gather not just surface political news, but to penetrate to the real motives and political forces that lay beneath.[13] He got to know many politicians personally and claims that he always respected their confidences; consequently they trusted him and he began to be made privy to inside political information. Soon he was priding himself on his knowledge of the inner workings of the city's complex political mechanism.

During this period Ickes became acquainted with the reform element in Chicago, the men and women who had led the Municipal Voters' League and backed Harlan's 1897 campaign, and who, Ickes says, were devoted to the public interest. They were beginning to enjoy great success, with Harlan and Billy Kent campaigning within the city council and movements emerging in the wards to elect upright citizens to that body. Money flowed in to the reformers' coffers, Victor Lawson's newspapers backed them, meetings of the council were crowded with concerned citizens, and before long the reformers had won a majority there.

In the political columns of the *Record* Ickes joined this campaign by hitting out vigorously at municipal corruption. He did so willingly, conscious of a strong sense of moral rapport with the reform community of the city. At heart, he felt, he belonged to this group, and from this time he was recognized as being one of Chicago's political reformers. But while he fought alongside the reformers, he also grew to know the bosses. He ought to have disapproved of these men, but, as his writings make clear, he found their habitual bonhomie and unabashed exercise of raw political power compelling, an echo of those sympathetic feelings toward his father which he had had to suppress. They were colorful and attractive figures, whom he could not help liking. The friendship between Democratic boss John P. Hopkins and the other members of his faction intrigued him. They were devoted to one another, but the way in which these rough Irish politicians showed it was by mocking and abusing each other. The reporters who gathered in their offices enjoyed the quick sallies of wit, the rollicking exchanges. Ickes maintained his links with some of the bosses for many years. Their empires may have been built on graft, but he would later confess that he "liked and enjoyed the company of the crooks." They tore each other to pieces in their power struggles, they were ruthless, but "they had real human qualities."[14] (He made similar comments to William Allen White in September 1927, when the Kansas editor sent him a copy of his latest book, *God Got One Vote*. An unusually good political novel, was Ickes' verdict. "I have always had a personal fondness for a certain type of political boss and to me Patrick Van Hoos is a lovable character."[15]) Although he was with the reformers in principle, he often found them aloof and forbidding. They may have possessed a polish that the Irish bosses lacked, but "it was like the polish on a slab of granite, and contrasted with the warm joviality of the Irish political chieftains."[16] Later, when Victor Lawson suddenly sold the *Record*, leaving Ickes without employment, it was the bosses who offered him help. The reformers, without exception, stood back.

In 1900 Ickes had his first experience of covering important conventions, first the Republican and Democratic state conventions; then the Republican National Convention in Philadelphia, which renominated McKinley for President and a reluctant Teddy Roosevelt for Vice-President; and finally the Democratic National Convention in Kansas City, Missouri, which again chose William Jennings Bryan.

Ickes' overriding concern with a candidate's character, especially his aggressive masculinity, rather than his policies or principles, is easily seen in his description of these campaigns. When a behind-the-scenes deal at the Republican State Convention delivered the party's nomination for governor to compromise candidate Richard Yates, Ickes was disgusted. In his eyes, Yates was "a weak, easy-going nonentity with few ideas, no real purpose and little charac-ter." During his speeches this "shoddy sentimentalist" would "ask his auditors to take their handkerchiefs from their pockets and wave them as he uttered some maudlin sentiment about some issue or na-tional party saint who had been dead and buried long enough to be a perfectly safe topic for discussion." At a gathering after the con-vention reporter Ickes put an embarrassing question to the nominee, who was greatly disturbed. Ickes comments: "Drawing me aside, he said with 'tears' in his voice: 'I hope you are not going to start in to hammer me.' He was as plaintive as a child . . . I formed an aversion for him that, while it softened somewhat as I grew older, never en-tirely disappeared."[17]

At a national level Ickes saw McKinley, who was assured of the Republican nomination, as a drab and uninspiring man, so different from Theodore Roosevelt, whose vivid, forceful personality and re-cent dramatic deeds made him the real center of attention at the convention. Because the bosses could not "handle" Roosevelt they got rid of him, as they thought, by making him Vice-President. But Roosevelt, young, aggressive, virile, had time on his side.

During the campaign that followed Ickes toured the West in the party of newsmen accompanying Republican strong man Mark Hanna. The purpose of Hanna's trip was to counter Democratic propaganda to the effect that he represented the money interests and little else. Although Ickes had no doubt that this was precisely what Hanna did represent, he nevertheless felt that Hanna had done well, talking to the people in a frank and straightforward way, unafraid to look men in the eyes. Ickes liked him, and came to the conclusion that he was not so much immoral as unmoral, frankly buying politi-cal support where he needed it.[18] The attractiveness of amorality in others was a legacy from childhood, when Ickes had chafed under the weight of his mother's strictures. But she had imposed her stan-dards too firmly for Ickes ever consciously to embrace amorality himself.

Although Ickes loved the work, his newspaper career was not to last long. After the *Record* was sold and the staff lost their jobs, he went to the *Chronicle* as a general reporter, but found that newspaper's political tone uncongenial. Briefly he was secretary of the Citizens' Association, the oldest reform organization in Chicago, charging itself with responsibility for checking extravagance, waste, and graft on the part of the public officials.[19] But he had become dissatisfied with his lot by the time John Harlan approached him and asked him to prepare the way for the attempt he planned to make to capture the Republican mayoral nomination in 1903.

While working on the *Record*, Ickes had become quite well acquainted with Harlan, whom he saw frequently and whose devoted follower he had remained. He accepted the offer with alacrity and, having rented an obscure office, began to build up a store of ammunition on political questions, particularly on the traction issue, which Harlan could eventually fire at his opponents. He also maintained his contacts with politicians at all levels of political life and continued to mix with the journalists who reported their activities.

The Republican boss who controlled Harlan's ward, and who initially agreed to back his candidature, was Fred Busse. But as the time for the campaign drew near Ickes became increasingly suspicious of Busse and finally concluded that he had withdrawn his support from Harlan, had in fact "betrayed" him by secretly switching his support to another contender. Eventually, Ickes was able to convince Harlan of this and to force a confrontation with Busse, an encounter which he described in familiar terms: "At first he [Busse] tried to bluff and hedge but finally, under pressure, he admitted the truth of what I had been telling Harlan. Instead of breaking him in two right then and there, as he could have done, Harlan stung him with a few verbal jabs and we contemptuously left the miserable creature cringing in the middle of the foyer."[20]

With the defection of Busse, which meant that Harlan would not even have the support of delegates from his own ward, Harlan decided that his attempt must be abandoned. But Ickes argued against such a decision. Should Harlan withdraw, the support which he had built up in 1897 would drain away, and he would be finished as a political force. Harlan could not win, Ickes conceded, but by a direct appeal to the voters he could mobilize sufficient public sentiment to establish himself as a man to be reckoned with in the future. Ickes' strong commitment to the cause of reform (not to mention his dependence on Harlan's continued political success) cannot be questioned, yet the satisfaction he achieved from fighting "for principle" against seemingly impossible odds would appear again and again in his political life. It was in line with his tendency to exaggerate the difficulties he faced in obtaining a college education and probably represented, in part, the playing out on a larger stage of his childhood role as a member of an embattled moral minority.

It was in this 1903 campaign that Ickes first revealed his talent as a politician for dedicated and efficient household management. He assembled a group of volunteers, ran campaign meetings, and handled publicity. Drawing on his newspaper experience, he arranged for advance copies of Harlan's speeches to be given to reporters before the speeches were delivered. Often he wrote the candidate's speeches himself. He worked from 9 A.M. until 11 or 12 at night, renting halls, organizing the printing and distribution of campagin literature, finding respectable citizens to sit on the platform at Harlan's meetings. Using the names on the petition that had called for Harlan's independent candidacy in 1897, he built up a rudimentary organization in some of the more promising wards. With characteristic thoroughness, he had made a card catalog of the names of these people while he was working secretly for Harlan so that he knew in which wards and precincts they resided. Understandably, Ickes found that this political campaign excited him and released his energies, though he could offer no real explanation for his dedication: "I showed in that campaign the same capacity that I demonstrated many times later of ability to work under great pressure for cruelly long hours at a stretch, day after day. It was my intense interest and my innate inability to give up that kept me going."[21]

For a time the campaign languished, but when Harlan, in a typically audacious move, decided to step up the number of meetings he was holding, support dramatically increased. Ickes saw this as a superbly heroic gesture by a man fighting for his political life. As crowds built up, the number of meetings was increased, until eventually the candidate was speaking six times a night. Ickes asserts that Harlan was deceived by this widespread and enthusiastic popular support into thinking that he could win the nomination. For his part, Ickes was satisfied that they had made a great fight, even though there was no realistic chance of success. When Harlan was eventually defeated by the Republican organization's candidate, Ickes was praised for his efforts. Harlan's brother, James, congratu-

lated him on his fine management of the campaign, and another political associate wrote that Ickes had played a near faultless game.[22]
Whatever the origins of Harold Ickes' political skills, they were undoubtedly considerable.

After that 1903 election Ickes decided to go to law school. He still
had no money, largely because he had been sending his sister Mary
to college, as well as repaying the debts that he had accumulated
during his own undergraduate career, but his deepening involvement with Anna meant that help was at hand.

Ickes' account of the events in his private life at this time appears
in his personal memoirs at a point when he was resuming after a
lapse of some three or four years in his dictation.[23] He recalls in a
rather prim and stilted fashion that he was at that time making his
home with Professor James Westfall Thompson and his wife. Anna
suggested that her mother might lend Ickes money to pay for his law
course, and in fact he borrowed sufficient funds from her at 5 percent interest. But what interests us here is the question of how this
situation had arisen. The circumstances in which Ickes had come to
live with the Thompsons were unusual to say the least, even when
one follows their gradual development.

Ickes certainly had been disappointed and piqued at Anna's marriage to Thompson, though hardly crushed. It is a blow to a young
man's ego when a young girl to whom he is attracted and who seems
to return that feeling chooses another. Ickes had consoled himself in
a tepid romance with Miss Lora Hieronymous, of whom he still
writes kindly, and to whom he was briefly engaged. His relief when
she decided that it was a mistake was quite conscious. He says that
his proposal was mainly a reaction to his disappointment over
Anna's marriage.

After the Thompsons returned from their honeymoon in Europe,
and after that first contact in the Hotel del Prado, Ickes continued to
see them formally and infrequently. They had moved into their new
house at 5747 Washington (now Blackstone) Avenue. Ickes writes
that the Thompsons' situation was not painful to him emotionally.
He had never been on intimate terms with Anna; they had not even
progressed to calling each other by their first names. Ickes says that
he had never liked Thompson, and that Thompson was unpopular
with the other men at the university. Not only was he arrogant and a

social climber (his true motivation for marrying the rich Miss Wilmarth, Ickes believed), but his masculinity was suspect, although Ickes finds it hard to say this outright. He comments unfavorably on the length of Thompson's hair on his return from Europe and muses over why it is that men dislike those of their fellows whose hair is long and why it is that artists and musicians are exempted from such negative feelings. Yet he says elsewhere that Thompson was regarded as a sissy and that men on the campus spoke of him in an unusual way.

In 1899, two years after the marriage, Anna gave birth to a baby boy, Wilmarth. Because of Ickes' affection for children this led to his visiting rather more frequently. Thompson already took little part in the daily life of the family, preferring to seclude himself in his study and pursue his work in history; the entertaining was left to Anna.

When the baby was about two years old (Ickes misdates this as 1899, though other sources agree that Wilmarth was *born* in 1899), the Thompsons asked Ickes to spend a weekend with them at the house of Anna's mother (who was abroad) at Lake Geneva. Although he considered them somewhat stilted and formidable, he accepted. During the weekend an incident occurred that some thirty years later still mystified Ickes. After the Thompsons retired on Sunday evening, Ickes sat up for another hour talking to his fellow guest, a beautiful young undergraduate called Lina Small. He insists that there were absolutely no romantic exchanges between them. But at breakfast the next morning—Ickes was returning early to Chicago on the businessmen's train—neither of the women appeared. James, who was rude to Ickes and made perfunctory excuses for Anna, made it clear that their sleep had been disturbed by Harold and Lina's talking on the porch the previous night. Ickes decided that if his hosts chose to be offended by such innocent behavior it was no concern of his, but the incident eventually proved to be crucial in sharply increasing the intimacy between Ickes and Anna, with all that it portended.

Not long after this, according to the personal memoirs, Ickes came down with a severe attack of appendicitis, which kept him in bed for several weeks in the fraternity house where he roomed with Stacy Mosser. Somehow Thompson heard about his illness and came in one day to see him with profuse expressions of friendship, quite at odds with the cold estrangement that had been initiated by the holiday weekend. He and Anna were desolated by Ickes' illness. He wanted to take him immediately to stay in their home, as if they had been the closest possible friends. Ickes politely refused, but Thompson left saying that when he was able to be about, he must come there to convalesce.

Courtesy prompted Ickes to call on the Thompsons after his recovery. James as usual was not in evidence, but Anna was very kind to him. Emboldened, Ickes asked her why she had taken offense at Lake Geneva. She claimed that Lina had told her the following morning that Ickes had importuned her to return to Chicago with him on the early train and had in general been very ardent. Anna and James both thought so highly of Ickes that they just could not bear to think that he had behaved in such a demeaning manner. These two overreactions—one of taking offense and the later one of excessive generosity—suggest an almost pathological possessiveness and need for dominance on Anna's part. Ickes, never the most perceptive of men where women were concerned, simply found them puzzling.

The next step toward greater involvement came, Ickes recalled, in early spring 1903. Thompson called at the fraternity house and asked Harold to come and stay with *him* for a few weeks while Anna and the child were away on holiday. Ickes was dumbfounded, and one cannot blame him. It is quite implausible that this cold and self-satisfied man would have generated such an idea for himself. Hindsight strongly suggests that Anna was initiating a long-term plan. Ickes demurred as long as he could but was persuaded in the name of forgiveness and understanding.

James was a cordial and hospitable host, but as the time for Anna's return approached, Harold announced that he would leave the day before she and her young son arrived. To his great surprise James then told him that Anna and he had reached the conclusion by correspondence that they wanted Harold to make his home with them until he should marry. This offer alarmed him because, he says, he placed too high a value on his independence to be prepared to surrender it in this fashion. But when he protested, James appeared very hurt and objected that Wilmarth loved Harold, also that both he (James) and Anna greatly admired him. Would he consent to stay at least for a short time after Anna returned? Of course, he acceded, and was lost. After Anna returned they both assailed him, and he finally gave up the struggle. He explains his surrender by protesting that his hard-boiled appearance actually conceals a great reluctance to hurt those of whom he is fond, and claims that Anna used what he refers to as the feminine tactic of suggesting that he wished to leave merely because he disliked his hosts.

Thus began a major episode in Ickes' life in which his self-righteousness almost destroyed him, and his future wife with him. He protests his rugged independence (as usual), believing that he yielded only from altruism, to avoid hurting someone whom he cared about. Yet the only hurt would have been to deprive them of his presence, and this shows an inflated estimation of the value to others of his companionship, affection, and loyalty. That is a common enough form of narcissism, but in Ickes' case it also prepared the ground for the flowering of his moral masochism, which eventually compelled him to continue year after year in a mutually destructive symbiotic relationship with Anna, unable to terminate it for fear (as he saw it) of a psychological catastrophe for her. Whether that image, which he maintained unshaken to the end, of himself as a blameless martyr to conscience and human decency was well-founded is a question that needs serious contemplation.

This flattering self-image enabled Ickes to persuade himself that by going to live with the Thompsons he was putting them under an obligation to him, by unselfishly making their lives happier, whereas the material aspects of the matter were in fact all in the other direction. His offer to pay for his food and lodgings was turned aside when James and Anna pointed out that there were unused rooms in the house and that they did not wish to be seen to be taking in a boarder. Furthermore, Ickes realized that what he could afford would not approach the value of what he was to receive.[24]

Thus, it was essentially a dependent relationship, rather like that of a distant, disadvantaged family member. Harking back to it in a later section of the memoirs, Ickes remarks that his decision to enter law school ensured his dependence on Anna and her mother, and reassured Anna that he would not leave 5747 Washington Avenue. Perhaps it was his perception of this that caused his memory to play him false later in trying to date these events while compiling his memoirs. We have seen that he unconsciously tried to push the date of the offending Lina Small incident at Lake Geneva back to 1899, although it occurred in 1901. The effect of that would be to increase the lapse of time between his washing his hands of the Thompsons forever and his entering their house as a nonpaying boarder.

There is a similar uneasiness about the exact date that he became a member of the household. If the foregoing account is correct, that James approached him early in the spring of 1903, when Anna and the baby Wilmarth were about to go on holiday, then presumably they would have returned and persuaded Harold to stay on perhaps in June or July 1903. Yet only a couple of months later, by September 1903, some serious trouble had developed between James and Anna, which, if not caused by, had at least come to focus on, Harold's presence in the house. On 19 September, James's younger brother, Wayne, who had also been living in the house but had left to take a position with the Western Electric Company in New York, wrote a dismayed letter in reply to one he had just received from his sister-in-law. Presumably James had got into a violent rage with Anna. Wayne says he had been afraid of what James might do, and concerned about his attitude toward Clair (as Harold was then known), for whom he professed a very high regard. Wayne insisted that, no matter how unpleasant matters became, she not allow Harold to leave. Harold would surely understand how things were between the couple and give Anna moral support and, should she require it (he obviously believed that she might), physical protection as well. Wayne lays great stress on the need for Harold to remain as her protector.[25]

Evidently Anna did confide in Harold about the trouble, because five days later Wayne was again replying to letters he had received from both. He suggested to Harold that were he to leave the house but remain in Chicago (unless he immediately married), scandalous speculation concerning the situation in the Thompson household might follow. Anna wished him to stay and would be in peril if he did not. As for James, since Anna owned the property and paid for its upkeep, there was nothing he could do. Moreover, Wayne asserted, James did not really wish Harold to leave.[26] Wayne's reasons for telling Harold this are a matter of speculation, but the reference to economic considerations carries more conviction.

An undated letter to James from Anna presumably related to the same contretemps. She writes that she cannot withdraw her friendship from Mr. Ickes nor stop caring, even though he may make her suffer some day. If James had withdrawn his friendship and loyalty from Harold, then it was only right that Harold should go from "his" house, but it seems plain that she did not expect James to take her up on this.[27]

Perhaps the period from June to September may have been sufficient for James to become restive about Harold's presence in the house and Anna's feelings for him, but one would think that the fuse for this explosion must have been smoldering for a long time. There is no reference whatever in the private memoirs to this episode, which plainly evoked powerful emotions at the time. Evidently the quarrel was patched up somehow, but its occurence and subsequent forgetting must make us cautious about accepting Ickes' later descriptions of the seemingly placid and civilized manner in which the trio continued to exist for some years after this. It may have been only right, as Anna suggested, for Ickes to leave what she politely called James' house, but that did not come about. He stayed on year after year until at long last it was Thompson who was displaced.

A related error in Ickes' memory might have tended to ease his consciousness of the interminable length of this occupancy and increase the gap between the earlier estrangement and the reconciliation. He says that the appendicitis which brought about the reconciliation prevented him from attending the state convention at which Charles Deneen was first a candidate for the Republican nomination for governor. That convention was held in 1904, and it is clear that Ickes was already resident in the Thompson house, following on his appendicitis, when he began his law school course in 1903. The illness that did prevent him from going to that convention was mastoiditis. In a later section of the memoirs he dates this as 1904, the year of the St. Louis Exposition, and he recalls the attendant circumstances with great bitterness. It was an acute mastoid infection, and the ear specialist Melville Hardie insisted on an immediate operation. Because of Ickes' aversion to hospitals, the operation was performed at home, that is, in the Thompson home. While Ickes was recovering, but still confined to bed, Anna came into his room one night, and a terrible argument ensued. Ickes, lying prone on the bed, tried hard to control his feelings, but before long blood began to gush from the wound behind his ear. It was some time before Dr. Hardie could be located and when he came it took him a couple of hours to stop the hemorrhage. Ickes felt that he could well have died without this expert care and, by his later account, would not have cared. Anna's cruelty in assailing him at such a time almost made him wish for the death that would constitute his own terrible revenge on her.[28]

Though Ickes says in his personal memoirs that he recounts this incident because it had an important bearing on his relation with Anna, he does not explain further. But if we entertain the possible interpretation of it as Anna's having inflicted (or reopened) a wound, and if we allow wounding its symbolic sexual connotation of emasculation, then this scene foreshadows Ickes' desperate struggle to preserve his self-image of masculinity and potency in his sexual relations with Anna, a struggle that would have profound implications for his political life.

Given what we already know of Ickes' personality, this relationship of dependent attachment was destined to become intensely ambivalent from the time he joined the Thompson household. In many ways it recapitulated his relationship with his mother, and that may well have been the reason he could not simply break away. Since his mother's death Ickes had been finding substitute mothers in the families of the friends of his adolescence—in Charlie Mosser's mother in Altoona and in Henry Adkinson's Aunt Sylvia in Chicago—and although Anna was only a year older than he, she belonged, as he was keenly aware, to a more powerful social class, was a dominant, morally judgmental woman, and was already a mother in her own right.

Although he had formerly been her suitor, his role was now an emasculated one. It was many months before the trio began calling each other by their first names. Wilmarth, however, always called him "Uncle Clair" and came to him to have the Sunday funnies read, to have his bumps kissed, and to be taken for walks. When the child went on holidays, he wrote affectionately to Ickes; in one letter, before sending his love to everyone and especially to Harold, he asked poignantly why his father did not answer his letters. (Later, Ickes would take the boy on holiday trips.)[29] James was never jealous of this, Ickes felt. They all lived peacefully together, with Anna and Harold retiring to the living room after the evening meal to play the victrola or talk impersonally, while James went to his study. Ickes says he was regarded as one of the family when friends of the Thompsons called, and that sometimes he, James, and Anna would go to the theater together and sometimes he and Anna would go alone.[30] James's frequent absences at academic conferences were not allowed to interrupt Harold's residence; he acted as if there could be no question of any relationship springing up between Ickes and Anna. This veneer of civilized placidity was retained pretty well uncracked for some four or five years, although by 1904, as we have seen, Ickes and Anna were already capable of vicious lover-type quarrels.

Having repressed the memory of the dispute between James and Anna in 1903, Ickes in his personal memoirs conveys the impression that only slowly did he become aware that there was tension between the two and that he was being used as a buffer, but that he had discovered this too late to do anything about it. Yet the correspondence referred to above proves that this is untrue; he had known these unpleasant facts since September 1903. Rather than becoming entangled by imperceptible degrees in a relationship from which he could not then escape, Ickes had (or so it would appear) attached himself to this conflict-ridden couple more or less in the expectation that they would eventually separate and he would be left with Anna. Was this selfless love or was there an economic motive? Ickes often must have been in agonies of indecision. He says that his sympathies sometimes ran in James's favor. Anna was quick-tempered with James and often seemed unfair, which echoes the disloyal thoughts that Ickes as an adult occasionally entertained about his mother's behavior toward his father and which colored his view of all his friends' marriages. When Anna spoke sharply to James, Harold would be depressed and embarrassed, yet these storm signals for his own possible future with her were obstinately ignored. (Perhaps it was her link with the image of his mother that caught him in this fatal attachment.) Whatever the cause, as far as his emotional rather than economic well-being was concerned, he had set his foot upon a slippery path; his self-destructive impulses were out of control. No wonder he could not later bear the thought that he had gone into the situation knowingly.

During these years, from 1903 to 1907 or 1908, Ickes was not only successfully pursuing his law course, but dramatically increasing his activity and effectiveness in politics, in sharp contrast and perhaps therefore in reaction to his dependent domestic position. Yet he always preferred to exert power from the background rather than set himself up as the front man, just as he would always strenuously deny that he possessed any personal political ambition or was interested in running for office. This prompts speculation that it was just this dividing line that he was inhibited from crossing by the underlying doubt of his male potency that we have had occasion to postulate, and of which there will be many further evidences in his married life with Anna.

We have seen that he boasted of his ability during Harlan's 1903 campaign to work under great pressure for many hours at a stretch, day after day, kept going by his "innate inability to give up." Whether or not he had taken up residence in the Thompsons' house during that campaign, he was certainly a satellite to the family and a courtesy uncle for the child of the woman he had hoped to make his wife. The emphasis on his driving political energy and growing power as the mastermind behind whatever campaign he undertook is a constant theme throughout the following years, and not unconnected to his strong commitment to the reformers' cause. But his "innate inability to give up" did not manifest itself in his domestic life—in entering the Thompson household he gave up his vaunted independence with hardly a struggle, and this demonstration of his inner vulnerability added to his need to attach himself as indispensable organizer to independent candidates of manifest strength and integrity, candidates who nobly rejected the encroachments of the established machines.

This suggestion is strengthened by the observation that Ickes' major motive in many of these campaigns seems to have been to act aggressively, rather than to fight for some particular reformist principle. We have seen this in the 1903 campaign, when Ickes, though certain that Harlan would lose, was satisfied that they had made a great fight. In Harlan's next campaign, this attitude was thrown into sharper relief.

In 1905 the Republican organization adopted John Harlan as its mayoral candidate, so that this time the only fight to be made was against his Democratic opponent, Judge Edward Dunne. The time appeared ripe for a favorable resolution of the traction question since the refusal of the traction interests to accept a new and more equitable ordinance had produced a ground swell of support for municipal ownership. Ickes discontinued his legal studies in the spring of 1905 to join Harlan's campaign ("A fight was, after all, a fight and I had not had a good one for a long stretch.") Yet Ickes makes it clear that although the Republican leaders had chosen Harlan, they had done so only to get rid of him forever. Hypocritically they pledged their support but, Ickes knew, would work for the candidate's defeat: "Harlan fell for their blandishments and called on me again to go down with him. I had no thought even of hesitating."[31] He urged Harlan to begin his campaign before his opponent, deliver a slashing speech on traction, and make the issue his own. But to his dismay Ickes found that Harlan's attitude toward the traction question had softened. His opening speech was a failure, and Dunne, by attacking the traction interests in a forthright manner, seized the initiative.

In the midst of this campaign, Ickes received word that his brother Felix was desperately ill with typhoid. Felix had assumed a false name and, without telling Harold, had gone to Nevada to prospect for gold. Since the campaign was nearing its climax Ickes decided that he could not go to Felix; Anna went instead, and after Felix had died she brought his body back to Chicago, whence Ickes took it to Altoona for burial. When he returned to Harlan's campaign headquarters a few days later, Ickes writes, he was profoundly depressed.[32]

Ickes' depression related to Harlan's prospects rather than to Felix's death. From what we know of it, Felix's history after Harold left Altoona in 1890 had been an unhappy one. Apart from the bullying he suffered at the hands of his older brother, it is clear from Jesse Ickes' letters to Harold that Felix was in some way disgraced in Altoona. He was sent to Chicago, where he was evidently under Harold's vague protection. Some time later he had gone on this ill-fated adventure. Nevertheless, the callous and unfeeling way in which Harold refers to his death and to his own "inability" to go to Felix when he was afflicted is striking. But it is not uncharacteristic. Ickes could never bring himself to express in his writings, political or personal, regret over the death of a close relative, even that of his mother. All his intimate relationships were very ambivalent, and the negative side of his feelings precluded any real experience of grief.

In any event, Harold informed Harlan that the campaign was in a very poor state. Harlan's response—that he would try even harder—won Ickes' admiration. Here was the courageous fighter, whom he had always loved to follow. Then came an important

break. At a public meeting Dunne evidently put his arm around notorious Democratic ward boss Mike "Hinky Dink" Kenna, remarking that Kenna was his friend, and paying tribute to his human
qualities. Ickes saw his chance and took it. When Harlan arrived at
campaign headquarters the following day, he was at work on a
speech that would change the whole character of the campaign. He
was denouncing Dunne with all the verbal force at his command for
throwing in his lot with this notorious ward boss. From then on
Ickes and Harlan dropped the traction issue entirely and tried to exploit the supposed connection between their opponent and Chicago's political underworld.

What is surprising is not that Ickes should have seized with such
alacrity a political opportunity which presented itself, but that he
could not see that, in having done so, he had casually jettisoned the
great question of principle on which he had sought to base his campaign: the issue of the public ownership of the city's transport systems. This is one of many instances of that fluidity in the content of
his ethical principles that we noted in Chapter 1. If, on the other
hand, Ickes really believed that the issue of principle was the question of corruption, rather than transportation, his attitude is equally
puzzling. For the sentiments toward the bosses that Dunne had in-
discreetly expressed in public were precisely those Ickes held in private. He, too, liked the bosses' human qualities. Either Ickes
maintained a rigid distinction between personal tastes and public
morality, or the new issue was largely a manufactured one. It is hard
to believe, in the light of his generally favorable remarks about
Dunne's character, that he really expected Dunne to ally himself
with Kenna, should he be elected; yet, even thirty years later, Ickes
could not see the discrepancy between the principle he espoused and
the practices he had adopted. Though Harlan again lost, Ickes took
pride in the fact that he had instigated the crucial change in tactics
that had allowed Harlan to take the offensive, as Ickes loved to see
him do.[33]

After the campaign Ickes' restless reforming energy, a counterpoint to his increasingly stressful situation in the Thompson
household, continued to manifest itself. He supported the city's
progressive school board, under attack for its enlightened educa-
tional policies. He became secretary of the Straphangers' League,
which agitated for improvements in the city's transport system. He

also helped to organize a campaign, eventually joined by the Teachers' Federation and other labor organizations, to force a referendum on a proposed traction ordinance.

Ickes had obtained his law degree cum laude in 1907 and, after a brief period with John Harlan's legal firm, had set up his own practice. But, as would always be the case, his purely legal work was subordinated to his political and social reforming activities. He gave priority to the settlement workers' calls for help and to assisting groups such as the Women's Trade Union League, as well as enlisting in an unending series of political campaigns. This pattern would continue. In 1913 he joined Donald Richberg and his father in a law firm, Richberg, Ickes and Richberg (later Richberg, Davies, Lord and Ickes); but Richberg, who left the firm in 1923, objected to being drawn into Ickes' unprofitable political and social activities. John S. Lord, another partner, has said that Ickes' heavy involvement in politics meant that his contribution to the firm was minimal. A brief perusal of his prodigious political correspondence during these years quickly confirms that this must have been so.[34]

Ickes was busily attempting to extend the web of his political influence. During 1907 and 1908 he wrote frequently to John Harlan's brother James, then chairman of the Interstate Commerce Commission, briefing him on the political situation in Chicago and Cook County, putting himself forward as a man who understood that situation and, as he hoped, bringing himself to the attention of Theodore Roosevelt and his likely successor, William Howard Taft. In May 1907 he told James Harlan that he had carried out his own investigation of the local political situation and the way in which it related to the national scene, discussing these matters with very important persons, whose names it would be imprudent to disclose. The Cook County Republican machine was opposed to Theodore Roosevelt and to any candidate whom he might favor in the coming presidential election. But if its bluff were called, an effective campaign could be organized for Taft or for some other candidate whom the public associated with Roosevelt. Such a fight would have to be vigorously waged, with Roosevelt involving himself heavily in it. The administration, Ickes remarked pointedly, must cease appointing to office men who, once the battle began, would be found in the ranks of its opponents.[35]

Ickes also helped organize a bipartisan conference, which met at

Peoria in 1910 to consider an agenda for political reform; there he delivered a speech on the initiative and recall. He supported the conferees' liberal stand on social issues and the demands for the direct election of senators and an end to political corruption. He later became a member of the "Committee of Seven," set up by the Conference to work for the adoption of its program, testimony to his growing reputation among the reformers.[36]

The following year he managed a campaign which he would always regard as a great personal triumph. This was the attempt by University of Chicago political science professor Charles E. Merriam to capture the Republican nomination for mayor. By Ickes' own account, it was he who persuaded Merriam to run. They had gone together as delegates to the Republican State Convention in 1910, and on the way back fell to discussing the mayoralty situation. Ickes suggested that Merriam oppose Fred Busse for the Republican nomination. Merriam, whom Ickes describes as "forceful and determined . . . capable and strong,"[37] finally agreed to do so on condition that no one else could be found to run and that Ickes manage his campaign. Ickes informed a group of potential financial backers that Merriam could be nominated, but not elected; independents within the Republican Party might achieve the former, but if they did the Republican machine would switch its support to the Democratic candidate rather than see an independent triumph. For Harold Ickes, the political pieces were falling nicely into place.

Shattering precedent, Ickes announced Merriam's candidacy well before it was customary to do so, which intrigued the press and amazed the politicians. Equally audacious was the decision to begin campaigning before Christmas for a primary election that would not be held until February. Still, the situation looked unpromising, recalling to Ickes those earlier campaigns which Harlan and he had begun in midwinter in half-empty halls. The same fighting spirit was in evidence now. Another similarity of course was that the cause could not ultimately succeed. Ickes refers to Charles E. Crane, one of Merriam's financial backers, as one of those rare people—a very rich man who was sufficiently public spirited to support a cause he knew to be hopeless.[38]

By now an experienced and highly skillful political manager, Ickes built up what he enthusiastically described as "the finest volunteer organization that has ever been knit together in Chicago—or anywhere else."[39] He used the Harlan team as a nucleus, bolstering it with young volunteers, some from the University. He handled publicity and ran the speakers' bureaus. The professional politicians, who had greeted Merriam's candidacy with derision, began to observe his progess with alarm. Mayor Fred Busse, the Republican incumbent, declined to stand against him, as Ickes had predicted, and the various warring factions were united only in their opposition to Ickes' candidate. As they dithered, popular enthusiasm for Merriam rose. More volunteers poured into headquarters, eagerly offering support. Some of the larger city newspapers declared for Merriam. This time, by contrast with the situation in earlier campaigns, there was no shortage of money; characteristically, Ickes is quick to say that it was run on the lines of strict economy and much more cheaply than any professional politician could have managed. The need for strict economy was always paramount with him.[40]

Merriam not only won the nomination, but he received a majority of all Republican votes cast. Ickes was exultant. "Chicago was stunned," he would later write. "The eyes of the professional politicians were bloodshot." Never before had there been "such a sweeping aside of the professional politicians of Chicago." As on earlier occasions, praise for Ickes' efforts followed. Senator James Hamilton Lewis, for example, wrote that, although he had never met Ickes, he greatly admired the way he had run Harlan's campaign and wanted to put on record his congratulations for a great piece of political strategy.[41]

This confirmation of his own powers and the public recognition of his enterprise and skill in politics must have been doubly sweet to Ickes because precisely at this time, 1910 and 1911, his involvement with Anna Wilmarth had reached a fever pitch of expectation and despair. In fact, all his increasing political involvement and ambition of the previous few years—his seeking in 1907 and 1908, for example, to extend his political influence to the presidential campaigns—gains an added psychological dimension when seen against the background of, and in part as a response to, his anomalous, invidious position in the Thompson household.

Ickes' sympathies in the Thompsons' marital discord may have at first been with James, who was not only a fellow male but had also started from a financially weak position. But it was not long before

Anna reversed the balance. One evening when she and Ickes had returned from the theater, James being away from Chicago, she began to tell him that she had been unhappy from the day she had married James. He had been not only inconsiderate but even brutal. Anna now believed that he had married her for her money, which would allow him to enjoy the sort of life he wished. During their quarrels he had sometimes struck her. Ickes writes that his sympathies were easily aroused by such disclosures because he had earlier been keenly aware of the suffering his father had inflicted upon his mother. Such a situation had always aroused his latent chivalry.[42] This last admission is precisely the sort of thing Ickes says about instances of disadvantaged minorities being deprived of their civil rights—the sort of cause that aroused his chivalrous instincts. We have seen that it was his father's treatment of his mother that first elicited Ickes' sympathy and indignation concerning the deprived and exploited. In trying to protect her from his father, he was in effect constituting himself a better and more just father figure, and there was to be more than a little of the benevolent father, promoting the healthy growth of those under his protection, in his civil-rights activities. It is not inconsistent with this interpretation if we foreshadow also a significant component of *maternal* protective attitude in him. He identified very strongly with his mother, and identification always includes an element of wishing to displace the identification figure and enact his or her role even more virtuously, as Harold had done in miniature over Sunday observance.

Although Ickes' commitment to civil rights and social justice remained a lifelong one, his feelings about the first exemplar, the apparently persecuted wife, underwent a profound reversal during the years with Anna. From now on, in most cases, it would not be very long before he came to blame wives for the greater part of their difficulties. After he and Anna finally married, he blamed her almost entirely for their marital problems, though in more judicious moments in his memoirs he offers a psychosocial explanation for her failings. These he felt originated in her relationship with her mother. Though a woman of culture and intellectual distinction Mrs. Wilmarth had, Ickes felt, been an unsatisfactory wife and mother, just as Anna proved to be. Neither could establish normally happy relations with their husband or children. He even blames Mrs. Wilmarth for her husband's alcoholism and early death. This last was pure speculation on Harold's part, and it was the kind of image that he held of an unusually high proportion of the marriages of his family and friends. It is easy to see it as a projection of his own attitude toward Anna.

Ickes writes, still contriving to forget the revelations of September 1903, that after Anna's disclosures of James's brutality, she and he developed a much more sympathetic and intimate relationship, but he implies that they did not become lovers, without actually disclaiming it. Early in 1905 James had proposed to take six months' leave in Paris, to pursue his historical studies. Both Ickes and Anna felt that Ickes should not continue to live in the house during this period for fear of gossip, but James and Mrs. Wilmarth pooh-poohed their anxieties. Ickes says that, as the time for James's departure approached, he and Anna realized that they were in love. The situation looked hopeless. Divorce was abhorrent to Anna, and Ickes recoiled from the thought. Yet, he says, it was only natural for him to want Anna to leave James. He had always believed it inexcusable—a species of prostitution no less—for a woman to continue giving her body to a man she no longer loved, just because it had become habitual or because she depended on him for economic security.

It becomes apparent that when Ickes says he wanted Anna to leave James, he does not mean that she should have set up a separate domicile; he simply means that he did not want her to live as James's wife, that is, to continue having sexual relations with him. Anna in fact went on having sexual relations with James right up to the time he sailed for Paris and did not seem to find it especially repugnant; nor of course was she economically dependent on him. The continued physical relationship between Ickes' own parents despite the fact of his father's infidelities, manifested in his mother's steady sequence of pregnancies, was one of the things that Ickes as a boy had found hard to accept. Oedipal feelings may not have been the sole ground of his moral preoccupation with this matter, but his arguments about Anna's position lack something in realism when he says that after James had departed he pressed Anna to agree that, even if they could never marry, she should at least promise never to be intimate with James again.

Why Anna should renounce her sexual relationship with James if she and Ickes were *never* to marry is not compellingly clear. She disputed the issue, saying that her New England conscience dictated that she should fulfill all the duties of a wife. In the face of Ickes' pressure, however, she promised that she would never submit to James again if she could possibly avoid it, and Ickes says confidently that she never did.

That summer of 1905 Anna, Wilmarth, and the nurse sailed to join James in Paris. Ickes spent a miserable August wondering whether James would demand his rights as a husband, which Anna would feel it wrong to deny. He developed insomnia, from which he was to suffer for the rest of his life, becoming dependent to some extent on sleeping drafts. As it turned out, he had no cause to worry. James's masculinity, Ickes says, was weaker than either of them expected. Though initially surprised, he acceded calmly to Anna's request, and indeed seemed more content with their new relationship.

After Anna's return Ickes protested to her that he was living in an impossible situation—sharing a house with the woman he loved and her husband. Anna sympathized and promised that if he would endure it for just two more years (from 1905), she would then divorce James. But the two years passed, then three and four, and she still made excuses, partly on the ground that a medium had told her that James would soon die. (As he dictated these memoirs in 1938, Ickes reflected that Anna was dead and James was teaching history at the University of California.)

During these years Anna had become very active with outside interests. She held office in various clubs or societies of a middle-class feminist or charitable nature, such as the Fortnightly, the Young Fortnightly, the Women's City Club, and the Chicago Women's Club. One which played a special role in their personal affairs was the Home for the Friendless, of which Anna was a member of the board of directors. Ickes reports that one day, probably about 1907, she brought home a young girl of eleven or twelve years of age named Helen S——, a pretty girl with lovely blonde hair, as he describes her, who had been left at the institution for a short period until her mother could afford to take her home again. Anna had a penchant for taking people into her home and under her protection and governance. In addition to Ickes, James's brother Wayne, prior to 1903, and Anna's first cousin Tom Gilmore spent several years as members of the household (Gilmore's stay extending after the Ickes' marriage); now it was Helen S—— and, some years later, an orphaned child, Robert. But Helen was to prove crucial in rearranging the family structure. After a few days, Anna decided that she wanted to keep the child for good; despite James' and Harold's doubts and reservations she did so, although the question of adoption was put off for the time being.

Alongside Ickes' political reformist activities, he was engaged during these years in various struggles for social justice, and the consciousness of disinterested altruism must have helped him endure the unpleasant emotions at home. Among other things, he enlisted in campaigns against juvenile delinquency and child labor and supported plans for school reform. In 1907 he assisted in the formation of the Women's Trade Union League and from that time became its legal adviser. In this capacity he was instrumental in securing the passage of the Ten-Hour Law in Illinois. In 1909, when Chicago clothing workers conducted their historic strike against Hart, Schaffner and Marx, Harold Ickes as well as Anna joined the representatives of the Women's Trade Union League and others who supported the strikers, taking up again the cause of underpaid and overworked women. He also defended Ellen Gates Starr, co-founder of Hull House, against legal charges arising out of the strike.[43]

But, as we have foreshadowed, persecution of the weak stirred him particularly. He was outraged over an incident, reported to him by Anna's maid, which occurred in 1908 on the street outside his fraternity house. A Jewish peddler had knocked at the door of the house; it opened, the man was drenched with water, and the door had been closed. Whereupon, Ickes pointed out in his letter of complaint, members of the fraternity had laughed at the unfortunate victim from the windows. The action, he declared, amounted to Jew-baiting and was especially deserving of contempt since it exploited weakness in the interests of fun.[44]

The Averbuch case was much more dramatic. Lazarus Averbuch was a young Russian Jew, who at the time of his death had been in the United States just three months. Early in 1908 he was shot dead at the home of the Chicago Commissioner of Police. First press reports of this sensational incident stated that Averbuch was an anarchist, an especially damaging charge in a city that still recalled the Haymarket bombings of two decades earlier. Police were said to have discovered anarchist literature in the small room Averbuch shared with his sister, and this helped to establish the motive for what was assumed to have been an assassination attempt. Mounting anger among Jewish residents of the slums surrounding Hull House, along with the fear that this might lead to violent clashes with the police and even to another anarchist scare, induced Jane Addams to summon a conference of reformers at Hull House to discuss what might be done.

None of the eminent lawyers present would agree to act for the dead man's sister, who was determined to clear her brother's name. One, who had been junior counsel in the trial of an anarchist, reported that he had spent years attempting to rehabilitate himself professionally. Though barely a year out of law school, Ickes agreed to take the case.

If he knew little about the law, Harold Ickes knew a great deal about the way the city of Chicago worked. Secretly he obtained a permit to disinter the body and arranged for leading specialists to perform a second autopsy. During their examination of the body the doctors made the sensational discovery that the Chicago police had permitted Averbuch's brain to be removed and sent to a medical center for scientific study. With the inquest a few weeks away, Ickes went to see the city coroner. He asked the man whether he was prepared to allow the police to raise the issue of Averbuch's supposed anarchist beliefs; when the coroner said that he was, Ickes threatened to reveal what had happened to the dead man's brain. The coroner blanched and asked Ickes piteously whether he was trying to defeat him for reelection.[45] As a result of Ickes' intervention, no attempt was made at the inquest to show that Averbuch had been an anarchist, though Ickes could not prevent a verdict that the Commissioner had fired in self-defense.

In a speech that he made in Chicago in 1937 on the subject of Roosevelt's plan to reorganize the federal judiciary, Ickes declared:

> I am and always have been deeply concerned about personal liberty . . . Nor have I merely given lip service to these ideals. My small law office in Chicago would experience its greatest thrill when Jane Addams would telephone us from Hull House . . . that some poor devil was in trouble.
>
> Without boasting I can truthfully say that whenever a case involv-

ing civil liberties was brought to my attention I never refused it because of any demands of private practice.[46]

There is no reason to doubt the accuracy of these remarks.

Yet the case of the Jewish peddler and that of Averbuch, coming as they did from the period in Ickes' life when, waiting for Anna to make up her mind about divorcing James, he was in mental torment and suffering agonies of indecision, suggest a link between his personal circumstances and his public behavior. The incidents referred to above were inhumane and contemptible, the more so to a dedicated reformer like Ickes, but not everyone who shared that opinion was prepared to risk his legal career by defending "anarchists," as Ickes was prepared to do in the Averbuch case. Not only was there danger of guilt by association, but Ickes also acted without prospect of financial reward. Yet he was certainly not indifferent to material concerns. Years later, when he fell out with his law partner Donald Richberg over a matter of the fair division of fees for work, Ickes recited in a long and passionate letter the most intricate details of a series of previous obligations, denying all the time that he would bother to cast up accounts of such mercenary aspects of his dealings with his friends.[47] We have already noted Ickes' rooted aversion to bullying and brutality, and some of the factors that lay behind his response; but some of the motivation of his indignant intervention on behalf of the two persecuted Jews may have come from his fellow-feeling. He, too, was an indigent outsider in one of the homes of the rich, and certainly felt that he was not getting his rights and privileges. Anna, he agrees, also was having a bad time, but it lay within her power to end this unnatural and personally destructive situation. However, the crisis finally arrived.

At some time before she brought Helen S—— home Anna had moved out of James's bedroom to a small one some distance away at the back of the house. The pubescent Helen was installed in a bedroom, formerly young Wilmarth's, opening onto a bathroom which in turn opened onto James's room. One evening early in 1909 Harold arrived home to find Anna in a highly agitated state. During the day Helen had reported to her that James had entered her room the previous night, drawn the covers from her bed, and placed his hand between her thighs. When she awakened, he quickly returned to his own room.[48]

Anna felt some self-reproach. If she had been sleeping with James this would not have happened; her self-reproaches, however, were concerned not with James's deprived state but only with Helen's being exposed to risk. Neither she nor Ickes believed that the girl was in any danger of being sexually assaulted by James, whom they believed deficient in physical passion. Nevertheless, this act became the exciting cause of the divorce. Ickes persuaded Anna to brief his friend James Harlan, who, he says, expressed great indignation when Anna told him about her husband's indiscretion. James and his lawyer, Clarence A. Burley, put up a posture of defense, but when Harlan threatened more serious charges against James, involving Helen, they resisted no longer and the bill was drawn on the grounds of cruelty. Harlan managed to have the case brought on at a time when the court was almost empty and the reporters had gone. The decree was granted and a carefully prepared announcement was given to the newspapers.

Ickes says that even before the divorce was finalized it was understood that Anna and he would marry, but there was an interim period of some two years, largely because of Anna's conflict of feelings over the fact of divorce, and because of her concern for appearances. He says that Anna regretted the necessity for divorce, which was entirely contrary to her upbringing, and was self-conscious about it for a long time. They both believed that when they did marry, people would assume that their relationship was the real reason for the divorce, and that the longer they waited the less this would be so. Ickes had moved out of the house before the divorce took place, and as soon as she could make arrangements Anna sold that property, 5747 Washington Avenue, and moved into a house that she had had built at Evanston. She lived there until after they were married, on September 16, 1911, and until their new house at Hubbard Woods was completed, in 1916. In the period between the divorce and remarriage, Ickes lived mainly in the University Club, and, although he visited Anna at Evanston two or three times a week, he claims he rarely stayed for meals and never remained overnight.

Along with this awkward preservation of respectability, powerful intrinsic tensions were developing between the two. Ickes had begun to realize that Anna was exacting and used to having her own way, whereas he had the conventional idea that a woman should be submissive unless the man behaved unreasonably. This last profession sits very strangely alongside his sympathy with his mother's mal-treatment by his father and his conscious embracing of minority rights and the in-principle equality of all kinds and conditions of men and women. It shows how profoundly difficult it is for a man brought up in any rigid morality that condemns the lusts of the flesh, especially the sexual ones, to overcome the alienation between the sexes and to relate to women in a simply personal rather than preconceived sexist way. In Ickes the attitude derived from the neg-ative side of his relationship with his mother. We have seen that he had a sneaking sympathy with his father, thoughtless and unfaithful though he may have been, because Harold's mother constantly held her husband up as an awful example of moral failing. When he wishes that instead of being so censorious his mother might have been "just a bit more of a good fellow," the gender of the laudatory image is not accidental. He did tend to see women as being severe moral critics almost by nature. In later years he advised Clinton Hazard, the despondent husband of Ickes' stormy yet highly moral younger sister, Julia, to go out and get drunk, even flirt with other women—a cliché male chauvinist image of the right way to protect oneself from a wife who is exacting rather than sweetly submissive.[49]

For a man of Ickes' personality, the relation between the sexes is likely to become a fierce struggle because he projects into it the in-ternal conflict between his masculine and feminine tendencies, the former stereotyped as dominance and the latter as submission. Cas-tration-anxiety heavily reinforces masculinity as against femininity, but the latter remains as a constant temptation. To be dominated by anyone, but especially by women, is felt as emasculation and as ex-posing one to ridicule. The same internal conflict can be activated also in competition with men, which partly explains Ickes' quarrel-some behavior with his political colleagues. But it reaches its great-est bitterness with women because of the disillusioning contrast between the initial romantic overidealization of the loved one and the everyday actuality of clashes of interest, experienced as betrayal.

That ancient conflict was viciously acted out in Ickes' relations with Anna. Though there were personality problems on both sides, it is difficult to avoid the suspicion that at this stage of his life, a stage at which his sexual relations had subsisted in a world of con-vention, stereotype, and fantasy, hardly at all in physical intimacy, Ickes was unconsciously prepared to see any wife as an enemy of his own personal development. In one significant passage in his personal memoirs dealing with their quarrels in the interregnum period, the reasons he finally settles on for having persevered with the marriage plans hardly offer a promising prospect for a happy marriage. Their violent arguments had occurred too often and, although usually smoothed over, should have warned them against marriage. Nevertheless, he says, he and Anna were sincere in their devotion to each other and felt that their destinies were linked. Harold felt a particular obligation to marry Anna, so long as she wished it, and believed that it would be dishonorable to refuse. Given a similar situation, he would do the same again, even with the knowledge of the long years of torment and unhappiness that the marriage had brought.[50]

One wonders what the concept of sincere devotion refers to here. When Ickes says that even now he would *knowingly* enter into years of misery in the same circumstances, it appears that the devotion was no more than his sense of duty, of being nobly but hopelessly committed. Such moral responsibility regrettably brings moral sadism inevitably in its train, and Anna was to feel the lash of this many times in the years to come.

Yet other powerful factors held Ickes close to Anna during the period between her divorce and their marriage. After all, in other spheres of life he had demonstrated an ability to change course and to rationalize behavior that to others might seem unscrupulous as being justified in the long run by some morally sound outcome. The fact that he had moved out of her house before the divorce and was acting the role of a respectable family friend could have opened the way for a decent termination of their relationship. But, on the one hand, Anna was part of that circle of high-minded, public-spirited, and wealthy women with whom so much of his professional life was now bound up, and, on the other, there must have been a powerful sexual attraction between them. He claims that after they were married the reconciliations that followed their quarrels were accompanied by physical transports almost beyond the bounds of nature. Yet he was now being denied any physical intimacy because of her concern for appearances.

Positive feeling for Anna is demonstrated in letters from Ickes to another of James's young brothers, Maurice, and to Anna's mother. To the former he complains that Maurice and his wife, Betty, had written hasty, angry letters to Anna, condemning her without a hearing. Harold claims the status of a brother to Maurice (presumably because Maurice had been Anna's brother-in-law, and Harold was to marry Anna), and argues that as his brother Maurice is under a special obligation to believe that he had acted solely out of a sense of duty.[51] To Mrs. Wilmarth he writes that he was shocked and disappointed to hear indirectly that she had in conversation expressed opinions favorable to James, saying that Anna was at fault in the divorce because she had an ungovernable temper and had rebelliously resisted her mother's attempts to control her. (Harold himself held exactly the same opinions of Anna.) The letter goes on to say that Anna had behaved with appropriate dignity in the whole matter and, because she had refused publicly to vilify James, had been subjected to unfair criticism when she might easily have won general sympathy.[52]

In view of all this strain and frustration, it is easy to understand the passionate energy with which Ickes threw himself into the Merriam mayoralty campaign and the pleasure he got from his personal success in it. He had initiated the whole thing, even to selecting Merriam as candidate and inciting him to run. He congratulates himself on having been "the spider at the center of the web" and the "dynamo running the machine."[53] His energies were here fully released, free from ruminations and self-doubt. One component of the fascination politics held for him is again revealed in his account of a trip that he took to New York early in 1911 for a break of a few days in preparing Merriam's run up to the finals, after the grand success in the primaries. Three old friends Democratic Irish political bosses Sullivan, Hopkins, and Brennan—were on the train. Their official nominee was Carter Harrison, but they soon had Ickes in their drawing room, telling him just how they would try to defeat Harrison, whom they actually detested, if they were in Ickes' position.

Until late at night in that drawing room, opaque with heavy cigar smoke, the sole topic was how, expertly but completely, to dissect the political carcass of Carter Harrison so that it could never be articulated again. It seemed to do Roger Sullivan's "regular" soul some good to insist from time to time that as the party nominee "he was for Harrison." Never once did he blink an eye. Then Hopkins and Brennan would chorus: "You goddamned fool, of course you aren't for Harrison, and neither are we." Roger would reiterate that he was, but all of the time the trio kept searching their brains for political wisdom to put into my hands, knowing full well that it was my job to win with Merriam if I could.

This vision of people going straight for what they wanted without being hagridden by moral scruples must have had a powerful attraction for Harold Ickes at this time, though to abandon principle in favor of conscious amorality was not a possible option for him. Politicians who appeared strong and decisive were always likely to win his regard, and some of his deepest disillusionment with Franklin D. Roosevelt would come when Roosevelt appeared to him to be vacillating and unwilling to act.

The next paragraph reveals a simpler, more immediate yearning. Ickes for a great part of his life found it difficult to have an easy, relaxed relationship with women, apart from clear-cut mother or daughter figures, sufficiently removed from him in age. In fact he did not manage to do so until after he had come to a position of power in Washington. In 1911 the insecurity and tension in his relation to Anna were at their height, so he found another reason to envy his companions on the train.

> These three big Irishmen interested me hugely. They were going off on a lark, as they often did, just their three selves. They would take luxurious quarters at the Waldorf Astoria Hotel and live off the fat of the land. They would go to the theater. They would spend long and late hours in their common sitting room "goddamning" each other through the smoke emitted from their own cigars. To hear them talk one would have thought that they were hereditary feudists. The fact was that they had so sentimental a feeling for each other that they felt called upon to shout insulting names and swear like pirates, in the belief that thus they could dissimulate their warm mutual affection. Any one of these men would have gone to the stake for either of the other two.[54]

This image of warm uncomplicated male affection struck an answering chord in Ickes' heart. But of course it is an unrealistic image. To call such a warm current of feeling "homosexual" is not for a moment to accuse Harold Ickes of unconventional practices.

We have seen enough of his furious indignation over bodily liberties by other males to realize that any thought of the physical expression of male affection would be absolutely repellent to him. Yet though such affections may have become entirely divorced from any bodily aim, they still provide almost as fertile a breeding ground for jealousy and possessiveness as heterosexual ones do, and we shall find evidence later on for their effect on Ickes' political relationships, especially with the men around Franklin D. Roosevelt.

In fact jealousy and possessiveness seem not far way in the Merriam mayoral campaign. Ickes wanted Merriam to go it alone with just himself and the volunteer organization he had built up. He distrusted the regular Republican machine. But by the time Ickes returned from his trip to New York, Merriam had decided to move into the Republican camp. Ickes continued as his manager and tried to take the move with a good grace, but found it hard to keep his hackles down, for example, with one Roy O. West.

> He had come back from Europe full of sweetness and light, perfectly delighted that Merriam (his candidate!) had won and oh, so eager, to help elect him. I pretended to accept West's proffers of aid at face value . . . He made himself quite at home in my private office, walking into it or through it without so much as "by your leave." He was completely "one of us." He was earnestly trying to create the impression that he and Merriam and I constituted a mutually trusting triumvirate that would win in April and make Chicago a second Garden of Eden—without himself offering the apple.[55]

Who is Adam and who Eve in this metaphor is not clear.

Tension continued to develop, and although, when Merriam was defeated, Ickes blamed the regular Republicans, Merriam and some members of his organization felt that Ickes' intransigence had contributed to the result. He says that for personal reasons he no longer wished to lead the eager band of reformers whom he had organized to help with Merriam's campaign (his marriage to Anna was now arranged) but also acknowledges a general feeling that he ought to be replaced.[56] Ickes may have unconsciously promoted Merriam's defeat precisely because he had lost control of this attractive candidate.

Over and above the stress of personal relationships, Ickes' attitudes and actions during these early years must have been significantly affected by the whole political and social context in which he was operating. As a young man in Chicago he had been caught up in the rising tide of municipal protest and carried into the ranks of the urban reformers. With them, from that time, he campaigned for political rejuvenation and fought for social justice. Through such struggles he had become an associate of the leaders of the reform community in Chicago, of Victor Lawson, the crusading press owner, for whose newspaper Ickes had gone to work, of Jane Addams and Ellen Gates Starr, the founders of Hull House settlement, of Mary Hawes Wilmarth, Anna's mother, a philanthropist and pioneer of the women's rights movement in the city, of Raymond Robins, the former settlement leader, who would be involved with Ickes in countless projects for social and political betterment.

Ickes absorbed the perspectives of these civic leaders, acquiring their resentment at the hapless condition of the immigrant poor and the oppression of women and children who worked in the city's sweatshops. He learned of cases of official discrimination because reformers like Jane Addams referred them to him, this blunt but sympathetic and apparently fearless lawyer who would take unpopular cases. He quickly came to share the reformers' determination to weed out the corruption and graft that shamed the city and frustrated plans for social improvement.

Ickes' inveterate reforming activity over these years cannot be seen merely or even mainly as an attempt on his part to work out, through political and social activities, certain frustrations and desires embedded within his admittedly complex personality, even though they help to explain why he responded with such fervor to the reformers' cause. The objective conditions of urban life presented a challenge to which many would respond. The wretched state of Chicago's poor could not be ignored. The political abuses so relentlessly opposed by Ickes were not a figment of the reformers' imagination. The bosses' empires did rest on graft. Electoral practices were corrupt. The alliance between big business and the city machines was real, and the people suffered from it. The city that Ickes and others would try for so long to improve was the product of rapid and chaotic growth and bewildering demographic change. It was the city of traction magnates Charles T. Yerkes and Samuel Insull, of the political boss Big Bill Thompson and the gangster Al Capone. In responding to its challenges Harold Ickes was not chasing shadows.

Elements of social ambition are bound up in the story. Ickes' seeming compulsion to set things right may not have been unrelated to the fact that he was, or became, an urban-based professional, whose contacts with the reformers brought him a degree of professional fulfillment and social prominence that he otherwise might not have achieved, and enabled him to shake free of the disadvantages of his early poverty, to which he had been so sensitive. By 1916 the poor boy from Altoona, who had been forced into a humiliating dependence on ungracious relatives and who carried about with him a keen sense of social inferiority, would be entertaining Theodore Roosevelt in his spacious and beautiful home.

But if the general nature of Harold Ickes' commitment to political and social reform sprang from the parlous state of urban life, from his association with the early Chicago Progressives, from the social advantages that such activities could confer, as well as more distantly from the strict moral training he had received as a child, its special fervor gained something from less obvious factors. His detestation of exploitation and of bullying in all its forms, whether by individuals, political groupings, or (later) nation-states, had originally been inspired by immediate personal experience in his formative years, in the physical intimidation of himself and Felix by the older brother John and in his father's callous treatment of his mother. The need to supersede and excel his own parents in the parental role, a need that was unusually strong in Ickes' case because of his specially intense relationship with his mother, similarly encouraged him to seize in later life the chance to act as protective parent to any oppressed minority. But a corollary of that need was his inability happily to cooperate with another competing parent-figure, and this, together with the acute sensitivity to any challenge to his competence and authority, led him into those highly charged contests with his colleagues that would characterize his career.

Ickes' experiences in Chicago had left their mark. The humiliation of having to accept the grudging and niggardly charity of relations after his mother's death, a dependency continued at a more subtle psychological level in his position in the Thompson household, gave him a firsthand acquaintance with the feelings of indigent and despised minority groups and strengthened his desire, as a reformer, to help them. The prolonged period of emotional stress in his relationship with Anna, the feeling of being symbolically unsexed with regard to her, and the actual financial obligations accentuating his questioning of his own masculinity provoked in reaction a great outpouring of vigor as he joined the Chicago Progressives in attacking the politically corrupt and protecting the weak against the vicious exploiter. But all this is not to accuse Harold Ickes of pursuing only paranoid fantasies. The corruption and injustices against which he set himself were real.

News that James Thompson had remarried finally brought an end to Anna's delays and indecision. Now she said positively that she and Harold could wed. He knew it was a mistake but did not hesitate, feeling that he loved Anna and that it was too late to change his mind.[57] Again we are driven to speculate about possible hidden motives, perhaps of a more pragmatic character, underlying the conscious professions of love and his conviction that it was too late to turn aside. They were married at Lake Geneva, on 16 September 1911, and a month later sailed for Europe.

THREE

Locust Years

IT WAS AN ODD wedding party that set off on the honeymoon trip: Anna and Harold, Helen, Wilmarth, and the children's nurse, Ida Erisman. Ickes, always a poor sailor, spent most of the passage in his berth prostrate with seasickness. One day Anna came into their cabin in a high temper and announced that she was pregnant. Thirty years later he still misunderstood the ground of her complaint. She believed that people would now conclude that they had had to marry because she was pregnant; he thought she was upset because it would be assumed that they had married so that they could have sexual intercourse.

Even when later in her pregnancy Anna conjured up the fear that she would have a seven-months baby—a surprisingly common if groundless foreboding among newly married women—Ickes still did not realize that she disliked the idea that her marriage would be regarded as a shotgun affair; he now thought it was just that she did not want people to think that they had had sexual intercourse before the marriage. He sardonically reassured her (or claims he did) that none of her acquaintances could ever believe her capable of giving in to such a human weakness. Whether he delivered that acid remark or not, his obtuseness about the focus of her anxiety argues a certain lack of sympathy and a readiness to misunderstand.

Anna's pregnancy spoiled the wedding trip. She did not want the child at that stage, and he resented her attitude. They landed in New York between Christmas and New Year 1911 and went back to the house at Evanston. Here the months of Anna's pregnancy passed. She continued to rage at him, and he resolved never to have another child by her if he could avoid it. However, he felt that in his overt behavior toward her he managed to hold onto himself exceptionally well. He described the period as a hellish one for them both, but believed it to be a hell of her making. The actual childbirth was a trauma for Ickes because Anna insisted that he be present while the baby was being delivered. She was adamant, he says, that he must see what agony she had to suffer because of his self-indulgence. This he put down to Anna's desire to be dominant, even during childbirth.

It is hard to know to what extent the sentiments Ickes attributes to Anna are a rephrasing of things that she actually said, and to what extent he is projecting onto her an image of martyred self-righteousness deriving from his own mother. One passage, given as a direct quote from Anna, stands out as a highlight of human feeling against this background of vindictiveness. Unexpectedly, when Anna was in her greatest pain, she faintly but sincerely told Harold that he had been wonderfully good to her during her pregnancy and she, by contrast, had been impossible, that she appreciated all that he had done and would try to repay him.[1]

Raymond was born on 12 June 1912. Ickes notes that the Republican National Convention had just broken up in great discord and the Progressive Party was coming into being at Orchestra Hall, but his feeling of duty, as well as his fear of her, kept him at home with Anna. He writes that something deep inside him was affected when the child was born, but he was not sufficiently introspective to be able to say what this effect was. Whatever it was, it allowed his energy to flow more confidently into political affairs.

During the first half of 1912, while Anna was still pregnant, Ickes had withdrawn from active political life.[2] But in the latter part of that year, after Raymond's birth and that of the Progressive Party (a happy coincidence), Ickes was back in the fray, more vigorous and confident than ever. He asserts that the dismal performance of the reform group's candidates in two recent electoral contests (in which he had declined to take part) led to a reappraisal of his own role in the Merriam campaign and to a corresponding rise in his standing within the group. Perhaps also this renewal of vigorous political activity reflected a new surge of faith in his masculine strength, inspired by the birth of his first child, a son.

The Progressive Party campaign of 1912 was perfect for Ickes in all ways. The party's national candidate, Theodore Roosevelt, was dynamic, courageous, and uncompromising. He embodied, it seemed to Ickes, the principles for which he had so long fought. Having dramatically defected from the regular Republican organization, Roosevelt now faced momentous odds. In recalling the events of those times in his political memoirs, Ickes recaptures the sense of excitement and enthusiasm that he felt. It was only natural that he should give his all in this new fight. He actually called Roosevelt the lady of his dreams—political dreams in this case—for whom he had waited for so long, extravagant and inappropriate imagery that accords well with our suggestion that politics was for him in part a substitute sexual activity, one in which he felt more confident than in the actual physical encounter.[3] It was a kind of imagery which sprang readily to his pen. For example, when the regular Republicans wanted to keep candidate Charles Evans Hughes from contact with the Progressives during the 1916 campaign, Ickes observed caustically that Hughes had not only had breakfast, lunch, and dinner with the Republicans but that he had almost slept with them as well. Ickes hoped that his whiskery chin would defend him in that event.[4]

There is no doubt of the strength of his commitment to this major movement in 1912 for political and social reform. Along with the other Progressives he saw this campaign as meeting the hopes of the people for a better life. For Ickes it was a profound spiritual rather than merely a political event, and he threw himself into it with total enthusiasm.[5]

Supplanting the ineffectual John Bass as Cook County chairman of the newly formed Progressive Party, Ickes ran a brilliant campaign. Again he was in complete control, and again he scored impressive successes. His organization carried Cook County both for Theodore Roosevelt and for the Party's candidate for state governor, though neither won downstate, where they might have been expected to be stronger. In addition, Cook County Progressives elected several local and county officials and a sufficient number of members to the lower house at Springfield to give them the balance of power there. Ickes wrote New York Progressive Amos Pinchot that the Merriam campaign and other independent campaigns had had much to do with the successes in Cook County, where people had been educated in progressive principles. Cook County possessed an established Progressive leadership, and the organization that Ickes had created for Merriam had again performed effectively. In all these matters, Pinchot was being told indirectly, Ickes had played a prominent part.[6]

There was much to these claims. By the close of the 1912 campaign Ickes had amply demonstrated that he was a tenacious and highly capable political organizer, even if his reluctance to share power meant that he was often embroiled in controversy. Many others shared Ickes' own opinion of his abilities. In the wake of the Progressive Party's eventual defeat in 1912, Raymond Robins, his friend and fellow reformer, told him that he was the most courageous, dependable, and gifted man with whom, in his many religious and political ventures, he had ever worked. Although Ickes had won few of the political struggles in which he had been engaged, he had fought for high principles and worthy goals; recognition must soon follow, Robins felt. Had the Progressives won the previous year, Robins would have done all he could to secure for Ickes a place in the new administration.[7]

If the birth of his son had given Ickes renewed confidence in his masculinity, evidently his sexual relationship with Anna during the next year or so also gave him no cause for self-doubt, despite his continuing wariness of her. Though they quarreled, their reconciliations were impressive. Ickes speculates that there seemed to be a sexual dimension to their fierce arguments and that the physical acts of love that followed their reconciliations were matched by extraordinary transports of joy. At such times they would vow never to fight again.

But the quarrels became more frequent and intense and the reconciliations less so. Ickes attributes to Anna a technique of working herself into hysterics until eventually she would become incoherent with rage. For years these states would reduce him to complete self-abasement. He was in a classic double-bind situation, faced with competing demands from Anna, each demand making the satisfaction of the other impossible. He used to tell her that she wanted only a pocket edition of a man—a lapman, not a real one—but she kept on insisting that she needed a man able to dominate her. He tried to do this, but she was too strong for him. If he took the other course and became submissive and subservient, something inside him would eventually cause him to rebel. No matter what he did, he was a failure.[8] He felt, too, that she seized control of his firstborn. He asserts that he had no say in the child's upbringing, yet at the same time complains that Anna was too busy with outside affairs to do the physical work of child care and devote to Raymond the time a baby needed. The child was brought up by nurses.

In later years, when journalists tried to make copy of the apparent divergence between Anna's and her husband's political alignments, Anna was to claim that politically she had always been an Independent Republican, and that as early as 1912 she had participated with him in the organization of the Progressive wing of the Republican Party in Illinois. If this is so, Ickes makes no mention of it in his memoirs, when he writes of her outside interests during the early years of their marriage. He prefers to concentrate upon incidents that seemed to reveal an underlying resentment of Anna's managerial style on the part of her fellow clubwomen. She became first an officer and then president of the Young Fortnightly, an intellectual and literary club modeled on the prestigious Fortnightly, which had Mrs. Wilmarth, Jane Addams, and their like as members. Ickes says that he never discovered what went amiss during Anna's presidency, but that something obviously did. He was approached by one of the members, Naomi Donnelly, to use his influence with Anna to persuade her not to be a candidate for a second term, although it was customary for a president to serve two terms. The impression Naomi gave, Ickes writes, was that Anna had been unpopular, and he professes surprise that she had managed to arouse such animosity within an organization of this kind. After this disingenuous remark Ickes says that, despite Naomi's urging him to secrecy, he felt that, in view of the circumstances, he had to tell Anna what she had said. Anna, hurt and angry, did not run for reelection and soon lost interest in the club.

After their marriage in 1911 Ickes and Anna lived in Anna's house at Evanston. Neither found the neighborhood very friendly, and soon they decided to move farther north. After searching for some time, they bought seven acres of woodland at Hubbard Woods. It was heavily timbered land with some magnificent oaks, two or three hundred years old. Ickes says that he had always loved woods and though Anna preferred lakes she generously gave in. This sentiment was one which Ickes frequently expressed and which was to find its greatest efflorescence in his concern with the Forestry Department. It had begun in the feeling of independence he had experienced in the woods as a lad. They began to build a house at Hubbard Woods and in this perhaps found their only episode of sustained mutual interest and fellow-feeling. It was some four years before the house was finished to their satisfaction. From an initial budget of $25,000, it expanded to an overall cost of $75,000; yet they had become so deeply engaged in it as a work of art that they could not bear to skimp or cut back. Originally all the financing came from Anna, but Ickes later paid off a mortgage of $35,000. No home, he says, in any way compared with this one. It was large and gracious with many unique features—a fine stone hall, which despite protests from the architects Anna insisted be built, a spacious library and a graceful staircase, which had been his ideas. Such was his love for the house that he could easily have devoted an entire chapter in his memoirs to its description.[9]

It was a great leap upward in status for a man who had spent his formative years in a frame house in Altoona, sharing a bedroom with three brothers, and had spent the greater part of his life since then living in a dependent relationship in other people's houses. But even his understandable pleasure at this social and material metamorphosis scarcely accounts for the rapt and obsessive care and minute supervision that Ickes exercised over every detail of the construction—a degree of concern which invites the conjecture that unconscious factors were involved. A notable example was his reaction on finding that the fireplace in the partially completed sun porch had been situated not in the center of the wall, but equidistant between one end of the wall and a doorway at the other end. Ickes immediately told the architect to shift the fireplace and says that he never grudged the additional cost, for "This house was part of me and I put everything into it that I had, not only carefully but lovingly."[10]

According to Freud's interpretive scheme, a whole house can unconsciously assume the significance of the entire human form, thus implying that Ickes' unusually passionate involvement in the house-building was in some measure a by-product of his maternal identification and his desire to assume the maternal generative role.[11] The plausibility of this interpretation is not harmed by his describing the joy he felt in watching the building slowly develop and turn into something with which he felt great intimacy, or "this house was part of me and I put everything into it that I had." Finally, one can only wonder at the remarkable volume, persistence, and itemization of his correspondence with the architects and builders. Some of his correspondence through 1916 and 1917 with the supervising architects, Perkins, Fellows, and Hamilton, and various subcontractors survives. For much of this time Ickes seems to have written about once a week, sometimes much more often, with a catalog of complaints. In this and other more important matters one sees the tone of Ickes' letters becoming steadily more hectoring, uncompromising, intransigent. On 12 May 1916 the exasperated Dwight Perkins was driven to protest about the injustices of a recent letter. Three days later Ickes sent a letter listing no fewer than twenty items demanding immediate attention, beginning with a hissing noise in the bathroom, a charge that the bath tub drained too slowly (meaning that all the drains needed testing), and the fact that the draft of the refuse burner was so great that chunks of paper of considerable size were drawn up and blown about the yard, to the failure or absence of drainage in most of the flower-boxes.[12]

Two days after that Ickes addressed a letter personally to Dwight Perkins, reproving him for his unreasonable reaction to Ickes' efforts to communicate. Ickes' admiration for the rationality and rightness of his own behavior was in full flood as he reacted to Perkins' having told Anna the previous evening that he could no longer discuss the progress of the building with her husband, because Ickes had hung up on him during their last two telephone conversations. Ickes had evidently told Perkins that he was too angry to talk to him, whereupon Perkins had replied that Ickes' anger was unjustified and that in any case he could not discuss the matter in dispute over the telephone. Ickes had then hung up. What else could Perkins expect him now to do? And so on.[13]

This uncommon degree of concern for minute care in housebuilding would be manifest again in his worried involvement with subsistence housing during the New Deal period. More generally, it reveals a need in this man who had grown up resenting being poor, who had never owned property, to have a domain of his own, a kingdom where everything would be just as he decided. This was exactly the attitude Ickes would always show to the enclaves he made for himself in political life.

Ickes and Anna may have found shared interests and mutual support over the house during these years, but in virtually every other regard their relationship was slowly declining into what Ickes came to see as a state of unrelieved and irremediable alienation. One gets a picture of an endless and bitter power struggle in the home, in which Ickes came to feel that he would never achieve the dominance he desired yet could not reconcile himself to the subordinate role that he felt Anna was thrusting upon him. At this distance it is difficult to tell who was the more aggressive or intransigent, and we must assume that, as in most such cases, there were failings in charity and in self-criticism on both sides. Yet even through the selective lens of Ickes' viewpoint, many of Anna's offenses against civil conjugal relations do not seem to deserve the weight of condemnation he gives them. A frequent complaint is that she was bent on improving his intellectual interests and his social bearing. Also, she wanted to know every detail of his daily affairs. She would ask him each morning what plans he had and whom he was going to see. She might phone him several times each day to ask what he was doing. At night she would minutely question him about what Ickes considered to be trivialities.[14]

Certainly this sort of interrogation could become very irritating, but Ickes' response, as described in his personal memoirs, seems excessive. He regards such detailed questioning as an expression of Anna's jealousy, of her determination to dominate every aspect of his life—a rather paranoid interpretation when we reflect that Anna herself must have had areas of self-doubt and insecurity, since by his own account she completely abandoned her judgment in favor of his in matters of business and political affairs. Probably at this stage of his life Ickes would have been primed in advance to suspect any woman he married of nagging and supervising him and limiting his freedom, because he would project onto her the bad image of his own mother and compare her unfavorably with the good image. Anna must have intuited that he was comparing her in both positive and negative aspects to Martha Ickes, and to Anna's disadvantage, because his mother was the subject of some of their most vicious quarrels—even though Anna had never seen her or known her except through Ickes' words. Ickes could only imagine that Anna, sensing his deep love for his mother, exploited his vulnerability on this point by saying unbelievably bitter things about her. He found devious, even paradoxical ways of hitting back. He says that he discovered that the only way to preserve a semblance of tranquillity was to gratify Anna's every wish. In this mood of passive aggression he would not attempt to discuss matters reasonably with her but just make it obvious that he was affected by her as by an unreasoning, insensate creature—a technique of retaliation that can be profoundly alienating.

Further, he began to withdraw his sexual favors. There is no doubt that Ickes initiated this and carried it through against Anna's slowly developing acquiescence, puzzled but not condemnatory or vindictive. They had started married life by occupying a double bed, but gradually, because of their quarreling, this became irksome to him. After some time Ickes' doctor decided that for the sake of his health he should sleep outdoors, which he did in the sun porch summer and winter. To begin with, he says, Anna attempted to sleep with him, even during winter, but after a time she had to desist. His bed on the porch was a welcome retreat. Anna, however, insisted that he should get into bed with her every morning after he came in from the sleeping porch, and, though she was usually at her most agreeable at these times, she would still, as they lay close, upbraid him and comment critically on his intellect or behavior.

Ickes claims that even in moments of passion she wanted to dominate him, not sexually but morally. He had always been repelled by the thought of sexual intercourse between a man and a woman who did not love each other, and when he finally concluded that he did not love Anna any more he determined to end their physical relationship. Anna, who Ickes says wrongly believed herself to be a passionate woman, began to question him about his changed attitude, but he offered one excuse after another and eventually she ceased asking. For several years they lived together with Harold getting into bed with Anna each morning for twenty or thirty minutes, but without making love to her. Harold learned later than Anna had concluded that he had become impotent.

In describing these events in his personal memoirs Ickes uses the word "omnipotent" for "impotent." This disarmingly naive slip occurs three times in succession while he is discussing his sexual relations with her, although he finally gets it right. The personal memoirs were typed by his trusted secretary May Conley, but since he read over the typescript and made many insertions in his own hand it must count as his error as well. It is a plain indication that Ickes was defending himself against his own doubts of his potency. There seems to be no physiological or behavioral evidence that would provide the smallest objective basis for this anxiety. It is, rather, a lingering consequence of the various threats from other family members to which he had felt exposed as a young boy. That feeling became a standard reaction to every other adult man or woman by whom he might feel challenged and would assert itself in his bellicose attitude to presumed rivals within the Roosevelt administration. With regard to Anna in particular, not only did he want to declare himself "omnipotent" rather than "impotent," but in speaking of their sexual relationship he is obliged several times to claim (without giving evidence) that it was she who lacked passion, and to point out that he managed perfectly well with other women when, after several years of abstinence at home, he sought sexual relief outside.

By the time the Great War broke out in Europe, Ickes had inured himself to a life that he had come to regard as a tragic one. He felt that he could not divorce Anna, not only because she was the mother of the son whom he profoundly loved and from whom he could not bear to be separated, but also because Anna already had been through one divorce and another would have been a grievous blow to her. A sense of duty ruled out that course. For years he was, from his own viewpoint, crucified by his Calvinist conscience. He sought relief in work and in politics, but even here, coincident with the decline in their marital relationship, matters had turned sour.

From soon after Raymond's birth, Ickes had been energetically and optimistically employed in the organization of the Progressive Party, and, although the fortunes of the party declined, his own influence within it rose. For several years he was in charge of the Cook County Progressive Committee, and in 1914 had been elected state chairman of the Party and a member of its National Committee. From 1912, too, he had held Jane Addams' proxy on the National Executive Committee and had regularly attended its meetings. During these years he invested his hopes in Theodore Roosevelt as the Party's prospective presidential candidate in 1916. But as 1915 drew to a close we find him urging Roosevelt to make "Americanism" the major issue of the 1916 campaign. The people were concerned not, as in 1912, with social reform, but with national honor.

He suggests delicately that some of the planks in their 1912 platform be laid aside, particularly the recall of judicial decisions, though protesting immediately his own long-term commitment to it and the remainder of their liberal doctrines. His chief interest at the time, however, was the relation of the United States to the current European situation. He felt ashamed that America had failed to respond decisively to the invasion of Belgium or the sinking of the *Lusitania*. Such lamentable weakness betrayed a decay of moral character. Many felt similarly indignant, and this sense of outrage should be directed into moral and altruistic channels.[15]

The question is not about the soundness of Ickes' view of Germany's aggressiveness, but of the source of his powerful feelings and his notions of what should be done. Among the moral and altruistic schemes he had in mind was universal military training as a preparation for armed intervention. The "Americanism" that he advocated does not sound so much like altruism as a demand that the United States ensure that it be respected for its strength and character rather than appear pusillanimous. Social scientists, aware of how extraordinarily difficult it is even with the help of professional pollsters to be confident of the majority opinion on any issue, cannot fail to be impressed at the ability so many politicians claim of being able to intuit the mood of the people. Such intuitions are likely to be affected by their author's own life situation at the time of utterance. Ickes, struggling to defend himself against his own conviction of being weak and pusillanimous in his relationship with Anna, was in desperate need of repairing his self-esteem and feelings of potency. Although his concern for social and industrial justice was never to die, and in fact reasserted itself as his guiding principle for the rest of his life, one can understand its burning less brightly at this grim stage in his personal life.

During this time there is more than a hint of desperation in his efforts to ally himself with strong men in the political world, who might carry him to a position of power of a kind which he evidently felt he could not attain without their aid. Ostensibly, it is true, he stood for principle. Striving to keep the Progressive Party together after its defeat in 1912, he reacted strongly when Medill McCormick, leader of the Progressives in the Springfield legislature, showed more interest in self-aggrandizement and in seeking an accommodation with the Republicans than in upholding Progressive principles. Bitterly, Ickes contrasted McCormick's behavior with that of those who, like himself, did not seek office, who wished merely to make the Party an instrument for social and economic betterment. He again saw Progressive principles being sacrificed when Chicago Progressives supported the candidacy of William Hale Thompson, the Republican candidate in the Chicago mayoral elections of 1915, and expressed his disgust. But in other respects Ickes' actions seem to betray a willingness to set principles aside if they might obstruct the emergence of a political champion.[16]

In his political memoirs he writes of his concern that Theodore Roosevelt might abandon the new party and accept the Republican nomination in 1916. Yet Ickes' correspondence with Roosevelt at this time makes it clear that he himself was prepared to cooperate with Roosevelt in such a course, and even urges him to adopt it. In May 1915, for example, Ickes wrote to the former president, asking whether he might come to Oyster Bay to give Roosevelt vitally important information concerning the Illinois political situation and how it might affect the national election in 1916. He spoke of the formation of powerful coalitions of Progressives, whose activities he could guide, if only Roosevelt would tell him how.[17] Roosevelt thereupon invited Ickes to Oyster Bay. But there they discussed Roosevelt's possible entry into the Republican, rather than the Progressive primaries the following year, and he later wrote telling Roosevelt that, with Ickes' invaluable assistance, he could win the Illinois Republican primary if he chose to contest it. In April 1916, following the Illinois Republican primaries, which Roosevelt did not enter, Ickes, pointing to the large write-in vote received by the former president, again assured him that had an active campaign been conducted on his behalf, he could have won the state.[18] Shortly after this Ickes held a luncheon for Roosevelt, to which he invited prominent local and state political figures, at his newly completed house at Hubbard Woods.

Ickes was bitter when Theodore Roosevelt, having been offered the Party's nomination in 1916, turned it down, but he could not bring himself to attach any blame to the former president and would later write a long article explaining that the machinations of George Perkins, chairman of the Progressive National Committee, had "killed" the young party. Ickes' subsequent selection as a member of Republican presidential nominee Charles Evans Hughes's campaign committee was a testimony to his influence. If Hughes were to succeed, he would need the Progressive vote. Ickes was given the task of persuading Progressives in the Midwest to support the Republican candidate.

But again, although Ickes' memoirs tell of his unhappiness at being forced back into the Republican camp, his letters to Hughes do not echo these sentiments. In July 1916 he told the candidate that, although he had been totally committed to the Progressive cause for the past few years, he was now back in the Republican fold, was completely and disinterestedly dedicated to Hughes's cause, and would do anything he could to see him elected.[19]

In view of his corrosive relation with Anna, it is not surprising that when the United States at last entered the war, Ickes' immediate desire was to get to France and take an active part. The loss of hearing in his left ear that had resulted from the series of mastoid operations meant that he could not play any part in the war as a soldier. For a while he served on the Illinois State Council of Defense, but then joined the YMCA, and set about getting himself transferred to France. The only restraining influence was his love for Raymond, not quite five years old, but he says that he had reached the stage where he had to get away from Anna. He also makes the startling statement that he fervently hoped he would never return, though he realized that this was cowardly, in view of his obligations to his son.[20]

His personal memoirs include an account of how Ickes got to France and of the genuinely exciting and active role he played, along with his friend Henry Allen, in bringing material aid and comfort to the troops in battle areas. His talents, sharpened by political campaigning, were exactly fitted to the catch-as-catch-can organizing needed in time of war. He was justifiably proud of their exploits, enjoyed this excursion into active service, and reveled in the warm masculine camaraderie, all leavened by frequent furloughs in comfortable hotels in Paris. But what is astonishing, in view of the declaration just quoted that he hoped never to return, is the outpouring of the most passionate declarations of love in his letters to Anna almost from the day of his arrival. These feelings are never mentioned in the personal memoirs, but Anna scrupulously kept all his letters and many of them can be found in the archives. For example, on 3 July 1918 he writes:

My Loved One:
    Why did I ever come so far away from you? Three more letters

have just come . . . and I want to come to you at once and take you in
my arms and assure you of my love and devotion.

Dearest, no one could influence me against you, if he tried to do
so. When I come home to you I will be spiritually improved. I am
trying to remedy my defects of character and temper over here—all
with a view to my homecoming. I want to make you happy and I
want you to find in me all the love and gentleness and consideration
that you would want in a husband.

I need not tell you, surely, that I love you and you alone . . . I am
writing all this deliberately because it is my sincere conviction. I
know I have failed where I ought not to have failed . . . I have
thought of how good and wonderful you have been, how unselfish,
brave and noble and my love has gone out across the wide ocean to
meet the love for me that I know is surely there.

. . . life can have no meaning for me, unless you constantly realize
that my love and deepest devotion are yours, dear, dear wife.

Semper,
Harold.[21]

Almost all the letters include such protestations of devotion, and
in many it is their main content.

The immediate impact of these sentiments is in such contrast to
the feelings later described in the memoirs that one is forced to wonder whether the letters were sincere. Yet the same tone is maintained
so consistently throughout the following months, even in reply to
letters in which evidently Anna had suspiciously accused him of deceiving her in some way, that skepticism is disarmed. There would
seem to be no reason for his self-abasement in admitting his character defects and in vowing self-improvement and reparation if he
really had become reconciled to a life that he knew to be tragic, if he
had hardened in his conviction that their relationship was beyond
repair. The letter quoted, like similar ones, must be taken as sincere,
at least in the sense that it is not a conscious pose or masquerade.
Yet with the best will in the world one must say that it is sentimental
and overwritten. Such romanticism is symptomatic of Ickes' unrealistic idealization of women and the estrangement from them engen-
dered by his boyhood. Further, it is decidedly masochistic, even
self-destructive in the name of virtue. During the preceding years of
bitter quarreling and attempted reconciliations Ickes must have had
many chances to discover that such a casting down of defenses, such

an unqualified declaration of endless devotion, positively inhibits a genuine reciprocation of feeling in the one to whom it is addressed. As Proust has it, if one person loves another a little too much, the other will not be able to love the one quite enough. Ickes must have been hoping to provoke in Anna just such an unconditional adoration as, across the sea, he was conjuring up in himself—the unrealistic demand of an infant on its mother, the demand he felt his own mother had refused. His method was self-defeating.

There may well have been a streak of paranoia in some of Anna's accusations against him, at least as it appears from replies in which he heroically restrains himself from telling her so. "Dear, dear Anna, I wonder why you assume that I have some deep laid political plans that Miss Gilmore knows of and you do not merely because she acts mysterious? . . . If my plans are unknown to you it is because they are equally unknown to me since I haven't any plans."[22] However, she also showed grains of shrewd intuition that seem very much to the mark as far as Ickes' inner life was concerned, however innocent he believed himself to be and may have been in his overt behavior. For example, Anna became very brusque and warned him not to waste time visiting Helen, whose introduction into the household as a young girl had led to James Thompson's sexual indiscretion and the divorce. Helen, in her early twenties, had gone to France as a nurse's aide before Ickes had gone there. In an emotional scene in New York just before she sailed, Helen and Ickes had become much closer than they had ever been before. He believed that like him she was desperately anxious to get away from home because the situation between her and Anna had become unendurable. He had failed her, paying little more attention to her than to one of the maids lest he arouse Anna's all-encompassing jealousy. Harold went with Helen to New York to see her off and they spent one night at the Belmont Hotel. He tried to show that he had genuine affection for her, but she was reserved and suspicious. In the evening, despite his solicitations, she went off alone to her room. He felt unhappy about her state of mind and followed her. They talked for hours, until finally he broke her down and she sat in his lap sobbing out her unhappiness and her resentment of Anna.[23]

This is very reminiscent of an earlier incident with Anna's son Wilmarth, who at the time was a high school student. There had been a furious altercation between Anna and the boy. Anna burst into Harold's room, declaring that she hated Wilmarth and wished he would die. Harold went to the boy and found him in a highly disturbed state. Though Wilmarth was really too old for such treatment, Ickes took him on his knee and let him sob out his resentment of his mother's cruel treatment.[24]

This encouraging of close body contact and emotional outpouring seems more typically maternal than paternal, especially with young people who are almost adult. In both cases Ickes, whatever his conscious intentions, cast himself in the role of sympathetic ally against the unjust Anna—that is to say, usurped her position as loving mother, a tendency we have seen operating in him before. The technique of encouraging childish dependency in return for protection against some uncaring oppressor is a useful one for any benevolent autocrat, as some of Ickes' critics later portrayed him.

Helen was nursing in Paris, and whenever Ickes was to spend a day or two there he would get rooms for the two of them at the Seville. Her hours were long, but after work they would have a leisurely meal in a restaurant; she would be off again early in the morning. They were companionable and at ease, Ickes says, and Helen felt free to talk about her hopes and expectations. One day there seemed a real threat that the German army would take Paris. There had been many stories of rape by German soldiers, and Ickes wanted to ensure that such a fate would not overtake Helen. He obtained from a friendly American woman doctor a small bottle of morphine tablets, sufficient to end her life. Helen was to keep this by her and swallow the tablets if the worst should come. When this fate did not eventuate and the danger was past, Ickes retrieved the bottle and kept it for years, in case he should no longer be able to endure his life with Anna. However, he almost admits that there was a degree of self-dramatization about this, for he would never actually have taken that way out.

Histrionic gestures of self-destruction by means of drug overdoses are reported to be more common among women than among men (who tend to make dramatic scenes with firearms in such acting-out). Ickes, then, in carrying the morphine was adopting Helen's feminine role, the enemy now being not German rapists but his wife. We have seen how wounded (literally) and horrified he had been some years before when his mastoid incision had opened and poured forth blood in consequence of Anna's verbal onslaught, or so he believed. Any surgical intervention is likely to be experienced unconsciously by men as an emasculation, and Anna had taken advantage of his weakened condition to reinflict the injury as he lay helpless in bed. Alongside his undoubted masculinity, Ickes had developed a competing current of femininity through his maternal identification, a current against which his male self must continually defend itself. Children of both sexes, especially those brought up in a regime of sexual obscurantism, tend to conceive of sexual intercourse itself as the infliction of a wound, and if a male person should adopt the passive feminine role, then it is the infliction of an emasculating wound. This was what Ickes feared, unconsciously and symbolically, through his involvement with Anna. The associative link, with the sexes reversed, to Helen and the imagined German rapists is not hard to make. It is tempting to elaborate this scenario, with Ickes standing, in his own mind, for the essentially noble American people, which had shaken itself free from a period of seeming cowardliness and regained its moral strength in France, and Anna representing brutal German imperialism.

In his letters Harold wrote Anna that he had been seeing Helen, but, he says, he never hinted that they enjoyed the closeness and intimacy that was, in his view, normal and natural between father and de facto daughter. This seems an inexact use of "de facto," for rather than Ickes' biological daughter, Helen was a young woman who had been brought into the household when a child of about eleven years of age. Ickes' conception of a normal and natural parental relationship is shown when he tells of a bombing raid that came very close to the Seville one night when they were staying there. Both had gone to bed, but, as was their custom, had left the door between their rooms open. When Ickes realized that Helen was awake, he entered her room and sat on her bed, and they gave each other mutual support until the raid was over.[25] There is not the slightest ground for suspecting any impropriety, and to suggest that there was an unacknowledged erotic tone to this degree of closeness is only to attribute to Ickes feelings that are not so uncommon as to be considered monstrous. But it is not surprising that Anna, who seems to have understood some aspects of Ickes' nature better than he did himself, expressed herself rather tartly about his spending more time than necessary with Helen.

Despite the dangers, Ickes enjoyed being in France, free of

Anna's censoriousness and faultfinding. He did not want the war to continue forever; he just hoped that somehow it would turn out that he could stay on there indefinitely. But the war came to an end and, as he sailed toward New York, he says, his depression deepened into black despair. The happiest chapter in his life had ended and he was utterly without hope.

The reunion with Anna was, predictably, a disaster. His written protestations of self-renewal and desire to fly back to her arms proved to be as unrealistic as they seem to a reader. Anna was waiting on the dock in New York, but he could not bring himself to go to the rail until the last moment. He saw her immediately. She appeared drawn and haggard, as if she were under great stress, but his heart could not warm to her. He kissed her when they met, but all that he could think of to say was that she looked poorly. Naturally Anna reacted badly and, Ickes remarks ruefully, his unfortunate words were to be dragged into many of their quarrels in years to come.

No sooner were they in the taxi on the way to the Belmont Hotel than she accused him of having a mistress in Paris. Ickes not only denied this emphatically but, he says, did so in good faith, and his denial carries conviction. Anna did not believe him for, she claimed, his letters from France had been detached and impersonal. This is impossible to square with the great majority of the letters unless we assume that Anna, too, could penetrate their self-deceptive sentimentalism. Or perhaps Ickes, as he was writing his memoirs, wished not to recall those vulnerable and passionate letters? In any case, the illusion collapsed. They made love that night, which seemed to soothe her for the moment, but she was up again in the middle of the night, storming about the room and berating him for his misdemeanors in Paris. He refused to respond, even when she threatened to hurl herself sixteen floors to the street. The future looked desolate, and he regretted more than ever that he had returned.

In the political sphere Ickes' behavior from this time was marked by growing bitterness, and even a sense of desperation. The virtual eclipse of the Progressive Party in 1916 and the draining away during the war of much of the reforming energy that had produced it had deeply disappointed him. There were strong personal reasons, too, why he should have turned with increased contempt against the corrupt and felt keenly that his salvation, in personal as well as political terms, lay in associating himself yet again with a vigorous, aggressive, courageous leader, whose ultimate victory might somehow rescue him from his fate.

He was not asked to participate in Charles Merriam's challenge to "Big Bill" Thompson for the Republican nomination for mayor in 1919. (His 1911 intransigence was still remembered.) Disdainfully he stood aside, watched the inept and amateurish efforts of Merriam's team go badly awry, and refused a belated request to take over. Predictably, Merriam's performance was derisory.

Ickes described the Republican National Convention of 1920, to which he went as a delegate-at-large, in characteristic terms. Former Progressive Hiram Johnson, who had made the best showing in the primaries and was therefore the choice of the people, was denied the nomination, which the bosses cynically delivered to Warren Harding. To Ickes, Harding was a weak character who lacked moral integrity. His running mate, Calvin Coolidge, was worse. The national reputation that Coolidge had won for his decisive handling of the Boston police strike was bogus; Coolidge had really displayed weakness and cowardice. Ickes could see no further point in Progressives continuing to meet or even to correspond.

In his political memoirs he describes at length his disgust at the abandonment of Progressive principles and the cynicism of the Republican bosses in putting forward a weak candidate whom they could control, before noting that a few days after the convention he went to see George Brennan.[26] Yet Ickes gives there no clear idea as to precisely what principles had been abandoned by his colleagues. It is possible that he had in mind the "principle" that party conventions ought not to be controlled by bosses, but his unselfconscious reference to his meeting with Brennan, the leading Democratic boss in Chicago, suggests that his major objection lay elsewhere. It is more likely that the personalities of Harding and Collidge determined Ickes' attitude. It was also characteristic that not even the fact that he was virtually alone among former Progressives in taking the "principled" stand that he had—that is, refusing to support Harding—did not for a moment cause him to question the correctness of his position. Ickes never doubted that he was right, that he alone understood what Progressive principles were. Others were blind; only he could see.

Through George Brennan, Ickes arranged a meeting with James Cox, the Democratic presidential candidate, and, having decided that Cox's general outlook on social and economic issues was the same as his own, he issued a public statement supporting him. The statement was sent to former Progressives, with the request that they comment upon it. Most, though by no means all, did so negatively, some with a good deal of vehemence. This did not prevent Ickes from giving a generally favorable account of their reaction to the man who had now become the object of his political ambitions.[27]

Relations between Ickes and Hiram Johnson, former Progressive Governor of California, vice-presidential running mate of Theodore Roosevelt on the Progressive Party ticket in 1912, and currently a United States Senator, had been strained by Ickes' failure to support Johnson in the Republican primaries of 1920. Ickes was intent on repairing the damage. From this time, indeed, he would be indefatigable in his efforts to persuade Johnson to contest the presidency. For example, in August 1920 he passed along to Johnson, Cox's remark that even if Harding were elected in 1920 he could not win again in 1924, and that Johnson would undoubtedly be president. In May 1921 he again urged Johnson to continue the Progressive fight; shortly afterward he assured him that a man of principle like himself would get no real help from the regular Republican organization, but that he was the only candidate whom those not dominated by the machine would support.[28] One obvious motive in all this was to put Ickes himself forward as an indispensable ally. The following July, Ickes sent Johnson more words of comfort and encouragement, words that he must have rather despairingly hoped to be true of his own situation as well. Those who stood for principle were bound to suffer temporary setbacks and loss of support, but the time would surely come when the people would turn to new leaders.[29]

Along with his growing admiration for Johnson went a strong feeling of revulsion for the administrations of Harding and later of Coolidge.[30] Ickes felt that the Teapot Dome scandal, which broke after Harding's death, should have forced the Republicans from office, and that only the general moral bankruptcy of the country had prevented it. But those who brazenly continued to sit in the cabinet could not escape his censure, and he pictured Herbert Hoover eagerly coveting the presidency and being prepared to do anything to get it. He was always skeptical about the value of Hoover's work as a food administrator in Europe after the war, and in September 1921 he wrote Herbert Croly, editor of the *New Republic*, urging him thoroughly to investigate suggestions that Hoover had played politics with food relief funds to the detriment of the starving peoples of Europe.[31]

When the general grubbiness of the Harding administration had begun to raise doubts about the possibility of the President's reelection, Ickes had begun to hope that the Republicans might turn at last to Hiram Johnson, whose electoral appeal had been amply demonstrated in the 1920 primaries. In February 1923 Johnson had encouraged Ickes by telling him that should he enter a national campaign, he would want Ickes by his side. Johnson admitted that he would like to be president, but believed that his candidacy could not succeed because of White House opposition. Undeterred, Ickes continued, after Johnson left on an overseas trip, to send him detailed analyses of the political situation and to importune him to run. But all this went unrewarded when he was not invited to assist in organizing a homecoming dinner for Johnson in New York, at which, the *New York Times* speculated, Johnson's campaign for the presidency would be launched. He could not bring himself to criticize Johnson directly, but he did point out that a more representative group of Progressives should have been invited, especially those from the Midwest and Far West, where liberal opinion and therefore support for Johnson was greatest.[32]

During the following months Ickes worked to put Johnson in his debt and to increase the pressure on him to run. In July, for instance, he told Johnson that Democratic boss George Brennan had been pressing him, Ickes, to accept a judgeship, and that Raymond Robins supported the idea, but that Charles Merriam had been generous enough to say that the public interest required that Ickes continue his invaluable work in the political sphere. Ickes would delay any decision until he saw Johnson.[33]

Under these generally encouraging circumstances, the death of Harding, in August 1923, and the elevation of Calvin Coolidge to the presidency were particularly unpleasant pills for Ickes to swallow. Not only did Coolidge seem relatively free of the odium of corruption beginning to settle around Harding and his cronies, but no sooner had he taken office than Johnson's support began to ebb as Republicans hurried to pledge their loyalty to the new president. In correspondence at the time, Ickes' invective against Coolidge reached a new pitch of bitterness.[34]

He continued to urge Johnson to enter the race for the Republican nomination, arguing that the Republican leadership would be unlikely to nominate Coolidge in 1924. But when he suggested that he might make some announcement on Johnson's behalf in Chicago, to avoid a threatened move by an unsavory faction within the Illinois Republican organization to adopt Johnson as its candidate, Johnson replied abruptly that such an announcement would be premature and that he did not wish to be offensive to any faction which might support his cause.[35]

Ickes was devasted when Johnson announced to a group of Illinois supporters that he had asked Frank Hitchcock to be national manager of his campaign. Although Hitchcock had been prominent in Theodore Roosevelt's 1904 campaign, had been Attorney General under Taft, and had held the position of Republican National Chairman, Ickes was skeptical about his suitability and suggested that Johnson take a chance on a newcomer who was able and aggressive, though without national experience[36] (a not inaccurate description of himself); he also pointed out that Hitchcock lacked support among many former Progressives. Johnson did not respond to this suggestion, nor did he clarify the situation in Illinois, where Ickes' role in the campaign had never been defined. After Johnson had formally announced his candidacy, in November 1923, there was press speculation that Ickes, who had been working with others to build up an organization in Illinois, would be named state manager. After all, he had an unrivaled knowledge of Illinois Republican politics and, better than anyone else, could mobilize Progressive support. But Johnson allowed matters to drift. Ickes' increasing frustration with the situation and his mounting criticism of Hitchcock's inactivity eventually produced a clash with Johnson, who evidently accused him of being rather too concerned with self-aggrandizement.

This was a charge to which Ickes was acutely sensitive, for it clashed with his self-image of disinterested commitment and suggested an ambition he could never admit. His response was heart-rending. How could Johnson believe him to be interested in preferment or personal reward? His family and close friends had always assured him that the reverse was true, that he had done the work while others had taken the glory. He would have been willing in this campaign to sacrifice himself again, but Johnson had never given him anyting but the vaguest of commissions. Hitchcock had proved himself utterly incompetent; virtually nothing had been done. He, Ickes, had now been unjustly accused. He must therefore withdraw his services. In a wounding conclusion Ickes declared that since 1920 he had subordinated everything to his desire to see Johnson win the Republican nomination and then the presidency. This he had done not only because the nation needed Johnson, but because he, Ickes, had a deep affection for him. But not even Hitchcock could stop him, though now only a spectator, continuing to cheer the candidate on.[37] On receipt of the letter Johnson moved quickly to place Ickes in charge of the Illinois campaign; but with only two months to the primary the position was an impossible one.

Most of Harold Ickes' fully developed political character is on display here. The open-browed sincerity of his declaration that he wanted only to serve, however modestly, a man the country needed; the actual but unacknowledged desire for a political appointment; the consequent desire to be the conspicuous central controller; the temperamental inability to share authority; the noble pathos of the resignation—all this is quintessential Harold Ickes, and typifies his political career from now on.

The collapse of Johnson's 1924 campaign deepened Ickes' disillusionment. In September of that year he savagely attacked a group of former Progressive colleagues who had publicly criticized Robert M. La Follette for claiming to be the candidate of the Progressives. Precisely what, Ickes wanted to know, had Raymond Robins, Ruth McCormick, Henry Allen, and the other signers done since 1920 to uphold the Roosevelt tradition, these erstwhile reformers who had failed to protest against the oil scandals of the Harding administration and who declined to support Hiram Johnson's bid for the presidency earlier in the year? Ickes told Johnson that he was thinking of supporting the La Follette campaign, though he realized that such a move would place him outside the Republican party forever.[38]

When Coolidge was elected, Ickes observed bitterly to Johnson that the country had returned not merely to normalcy but to subnormalcy. He had been foolish to attack the former Progressives, but did not regret what he had done because he was already beyond further hurt. He had no future in politics. There was no difference between the two major parties. Nor could he see any hope that the Progressive Party could be revived, because the country was still caught in the disillusionment produced by the war and there was no leader to rally the reformers or inspire the people. Nothing would change until people believed that there was more to life than making money.[39]

Nowhere was there an area of happy fulfillment to ease the sourness and grayness of Ickes' life at this time. An index of his domestic bitterness is to be found in an exchange of letters with Anna in 1925. A few days earlier Ickes had stormed out of the house after an argument that seems to have been a little more savage than usual. After leaving, he had given vent to some of his complaints against Anna to Wilmarth. When these were relayed to Anna, she took them as being an offer to return under certain conditions, which however she found unacceptable. She would not allow him to live in the house on the same basis as Tom Gilmour (this dim, distant relation) and refused to abandon her responsibility as a mother for Raymond. She could not subject herself to another such scene, which had humiliated her in front of the servants. Nevertheless, she closed by saying that she need hardly tell him how much she cared for him. Such an opening was irresistible to Ickes. He knew how much she cared: it was so little, and she was so deficient in wifely decency that he had become entirely cynical, friendless, ambitionless, and indifferent as to whether he lived or died. How could he respect a mother who would use her own child as an instrument against her husband, just because of her jealousy over his fatherly love?[40] But evidently the matter was patched up somehow.

At this time Raymond was thirteen years of age, Anna fifty-two, and Harold fifty-one. At such an age, when a man can see the close of his life not immeasurably distant, he may ask himself whether he has achieved the full unfolding of his powers, whether he has any chance of doing so, whether he can ever now achieve recognition and happiness. Ickes seemed to be staring down a very constricted tunnel with no light visible at the end.

Nor were there any developments in city politics to lighten his mood. In 1923 he organized an independent-Republican group to support William E. Dever, Democratic candidate for mayor, who was elected. He again backed Dever in 1927, creating a nonpartisan group to support his candidacy, but he quarreled with some of Dever's followers, accused them of jeopardizing the reelection of Chicago's finest mayor, and was sickened when he was defeated by Big Bill Thompson. Dever had honestly tried to enforce the prohibition laws and tried to control the criminals; under Thompson they would again have free reign. Once back in office, Thompson began to show favor to utility magnate Samuel Insull, and almost immediately Insull's lawyers presented new traction legislation to the Springfield legislature, that would allow him to control the city's transport systems. Ickes thought that public concern over civic affairs in Chicago had reached its lowest moral ebb. Disconsolately he reviewed his long history as an urban reformer, concluding that after thirty years of dedicated efforts things were worse than when he had begun.[41]

He had reason enough to despair. For three decades he had campaigned tirelessly for political reform and fought for civil rights and social justice, opposing the 1920 crusade by Attorney General A. Mitchell Palmer against so-called anarchists and communists, and attempting, during the 1920s, to assist blacks and American Indians, though not with equal commitment. His experience as president of the Chicago branch of the NAACP, a position which he accepted in 1922 and from which he resigned in 1924, was in general unsatisfactory and unsuccessful, with Ickes complaining repeatedly that when he had consented to become president he had done so on the understanding that the branch was well organized and adequately financed and that he would not be called upon to do a great deal. Actually he had discovered that the branch existed virtually in name only, possessing neither membership lists nor money.[42]

Admittedly his assessment was accurate; the passive attitude of the Chicago NAACP during the race riots of 1919 had greatly reduced its influence. Also, when Ickes did attempt to recruit prominent citizens to serve on the committee, responses were lukewarm. Although Robert M. Bagnall, director of branches, spent some time in the city conducting a membership drive and formulating a plan of activities, little changed. Even so, Ickes' attitude was defeatist from the outset, and his correspondence betrays a note of irritation, a sense that he had been imposed upon, even deceived. Although there were grounds for his resentment, it is not easy to escape the impression that his heart was never in the work. The fact that he was prepared, in a letter to Bagnall, to give currency to the speculation of branch secretary Morris Lewis that the real problem in Chicago was that blacks lacked substantial grievances betrays something about his attitude toward the problem.[43]

Ickes' commitment to the Indians, on the other hand, was wholehearted. Early in 1923 John Collier, executive secretary of the American Indian Defense Association, and a group of several Pueblo Indians from New Mexico, addressed a meeting in Chicago at which Ickes was present. Collier explained that the Pueblos, an ancient people whose agrarian culture depended on a centuries-old irrigation system, had been confirmed in their occupation of their lands first by the Spanish and later by a United States Government treaty. But, without government opposition, whites had been encroaching on the Indians' land and taking their water. A bill introduced into the Senate by Senator Holm Bursum of New Mexico, and backed by Secretary of the Interior Albert Fall, under whose jurisdiction the Indians were, now sought to confirm the rights of the new settlers. The Snyder Bill, which had been introduced into the House of Representatives, had a similar aim. Collier and the Pueblos were on their way to Washington to oppose both bills and to urge passage of the Jones-Leatherwood Bill, which would secure the Pueblos' rights to land and water.

Collier's story affected Ickes very deeply, and he wrote Hiram Johnson that the treatment of the Pueblos was something of which all decent Americans should be ashamed. These simple, defenseless people must be protected from rapacious whites.[44] By June 1923 Ickes was on the board of Collier's American Indian Defense Association. But, almost inevitably, conflicts began, as Ickes' sense of outrage at the Indians' plight began to collide with his unwillingness to share power and with the stirrings of a larger ambition. He began to agitate for the replacement of many groups interested in the Indians' plight with a single national organization. When the executive committee failed to respond to his plea for a conference of representatives of the various Indian rights groups, he accused Collier of blocking the plan, and a vitriolic correspondence ensued. Yet Ickes continued to work for Indian rights, urging Johnson and other Senators to oppose anti-Indian legislation, to press for an investigation of the administration of the Indian Bureau, and to agitate for increases in congressional allocations for food and clothing for Indian children. By 1933 Ickes, sensing that the change of government in Washington might somehow lift him out of his slough of despair, was ready to accept Collier's help in his plan to secure appointment as Commissioner of Indian Affairs in the Roosevelt Administration—a plan soon to be superseded by a more ambitious one. Still later, when his appointment as Secretary of the Interior relieved him of any need to compete with Collier, he was glad to appoint him to the office he himself had bypassed: Commissioner of Indian Affairs.

At the end of 1924 Ickes had resigned as a partner in Don Richberg's law firm to start his own practice. According to his personal memoirs, however, he was too dispirited by his poor relationship with Anna to develop much of a practice. He occupied himself with political affairs as well as Indian rights and encouraged his wife's already existing interest in such matters, because, he says, he had found that only when Anna was fully occupied with outside interests, with less time to devote to attacking him, could he tolerate living with her. He claims that she had developed an interest in politics because of his own heavy involvement and that she delighted in publicity. Anna, in his opinion, was also coming to feel that she would be dominant in their political, as in their personal, activities and that Harold was something of a spent force, though he might still be useful to her.[45]

But even at the lowest ebb there was a desperate, grim stubbornness in Harold Ickes that would never accept being written off as a has-been. Eventually the balance of power between himself and Anna was to be dramatically reversed.

Some time in 1926 Harold suggested that Anna might have a good chance of being elected to the state legislature, he writes that she took the bait immediately. When the time came for the 1928 campaign she ran as a Republican under his management. He says she was helpless and politically naive but that to her credit she accepted at once that he could not accompany her on speaking engagements; she must not appear to be running simply as his candidate. Once or twice during the campaign she asked whether he had suggested that she run just because he wanted to get rid of her, but he lied convincingly and said it was because he thought she would do a good job. Anna led her competitors in both the primary and the general elections, and this success was to be repeated in 1930 and 1932. Ickes says that, if she had not followed him to Washington, she could have continued being reelected as long as she wished. Her position was so secure that in 1932 he felt free to demonstrate his political independence of her. The incumbent state's attorney, a Republican, was up for reelection, but Ickes felt that his record was poor and organized an independent Republican committee to support Thomas J. Courtney, the Democratic candidate. This allowed Ickes to declare publicly once again that he was a political independent, even though his wife sat as a Republican in Springfield.[46]

In 1931 Ickes began one final attempt to persuade Hiram Johnson to contest the presidency, following a national conference of Progressives in Washington. In his political memoirs Ickes gives the impression that, faced with the reluctance of Johnson and Johnson's wife, he resigned himself to defeat. (When Ickes adopted Johnson's nickname of "the boss" for Mrs. Johnson, he was not jesting.) He bombarded the unwilling Johnson with a series of letters, between November 1931 and February 1932, which began by encouraging and ended by imploring him to run. Every possible argument was utilized. The *Chicago Tribune* had pledged its support. Sentiment was strongly favorable in Illinois, and if in Illinois then probably in other states as well. A person whom Ickes could not name, but who regularly traveled about the country, believed that Johnson could win three out of four Republican primaries against Hoover. (The man was Raymond Robins, whom Johnson had come to despise.) Senator Bronson Cutting of New Mexico believed that a fight against Hoover must be made and that Johnson was the strongest possible man to make it. Ickes was confident that Johnson would make a clean sweep of the Republican primaries, capitalizing on enormous latent support. The people were longing for his type of dynamic leadership. By January 1932 Ickes was assuring Johnson (and Johnson's wife, still hostile to her husband's candidacy) that he could be nominated and that, if nominated, he could be elected. Johnson had a patriotic duty to run. Progressive principles might die if he did not. On and on the letters went, until finally, in mid-February, a brief formal announcement by Johnson dashed Ickes' hopes.[47]

Disillusioned after his defeat in the Insull campaign and bitterly disappointed by Johnson's refusal to run, Ickes determined to take little part in the 1932 campaign. After the state elections he would do some writing, read a great deal, and attend to his stamp collection and flower garden. It was as if he had finally, though not happily, resigned his hopes for a major political career.

Harold Ickes always denied that he was ambitious. Time and again he dismissed the suggestion that he was interested in personal aggrandizement or political power. He had not sought elective or appointive office and never would. By contrast with party regulars, who might cut their political coats to suit any available cloth, he was the man of principle, the selfless fighter for the just cause, whose sole concern was with the general good. Compromise of principle in the interests of personal advancement or electoral gain was something he could never contemplate. Such was his firm self-image.[48]

But the record of Harold Ickes' ambition is eloquent beyond any denial. What becomes clear as his political activities are examined is that, in order to sustain the conviction that he was not interested in personal power, he employed a highly circumscribed conception of the nature of political ambition. If political ambition is to be equated with immediate electoral success, either for himself or for a candidate whom he had decided to support, Ickes was not ambitious; if, on the other hand, it is taken to consist in a sustained attempt to advance his own reputation as a political manager, an intense and jealous enjoyment of executive power, and a long-term strategy of placing candidates who might ultimately be elected to an important office deeply in his debt, in the hope that in their gratitude and admiration they might confer on him a just reward, he was ambitious. His inhibition against pushing himself forward as a public candidate betokens his old unconscious anxiety, that if he did expose himself to the public gaze, his mask of masculine ebullience would be penetrated and an underlying incompleteness, a symbolic emasculation, would be revealed.

His strategy of indirection, if that is what it was, almost succeeded in 1924, and after a period of despair was miraculously blessed with success in 1932. On the earlier occasion, had the largely discredited Harding not died in 1923, or had Hiram Johnson been his running mate (which, given Johnson's strong showing in the 1920 primaries he might easily have been), or had Johnson instead of the unimpressive Coolidge become the Republican candidate in 1924, it is highly likely that Harold Ickes would have entered the national government eight years earlier than he did. Now, in 1932, Ickes was about to be plucked from the political wilderness.

In his account of his appointment to the secretaryship of the Interior, Ickes comes close to admitting that at some level his aim had been to be carried to power on the coattails of a political champion.

He writes there that the thought had at least occurred to him that if Hiram Johnson became president and asked Ickes to join his administration he would like to be Secretary of the Interior. But, obviously uncomfortable with this near-admission of personal ambition, Ickes modestly disclaims the possibility as unrealistic. He had never, he says, believed that Johnson had any chance at all of achieving that goal and so had not wasted his time dreaming of the impossible.[49] But he had indeed believed that Johnson had a chance in the presidential election of 1924 and, in pleading with him to run in 1932, had repeatedly assured him that he could win both nomination and election.

Nor, in the wider sense, was Ickes' independent political stance, his refusal to ally himself permanently with one or other of the major political parties, necessarily inimical to his chances of political advancement, though he usually inferred that it was. Certainly it accorded well with Ickes' notion of himself as a man of principle, of strong and independent political convictions. But this independence might serve a larger, if possibly unrecognized, end. For if the pond of political independence was small, Ickes made a far bigger splash by repeatedly and noisily jumping into it than he would have done by remaining reliably within either of the major parties. The independence of which he was so proud allowed him to retain his own conception of himself as a man of principle, while at the same time bringing him to the attention of the power brokers of both parties as someone who could be treated with, who might help to deliver the independent vote. This is precisely what happened in 1932, when Franklin Delano Roosevelt's campaign managers asked Ickes to help organize the Midwest Independent-Republican vote for their candidate. This was his crucial chance, but the question was whether he would be able to seize it. He became chairman of the Western Committee of the National Progressive League for Roosevelt and Garner, but he still had to find an excuse for the stirring of ambition. His decision to support the Democratic presidential nominee, he says, was not well received by his wife, currently seeking reelection as a Republican to the Illinois legislature. To mollify her he promised that if Roosevelt won he would break his lifelong rule against seeking public office and attempt to secure the position of Commissioner of Indian Affairs.

Ickes points out, quite correctly, that Anna was intensely interested in the welfare of the Indians, particularly those of New Mexico and Arizona, about whom she had written as book.[50] From 1916 on she had spent much time in those regions, the climate of which brought her relief from asthmatic attacks, and she had recently built herself a house near Gallup, New Mexico, on the Santa Fe Trail. She had also been involved in the campaign to prevent encroachments on Indian lands. It is conceivable that she might have looked favorably on her husband's offer to seek a position that would enable him to assist a people in whom they were both interested.

Yet the very fact that it was her interests that he appeared to be serving created ambivalence in Ickes' feelings about his own proposal. In the memoirs he can hardly bring himself to admit that it was Anna who first broached the possibility of his appointment to John Collier and some other supporters of the Indian cause. Then he contrives to suggest that his own interest in the Indians was of even longer standing than hers, having begun through his studies of anthropology and ethnology in college during the 1890s (though it seems not to have expressed itself in any significant active concern before 1923). But gradually an ambitious conception of how he might preempt the whole issue and raise himself at one stroke from an ancillary status to an executive one began to form in his mind. He writes that he either had to make good on his promise about the Indian commissionership or come away with a richer prize—richer, that is, with regard to his own career.

The seed was sown at a Washington meeting with John Collier, Lewis Merriam, and Nathan R. Margold, all active on the Indians' behalf. They argued that a commissioner for Indian Affairs would not be able to do much without support from higher up and that Ickes should seek the position of first assistant secretary within the Department of the Interior, under whose control the Bureau of Indian Affairs was placed. Ickes had a grander idea. He would keep his commitment to Anna and secure an appointment that was greatly appealing to him if he could become not merely assistant secretary but Secretary of the Interior. Yet it seemed such a remote possibility that he scarcely had the temerity to contemplate it.[51]

Roosevelt had been swept to power and the problem for Ickes was how to draw himself to the attention of the President-elect. He knew that Roosevelt was thinking of including a representative of the Independent Republicans of the West in his cabinet, and he learned that both Hiram Johnson and Bronson Cutting had been offered and declined the position of Interior Secretary. He approached several Senators—Johnson, Cutting, Gerald Nye, and Robert La Follette, Jr.—and told them frankly that he would like to be Secretary of the Interior. All agreed that it was a fine idea but regretted that because they were not members of Roosevelt's party they could not volunteer suggestions to him about his cabinet. Appeals to personal and political acquaintances such as Gifford Pinchot and Donald Richberg also fell on stony ground despite favors they owed him, probably, Ickes thought, because they, too, had the possibility of a cabinet appointment in their thoughts.

When he had almost given up hope, he was telephoned by Raymond Moley and invited to a small conference in Roosevelt's New York home to review the economic situation. Moley had consulted the Independent Republican Senators in Washington, who had unanimously suggested Ickes as their representative. Others were introduced to the President-elect before the conference, though Ickes was not, but at one point Roosevelt had asked whether Mr. Ickes was there, and he had identified himself. Evidently, Moley or someone else had given Roosevelt not only Ickes' name but at least some short account of him, enough to pique Roosevelt's interest. Ickes must have looked incongruous in that gathering. Frances Perkins, soon to be Secretary of Labor, who saw him shortly afterward, described him as "a plump, blond, be-spectacled gentleman" who ignored her presence. He "didn't have any of that flip style about him that a New York City person has," none of the New York elegance, nor the Bowery or Broadway style. She assumed that he was from upstate New York. But Roosevelt later told Moley that he "liked the cut of his jib."[52]

During the conference itself Ickes said nothing but noticed that the President-elect was observing him closely. As he was about to leave, Roosevelt called him into his study. He told Ickes that the two of them had been saying the same thing for twenty years and shared the same attitudes on political and social questions. Cutting and Johnson had declined his invitation to become Secretary of the Interior. He needed a man from the West, an honest man, who could stand up to the interests. He had almost decided that he wanted Harold Ickes.[53]

Ickes was dazed with pleasure. It was true that the previous day in the Capitol building he had met Arthur Mullen, a Democratic boss in Nebraska and FDR's floor manager in 1932, who had willingly agreed to suggest him to Roosevelt for Interior, but Ickes never did know whether he had been able to get through by telephone in time. As we have seen, someone had called Ickes to the President-elect's mind, and it may even be true that Roosevelt had noticed something of Ickes' public pronouncements in previous times and was not just being polite when he said they had been saying the same things for the past twenty years. But Ickes, who admits he was not coy in accepting the offer (conditional on his acceptability to the new Attorney General and Secretary of State and the independent Republican Senators), was quite clear in his own mind as to why Roosevelt had "propositioned" him. He had watched him, weighed him, and chosen him during the conference, though Ickes had not said a word. He was sure that it was to Roosevelt alone that he was indebted for his appointment, something that he says he never forgot. Later Ickes wrote about another appointment Roosevelt had made: "He has these sudden crushes. The same thing happened to me in 1933."[54] So began a romantic attachment on Ickes' part, a relationship that even Roosevelt was to refer to as a marriage, which, despite its tribulations, was never to die.

Perhaps nothing that Ickes had done in his pursuit of the secretaryship of the Interior had directly affected the decision of the incoming President, but that was not Ickes' fault. In the short span of time available to him after he had seized the nettle of ambition, he had acted with speed, adroitness, and persistence. What had prompted this sudden outburst of undisguised power seeking, so greatly at variance with his behavior up to that point?

Deep down Ickes had always been politically ambitious, though certain neurotic inhibitions had kept him from attempting the direct path to political success. Political ambition was a corollary of his conviction of personal rectitude. It is widespread among politicians, if they are not merely adventurers or time-servers, to see themselves as rightful fathers of their people, rightful guardians of the social conscience, and benevolent directors of the masses because of their supposed special knowledge of the right way to live and their dedication to pursuing that way. That Ickes felt this is plain in many of his derogatory remarks about "the people." He lacked Roosevelt's faith in their basic soundness; they needed guidance. When Hiram Johnson was defeated in the California Republican primary in 1924, Ickes commented to him that the people lacked gratitude, too easily forgot, and ran after strange gods. They needed champions to lead them and protect them from themselves.[55] We have remarked on Ickes' desire to excel as a parent. After his own defeat in the campaign against the Insull traction ordinance (with some immediate reason for his pessimism), he complained that the young had no interest in public affairs and lamented that he and other reformers had been trying to win social and political gains for people who were indifferent. Chicagoans did not care about crime and graft and the suppression of their civil liberties, but about movies, jazz, and baseball.[56]

The very mass of autobiographical material he has bequeathed us is testimony to the duty Ickes felt to explain how he had become such a strong and idealistic character. But from where had the surge of nervous energy arisen to overcome the secret, nagging self-doubt about his personal competence as a prime actor, as distinct from stage manager? The most likely source is his feeling of desperation that he was at the point of being submerged and defeated in the long war of attrition with his wife. She may have entered onto her own legislative career with his superior professional assistance, but she had made such a success of it in her own right that she scarcely needed him any longer as campaign manager. His temerity in supporting Democratic candidates, one for state's Attorney and one for President of the United States, had prompted him in reparation to offer to seek a position from which he could assist her campaign for Indian rights. If he had gotten it, he would have felt little more than her assistant.

The fuse lit by John Collier and the others in encouraging him to look higher had fired a skyrocket of successful aspiration. Harold Ickes' position as Secretary of the Interior would easily eclipse Anna's in the Illinois State Legislature, and in fact, having served out her term she eventually resigned that independent career and came to Washington as his appendage. But a much sharper reversal awaited her. Harold was to take immediate advantage of his post to bring about a dramatic development in his intimate relationships through which he would deliver a crushing blow to Anna, one from which she would never quite recover. At fifty-nine years of age his powers were suddenly released in every major area of life. Of course he would encounter political thuggery, and of course his character defenses would lead him into unwinnable head-to-head contests that a smoother man would have evaded, but in contrast with the years since the Great War a period of unforeseeable self-realization had begun.

FOUR

Mr. Ickes Goes to Washington

ICKES' PRIDE in the Department of the Interior and the fascination which his new position held for him are revealed in a radio address that he gave on 8 May 1933, just two months after his appointment.

> The Department of the Interior, comprising within its jurisdiction as it does so many varied and widely divergent activities, is, to my mind, the most interesting division of the Federal Government . . . from supervising the social and business affairs of the approximately 228,000 Indian wards of the United States to keeping touch with the activities of hospitals and schools for the Negroes; from administering the 14,702,205 acres of the national parks and monuments and seeing that they are available at all seasonable times for the enjoyment of the millions of American citizens who visit them each year to passing upon such technical matters as are involved in the administration of the General Land Office, the Geological Survey and the Reclamation Service offer such a sufficient variety to engage the enthusiastic interest of any man.[1]

He went on to list, in addition to this avuncular caretaking role, the more substantial functions of the various bureaus within the department. First and perhaps closest to his heart was the General Land Office. "Land is the basis of our civilization. What citizen has not felt the urge of land hunger?" This bureau was the trustee of "the mineral wealth that lies in the bosom of the soil, of the undeveloped and undiscovered oil pools within the public domain, of the water-power sites of enormous financial potentiality." The Geological Survey was concerned with the discovery and appraisal of natural resources: "Coldly scientific in its interests . . . its opinion on any matter within its jurisdiction is recognized everywhere as being the last word." The Bureau of Reclamation was "charged with the responsibilty of developing the argicultural possibilities of the arid and semiarid regions of the United States," especially through such enormous dam-building projects as that on the Colorado River. The Office of Education researched the progress of schools and colleges and disseminated its data to educators. Interior helped to support Howard University, "the largest Negro university in the world," and ran hospitals for the mentally ill and the deaf. It had administrative responsibility for Alaska, Hawaii, and the Virgin Islands.

Some of Ickes' most glowing comments were reserved for the Bureau of Indian Affairs and the National Park Service. The policy of the former was "to help the Indian to help himself . . . to protect him in his property rights . . . to prevent further ruthless exploitation . . . to encourage him to live his own life in his own way." This would "encourage both races to live together in mutual tolerance and understanding." Speaking of the National Park Service, he paid tribute to various individuals (especially John D. Rockefeller) who had joined forces with the United States to preserve "those glorious areas of trees and wild flowers, of beautiful lakes and limpid streams, of towering mountains and expansive meadows, where vast herds of native animals graze, secure from the huntsman."

The common thread in all this heterogeneity was plain to Harold Ickes: "Our primary concern is the protection and enlargement of life and the conservation of natural resources." There is no need to seek a devious psychological explanation of these goals. If anything can be said to have intrinsic value, they can. There may be differences of opinion about what constitutes the enlargement of life, and about the dividing line between conservation and reasonable exploitation, but there was nothing esoteric or elitist about Ickes' notions of these things. By enlargement of life he meant improvement in the health, working conditions, and education of the mass of ordinary people, and for him conservation included the planned development and productive employment of the earth's resources. But, although these goals were commonly held and admirable, not every politician or public servant who nominally adopts them exhibits the dedication, extraordinarily sustained hard work, and obsessive concern with probity that Ickes showed.

We have referred before to his underlying need to be the most responsible and caring parent possible. For him the Department of the Interior exercised a protective, maternal function over the entire country, and he merged with and identified himself with that function to a profound degree. The people were his children, and his concern was with their material and psychological well-being in the daily business of life. He drove himself in their protective service morning and night, typically working a fourteen-hour day, six and even seven days a week. That is not to say that he was totally self-abnegating in his dedication. The more work he accomplished, the more he admired himself and the more convinced he became that his special ability and right to exercise these functions exceeded those of anyone else.

His feeling for Interior owed something of its richness and depth to a classical theme in oedipal fantasies. When he came to the department it was, figuratively, a fallen woman, besmirched by notorious scandals, its noble functions prostituted in the service of unscrupulous private interests by a succession of weak or venal administrators. As recently as 1927 a former Secretary, Albert B. Fall, had been convicted of accepting bribes to secure the leasing of two great oil reserves (the best known being at Teapot Dome in Wyoming) to commercial oil interests, and in general the Department of the Interior was considered almost irredeemably corrupt. Such a stigma was intolerable to a man who had always found it necessary vehemently to protest his own integrity, if ever it were called into question. But when Ickes, writing to Roosevelt in 1935, referred to an attempt to take from Interior some of its functions as "this new attempted rape," when he declared on another occasion that the "grievous hurt" inflicted by the Ballinger-Pinchot row had left the department "in no position . . . to withstand the criminality of an oil-besmeared Albert B. Fall," or when he described Interior as being "furtive and demoralized" and "shame-stricken and apologetic," he was evoking an image that had powerful, if unrecognized, emotional connotations.[2]

In his memoirs Ickes made clear his resentment of a situation in which his mother, though deceived and ill-treated by her husband, continued to have sexual relations with him—as evidenced by her steady sequence of pregnancies. It is not uncommon for boys, when they fully realize the facts of their parents' sexual life, to feel that their mother has been acting as a prostitute in relation to their father; and in Ickes' case his parents' partial estrangement, their lack of mutual respect, must have heightened this feeling.[3] In discussing Anna's relations with James, her first husband, Ickes had written of his belief that for a woman to continue to have sexual intercourse with a man she did not love was the worst type of prostitution. Explaining why he ceased to have sexual relations with Anna after his return from France, he states that he had always objected to prostitution within marriage, that the very notion of such a thing was repellent to him.[4] He was conscious that his very deep feelings about this matter predated his relationship with Anna. In family situations such as his, oedipal love typically takes the form of wishing to rescue the mother from this degrading connection and restore her to a state of grace. It was not unusual that Ickes, as a newly appointed public official, should have sought to assert his authority over his bureaucracy, or have wished to be seen working effectively. But if he also, in his unconscious mind, saw Interior's true function as being the giving of loving maternal care to the country and its people, and himself as the department's rightful husband, lord, and master, entering upon and taking possession of her, it is little wonder that he embarked on such a strenuous program to redeem her from her fallen state.

Ickes saw his first task as getting rid of the deadwood and bringing into the department men of integrity and strength who shared his convictions. The theme of providing genuine protection for exploited minorities was prominent. Nathan Margold, whose outstanding legal work for various Indian causes was well known to Ickes, was an early choice and was appointed the department's solicitor. Louis C. Campton, of the Bureau of Indian Affairs, who had once announced to the House of Representatives that eleven cents a day was sufficient for the feeding of an Indian child, departed. For the post of Commissioner of Indian Affairs, a presidential appointment, Ickes was determined to have John Collier, and he was delighted when Roosevelt supported him in this resolve, using his political wiles to secure Collier's appointment. Not only was Carl Witherspoon, a black, retained as Ickes' official chauffeur, but an early directive ended racial discrimination in the department's rest rooms and cafeteria. Robert Weaver, a black, was hired to advise Ickes on Negro affairs, and William H. Hastie, a young black lawyer, became assistant solicitor of the department. To help guard against exploitation of natural resources, Harry Slattery, recommended by Gifford Pinchot as a man solely dedicated to the public interest, was appointed Ickes' personal assistant. Slattery, who had been associated with Pinchot in his fight with Ballinger, had also helped to uncover the Teapot Dome scandal and later served as lobbyist for Pinchot's National Conservation Committee.[5]

In the first month of his administration Ickes had had occasion to send Louis R. Glavis, a special investigator attached to Interior, to Muscle Shoals to inquire into allegations of improper practices by power companies there. Ickes was impressed with his work on this mission; in addition, a special connection strongly inclined him to a favorable view of Glavis' ability and ideological soundness. Years before, in 1909, in another of the bitter public scandals of the Interior Department, Glavis had been a chief witness on the side of Gifford Pinchot, then head of the Division of Forestry, who had accused Interior Secretary Richard A. Ballinger of interfering with the government's conservation plans for certain water-power sites and coal lands, in order to aid private corporations. The case made Pinchot, sacrificially dismissed by President Taft for "insubordination," a hero of the conservation movement and was one of the crucial incidents leading to the formation of the breakaway Independent Republican Party in 1912. Ickes had been a member of Pinchot's National Conservation League during 1908 and 1909 and ever since had deeply admired him as a man and as a conservationist. Forestry had been removed from the Department of the Interior in 1905 by Theodore Roosevelt, who considered the administration of it by the Lands Office inefficient. In Ickes' view this was a mark of shame to the department and from the beginning he waged a vigorous, and in the end desperate, campaign to have Roosevelt restore Forestry to Interior. This, and his wider concern with conservation, gradually assumed a portentous and obsessional role in Ickes' mental life, until eventually he felt that all his work would have no meaning if Roosevelt, a prepotent figure in Ickes' conscious and unconscious thoughts, failed to grant him this evidence of faith and trust, the return of Forestry.

Glavis, who had acquired virtue by his association with Pinchot, was appointed Director of Investigations for the Department of the Interior and soon developed a complicated network of supervision and security investigations. Graft was to be made unthinkable in the operations of the department, and the threshold of suspicion of interested parties' motives fell dramatically when Ickes was made head of the newly created Public Works Administration. Although the intense and sustained pitch of investigation and surveillance kept PWA free of scandal and helped achieve Ickes' aim of restoring Interior's tattered reputation, in that in the years of his secretaryship not even one successful accusation of graft was brought against it, this was not without its psychological costs. Ickes eventually came to feel that Glavis had created a juggernaut that was out of Ickes' control, something not to be tolerated; further, Ickes' own business and personal affairs came under hostile scrutiny in reprisal from parties who had come confidently to dip into the great pork barrel of PWA and been sharply rebuffed for their pains. Many people wanted to "get something" on Ickes. Some pried into and misrepresented his own modest (and largely unsuccessful) dealings in real estate, claiming that he purchased land and then manipulated national park boundaries in such a way as to increase its value. None of this was made to stick.

The administration of PWA was a major part of Ickes' Cabinet career, and one which gave him an enormous sense of gratification and solid achievement. The Roosevelt government took office at perhaps the most desperate crisis of the Great Depression, dramatized by the fact that many of the nation's banks had closed their doors. The financial system, industry, and business in general seemed to have ground virtually to a halt, and doomsayers were in full voice. After Roosevelt's emergency measures to stop the run on the banks and the exporting of gold, a strong body of opinion in the Cabinet, though not a unanimous one, favored a massive injection of public money into the economy to get the financial system working again. This was to include a large public works program as well as work-relief. The relief program began in May 1933 under the Federal Emergency Relief Administration as direct relief with funds given through the states. In November 1933 an additional program of work-relief for men on the unemployed rolls commenced under direct federal control, administered by the Civil Works Administration. Both programs were directed by Harry Hopkins.

The public works program was begun by the Public Works Administration (PWA), set up by the National Industrial Recovery Act of June 1933. Harold Ickes was appointed its administrator on 8 July 1933, in addition to his major post as Secretary of the Interior. (To these was added a little later the post of Oil Administrator.) The sequence of events which led to his appointment to PWA throws an interesting light on the nature of Ickes' ambition. Writing years later in the *Saturday Evening Post*, Ickes said of his appointment as Public Works Administrator: "This was an entire surprise to me. I had not suggested to anyone that 'Barkis is willin'.' I already had a full-time job, and one that excited my interest. To be sure, one day when we were in conference with the President, Dan Roper, the Secretary of Commerce, had suggested my availability for Public Works, but the President had made no comment and neither had I."[6]

However, according to the entry for 5 July in the *Secret Diary*, which refers to that conference, the President "fell in with the idea" of Ickes' appointment "quite readily," and there was some general discussion of what supporting appointments there might be if Ickes were made Public Works Administrator. But, much more importantly, he had been preparing the ground two months earlier. On 16 May, after the Cabinet meeting, secretaries Perkins, Roper, and Ickes discussed with the President the final draft of the Public Works and Industrial Control Bill. Ickes made two suggestions that met with the President's approval. "The first was that there be a definite revision made to include conservation of natural resources among the objects of the bill; and the other was that instead of appointing an independent Public Works Administrator, the new official be assigned to some department." The import of these suggestions is clear. The conservation of natural resources was precisely what Ickes saw as the prime function of his own department, and the inclusion of this as one of the objects of the bill would naturally suggest that the "some department" of his second proposal would be the Department of the Interior. Even though the precise form of Ickes' suggestions was not incorporated in the bill, they helped to create a connection in the President's mind between Public Works and Interior. They further imply that from the start Ickes had his sights set on administering public works in what he considered the most appropriate manner.

While the National Industrial Recovery Act was being drawn up, Ickes had been concerned that the President intended to appoint

General Hugh S. Johnson as administrator of the program's Industrial Control section because Ickes believed that Johnson would try to take over public works as well. (Indeed events showed that that had been his intention.) In his diary entry for 8 June, Ickes notes that he telephoned Roper and Postmaster General James Farley and told them that in his judgment "the President would be making a terrible mistake if he should appoint General Hugh S. Johnson to have charge of the administration of the Industries Control section," evidently hoping that they would try to sway the President away from that course. In the event, Roosevelt did appoint Johnson to administer industrial recovery, but in his presence dictated executive orders making it plain that there was to be no overlap with public works. Ickes says that Johnson, "in his impetuous, high-handed way, has already set up a practically complete organization to administer public works, apparently on the theory that he would have control of this also." He enjoyed Johnson's discomfiture, though he himself had as yet been given only supervisory control of public works.

There was an interim period of about two weeks during which Colonel Donald H. Sawyer was appointed temporary administrator, under the supervision of a committee chaired by Ickes. At the first meeting of the Special Board for Public Works, Sawyer, who also cherished the hope of being permanent administrator, asked for approval of a list of federal construction projects that he, as chairman of the Federal Employment Stabilization Board, and his staff had been working on feverishly for the preceding two weeks. Sawyer was one of those who believed that speed in spending the public works funds was essential. But Roosevelt had gone on vacation, leaving instructions that no allotments were to be made until he returned; consequently, Sawyer was overruled.[7] From then on the policies of Ickes, and perhaps Roosevelt, intentionally or not, had the effect of slowing down the infusion of public works funds into the economy. Soon after Roosevelt's return a conference with secretaries Roper and Ickes was held, during which they managed to create a consensus of opinion that Sawyer's poor administrative ability ruled him out as Public Works Administrator and to persuade the President to appoint Ickes.

Why did Ickes falsify his memory of his appointment and claim that Roosevelt's gift to him of PWA was unsolicited and unexpected? The motivation is the same as that which prompted his claim that Roosevelt made him Secretary of the Interior simply because he liked him and intuited his worth on sight. In the years that intervened between those appointments and his reminiscences, Ickes had developed a tremendous attachment to Roosevelt. There is evidence for this in his growing rivalry with Wallace (over Forestry) and with Hopkins (over public works) for the President's trust and appreciation. The origin of this feeling lay most openly in his admiration for Roosevelt's enormously charismatic leadership, that demagogic power Ickes had so often admired in his favorite political candidates and felt so lacking in himself. But often, with once-admired leaders such as John Harlan and, later, Gifford Pinchot and Hiram Johnson, Ickes eventually turned against them and reversed his earlier estimate of their value. For such a personality as Ickes, relations with admired males always were ambivalent, because they were based in large measure on feminine feelings of dependency and physical attraction, against which he desperately defended himself when those feelings came close to consciousness. These unconscious fears of emasculation underlay much of his combativeness.

Symptomatic of these unconscious fears was, for example, his overreaction to the hazing to which his beloved son Raymond had been subjected at Culver Military Academy a few years before. In his memoirs Ickes wrote that Raymond, like himself, strenuously objected to hazing, that he just could not tolerate manhandling or interference with his person, though he would willingly meet any boy in a fair fight. To some extent this was a projection onto Raymond of Harold's own feeling. Raymond did resent the hazing but did not want his father to interfere. At the end of the academic year, when the hazing was at a climax, Harold could no longer restrain himself. He stormed out to the college, burst into the room of the Colonel who headed the Academy and gave vent to a tirade against him and his depraved institution; Raymond would be withdrawn forthwith, and Ickes would advise against Culver to anyone who asked.

Later, when Raymond was attending the University of Chicago, he found that all the fraternities required prospective members to do stunts seemingly calculated to cause physical and mental humiliation; with his father's approval, Raymond decided against joining one. Ickes again notes that, like him, Raymond found intimate physical contact repellent.[8] He digresses to say that even now, at the time of writing, he himself could not bear to have any person idly take his arm or touch his shoulder. For reasons dating back to his boyhood, Ickes was more concerned and suspicious than most men about the threat of aggressive bodily contact, which, we propose, he equated with attempted emasculation. By extension, through associative links, any attempt to challenge his competence or authority, or to encroach on his spheres of influence, was apt to provoke in him an angry bull-like response, as if his masculinity were threatened.

This complex was if anything potentially more explosive in his relations with revered leaders to whom he felt physically attracted. His tendency to be admiringly subservient to them was an internal rather than external force exposing him to the danger of being unsexed, and it was his defensive reaction to this that had made him turn against former heroes. But, although there were to be many occasions of bitter doubt over Roosevelt's loyalty to him, Ickes remained in thrall to the President as long as his life endured. And FDR, when the occasion demanded, did not hesitate to exploit that feeling by endearing, almost flirtatious cajolery (telling Ickes on one occasion that "That is mighty sweet of you and if I were a Frenchman I would kiss you on both cheeks").[9] Ickes felt keen pleasure in physical closeness with Roosevelt, even if he could not tolerate it with any other adult male. One gets the impression that every occasion when Roosevelt put his hand on Ickes' shoulder, or pressed his forearm, is faithfully recorded in the *Secret Diary*.

An amusing contrast of reactions is revealed within two pages of Volume II, in the entry for 24 December 1936. Ickes tells of an official dinner at which he sat next to Josephus Daniels, United States Ambassador to Mexico. "He has the habit, which to me is excruciatingly annoying, of prodding a person when he has a remark to make. This he varied by putting his left arm around my shoulders while he grasped my right forearm firmly with his right hand. This sort of physical contact simply makes cold chills run up and down my spine." With Roosevelt it was a different matter. Because it was the beginning of the second term Ickes had formally offered his resignation, in case the President wanted to be rid of him. Of course it was refused. When he went in to see the President, he was told to go ahead and move into his new Interior Department building (built with PWA funds). "I thanked him very sincerely for what he had said. He put his left hand on my forearm and in an affectionate manner said: 'You and I have a lot of things to do yet.' I told him how much I appreciated the opportunity that he had given me when he first appointed me and that it was difficult for me to express my real feelings at this continued evidence of his confidence in me."

Why was there no negative reaction to such physical contact or to Roosevelt's overpowering masculine charm? Perhaps Roosevelt's paralysis, the crippling of his legs, disarmed Ickes' belligerent defensiveness. For such a man as Ickes, this would stand, unconsciously, as the canceling out of Roosevelt's physical masculinity (though it was not so in fact). So the threat of too great a challenge to Ickes' own masculinity was decreased. Roosevelt was like a feminized father figure, attracting admiring dependency, and perhaps the physical tenderness Ickes would have felt for an ideal mother, or wife, without any accompanying danger.[10]

Whatever the unconscious forces may have been, there is no doubt that Ickes' feeling for Roosevelt was much more personal than mere admiration for a great political leader. Because of this he needed proof of Roosevelt's love; he needed to believe that the President had awarded him PWA out of the same personal regard which (Ickes felt) had led to his appointment as Secretary of the Interior. When Ickes wrote in 1948 in the *Saturday Evening Post*, "PWA was my baby from the moment that FDR had laid it so unexpectedly on my doorstep. I loved it passionately,"[11] his choice of imagery is not only a convenient cliché. Roosevelt had given him a child, thus creating him a parent, though an ambiguity in these fantasy sex roles often reappeared. Roosevelt as a male would have turned Ickes into a mother, but it is typically females who leave infants on doorsteps. In any case, Ickes plunged into the parental role of providing life-giving streams of nourishment for the people of his country, but with a careful eye to the healthiness of the diet.

A good indication of the value he placed on public works is found in his book *Back to Work* (1935). These sentiments were repeated many times:

Many billions of dollars could properly be spent in the United States on permanent improvements. Such spending would not only help us out of the depression, it would do much for the health, well-being and prosperity of the people. I refuse to believe that providing an adequate water supply for a municipality or putting in a sewage system is a wasteful expenditure of money. Any money spent in such fashion as to make our people healthier and happier human beings is not only a good social investment, it is sound from a strictly financial point of view. I can think of no better investment, for instance, than money paid out to provide education and to safeguard the health of the people. Sound and well-trained minds in sound bodies would add more to the actual prosperity of this country, measured purely in money values, than anything I can think of at the moment.[12]

Plainly this is more detailed version of Ickes' statement of aims for Interior—"the protection and enlargement of life and the conservation of natural resources"—and his laying claim to PWA is consistent with what he saw his role as Secretary of the Interior to be.

But even among those in the Cabinet who wanted to reflate the economy there were opposing views as to the most effective means of getting the money into circulation. Ickes' view was very characteristic of him, and of the thrifty attitude ingrained in him since childhood. Not only did he favor socially useful, permanent improvements but he wanted them to be financially self-liquidating, so that money borrowed from federal funds might be repaid into those funds within a modest span of years, thus creating a self-renewing, two-way flow of capital. Under PWA the Government advanced 100 percent of the money needed for a project, but only a certain percentage (45 percent for the most part) was a direct grant. The remainder was a loan at 4 percent interest, to be amortized as soon as possible and in no case more than thirty years. The contrary view was advanced predominantly by Harry Hopkins, administrator of FERA, who held that speed in getting the money actually into circulation was of critical importance, and that the PWA type of program, worthy though it may have been, was unavoidably slow in delivering funds because of the time-consuming investigations required to ensure that the proposed projects were financially responsible. Hopkins wanted projects that could be started immediately and would take men off the relief rolls as soon as possible. Such schemes could not call for the setting up of capital equipment and so were apt to be short-term in their effects. The exaggerated but convenient expression that came to be used by his critics for the projects Hopkins instituted was "leaf-raking and grass-cutting"—labor-intensive but largely unproductive jobs whose effects were soon nullified.

Both types of operation had a legitimate role; the difficulty was that before long these two powerful administrators came into competition for the limited funds that the Bureau of the Budget was prepared to allow them. Lewis Douglas, Director of the Budget, held the traditional conservative view that inflation was the great enemy of economic well-being and that the budget should be balanced and not in deficit. Since Hopkins' administration spent money more quickly than Ickes', it was he who usually was the aggressor in this competition. By November 1933 Hopkins, as Emergency Relief Administrator, was devising a plan that would "put anywhere from two to four million men back to work for standard wages on a thirty-hour-week basis," as Ickes described it in his *Secret Diary*. Hopkins would continue to pay on account of these wages what he was contributing toward relief, and the balance would be made up out of the public works funds, that is, Ickes' funds. "This would amount to a maximum of $400 million for the next sixty days. This would put a serious crimp in the balance of our public works fund, but we all thought it ought to be done." Ickes shared the view that the country was "really in a very critical condition and that something drastic and immediate ought to be done to bolster the situation." In this spirit of compromise he made no demur to Hopkins' proposal, and even helped him present it to the President at lunch the next day. The reallocation went through, and a few days later there was a meeting in Ickes' office to draw up lines of demarcation between Hopkins' projects and PWA projects, on the general lines described above. One can see the dawning of territorialism in the statement Ickes read to the newspapers after this meeting, that "any state or municipality withdrawing a project submitted to the Public Works organization for consideration in the hope or expectation that the Civil Works [that is, Hopkins'] organization would do the work instead, free of cost, would not only not have such work done by the Civil Works organization, but . . . might not again resubmit its project to the Public Works organization."[13]

A decided rivalry later developed between Ickes and Hopkins over appropriations of funds and over the power to approve works projects, but for the first year of the New Deal they worked harmoniously and cooperatively. Ickes worked unflaggingly in setting up his PWA organization and starting the machinery for determining the economic feasibility of projects and the credit worthiness of the communities applying for them. Complaints of slowness, stinginess, overcautiousness, and so on were leveled against him, but many of these seem to have originated from rivals within the administration or from local politicians disappointed that he had found their proposals insufficiently responsible. Ickes defended himself vigorously against such complaints. Writing in September 1933 to Heywood Broun, who had suggested in his column that the public works program had been unduly retarded, he protested that matters had progressed as rapidly as possible. Colonel Waite and his engineers had worked day and night on the approval of projects, consulting lawyers and accountants and then sending their recommendations to the Board of Public Works. From there they were taken by Ickes to Roosevelt, who rapidly gave his assent. Since his appointment three months earlier Ickes had selected regional advisers and put together organizations in every state.[14]

There is little reason to doubt that this was substantially true. In the *Secret Diary* entry for 11 July, Ickes tells us that at a recent meeting of the Special Board for Public Works, just three days after he was made administrator, "we went over a number of projects that had been certified to us with approval by a subcommittee of the board which has been working on the matter for the last week or ten days. Some items were approved and others deferred." The next day Ickes took the recommendations to the President, who "approved practically everything." That did not mean that the money began to be spent instantly, but Ickes had set the process in motion as rapidly as possible, given the procedures that he believed had to be gone through.

Whether all of those procedures were necessary is a different and perhaps more pertinent question. Complaints persisted, and even some of Ickes' friends expressed unease about the degree of centralization and the extensive network of financial and administrative controls with which Ickes, in his avidity for honesty and strict accountability, had encumbered PWA. Former Chicago Progressives Frank Knox and Charles Merriam urged him to move more quickly. Merriam, a professor of political economy at the University of Chicago, pointed out in August 1933 that, since as a Cabinet officer

Ickes had acquired unprecedented peacetime responsibilities, he must relieve himself of much detail, take only the most important decisions, and appoint subordinates whom he could implicitly trust. Two months later Merriam, by now gravely troubled about the slowness of the Public Works program, again urged a speeding up.

The real difficulty, Ickes told Merriam, was not in approving the projects, but in having the work started. Government agencies at all levels were dragging their feet. Far from attempting to supervise every detail, he put his signature to contracts worth millions with hardly a cursory look.[15]

But a later account, in which Ickes proudly reveals his passion not only for honesty but for what Frances Perkins referred to as his "punctilious, fussy scrutiny of detail," gives a different picture: "With the spotty record of Interior always in mind, I slaved away over endless mountains of documents, contracts and letters, refusing to sign anything that I had not personally read, lest one day it should rise to haunt me in the steam of another Teapot . . . I tried to compensate for my caution by working an average of fourteen hours a day." And again: "I read and signed in triplicate every Public Works contract—thousands of them . . . I never asked for large sums to be dissipated in blindman's buff fashion, through state and local administrators . . . who frequently had nothing to show in the way of accomplishment after the grass had grown again or the leaves had once more withered and fallen to the earth [an allusion to Hopkins' activities]. I am willing to pay the price of my newest derisive characterization of 'medicine-dropper spender.' "[16] Ickes' early training in household management had left him with an archetypal view of the proper husbanding of resources.

That PWA was able to function without graft was a significant achievement on Ickes' part, and his careful scrutiny of its operations undoubtedly winnowed out many unwise projects. His prudence probably helped, too, to deflect from the New Deal criticism which Hopkins' free-spending activities might otherwise have attracted. Certainly, PWA's effectiveness as a short-term recovery program is open to question—only $110 million of its allocation of $3.3 billion was spent during the first six months—[17] but Ickes never viewed PWA's activities solely, or even mainly, in these terms.

If claims and counterclaims about the slowness of the public works program are difficult to assess, criticisms of Ickes' conservative credit policy had more substance. The National Industrial Recovery Act, in giving PWA authority to lend to institutions, specified that the loans thus made should be "reasonably secured." Ickes interpreted this to mean that a municipality should not have exceeded its debt limit, that its corporate stock should be marketable. If its bonds were selling below par, then it seemed a bad risk to him. This had the effect of eliminating poorer communities from the public works program in favor of those already in a reasonable financial condition. Such indigent communities could then apply to Hopkins' work relief organization (CWA at first, then WPA), but Ickes' policy definitely restricted the scope of application of the public works program. In correspondence with Senator James Couzens of Michigan, he claimed it would be immoral to restrict some communities to a 45 percent loan plus a 55 percent grant and make a 100 percent grant to others. But it is not clear why it should be thought immoral if the discrimination were made not on the basis of political favoritism but on that of ability to pay. It seems, rather, that Ickes, perhaps not consciously, felt that municipalities that had shown themselves to be sober, thrifty, and responsible should be rewarded, while spendthrift, shiftless ones should not.[18]

PWA bore the strong stamp of Harold Ickes' character in other respects. He saw to it that blacks were added to the local committees set up to supervise projects and that black engineers and architects were employed. He specifically outlawed "discrimination against any person because of color or religious affiliation" within the PWA organization; when he found that this instruction was being circumvented, he, with Robert Weaver and Clark Foreman, his two advisers on Negro affairs, devised a formula by which firms signing contracts with PWA's Housing Division were required to pay a certain percentge of their total wages bill to blacks. Other contracts contained similar provisions.[19]

Blacks benefited directly from such policies, which Ickes, under the provisions of the legislation setting up PWA, was under no obligation to introduce. Their wages were raised, and they were admitted to Southern construction unions, which had previously excluded them. Approximately one-quarter of all PWA housing projects, which provided low-rent accommodation, were allocated to blacks, and many such projects outside the South were desegregated.[20]

Though he was unable to revise discriminatory contracts entered

into by the previous administration, Ickes did what he could to miti-
gate their effects. As a result of earlier political pressure a small
number of blacks had finally been employed on the giant Boulder
Dam project, but these workers were excluded from the newly established settlement at Boulder City and forced to make a thirty-
mile journey between the dam site and Las Vegas each day. When
he became aware of the situation, Ickes abolished the rule which excluded blacks from Boulder City, and provided housing for them
there. There was never anything equivocal about Ickes' official
statements on such matters. He told Robert Fechner, director of
Emergency Conservation Work, to cease his objection to the appointment of blacks to supervisory positions in CCC camps.[21] These
protective attitudes toward minorities can be traced in a continuous
line back to his attempts to protect his exploited mother.

Yet there were moral blind spots. Despite his great stress on rectitude and strict accountability, Ickes was not above giving, under
pressure of public criticism, a misleadingly favorable picture of the
progress of PWA, using statistics to his advantage. In a *New York
Times* article of 24 September 1933, answering criticisms of slowness, he declared:

> The President appointed me administrator on July 8. Since the In-
> dustrial Recovery Act was passed approximately $1,500,000,000 of
> the total fund appropriated has been allotted for work on socially
> beneficial public works . . .
> Allotments already have been made to practically every type of
> public works specified in the act . . . The two largest allotments were
> $400,000,000 for roads in all States and $238,000,000 for naval con-
> struction. Money also has been allotted for all types of construction,
> such as sewers, housing, water plants, schools, asylums, bridges, tun-
> nels and a whole variety of public works.

But those two large allotments for roads and naval construction,
totaling a little over 40 percent of the funds allotted, were not a
proper use of PWA funds, at least as the public works program had
been represented to the public. Roads and naval constructions were
the regular business of other departments or bureaus, and the
money for them should have come from seperate appropriations,
rather than from the recovery funds. PWA was supposed to start
projects additional to normal, recurrent expenditures—to be an infusion into the economy over and above the regular government ex-

penditure, which had proved insufficient. The claims Ickes was to make later about the numbers of people given jobs by PWA were inflated in the same way, for they included those who would have been employed by other agencies in any case. PWA's funds had been diverted to these other agencies, but that did not mean that new jobs had been created by them. This diversion of "recovery" funds continued throughout the life of PWA, but there is surprisingly little mention of it in the *Secret Diary*. It has been estimated that the maximum number of jobs directly provided by PWA was only 500,000 and that overall only about half the funds appropriated for it were actually spent on recovery projects.[22] But, as we have seen, when Ickes felt that he was in the right, which in politics was most of the time, he was prepared to allow a certain leniency in the means that were justified by the end. Dedicated to the success of Roosevelt's administration, he did not mind some well-meaning misrepresentation of the scope of PWA, if it brought credit upon the government.

In November 1934 a series of conferences took place between Roosevelt, Morgenthau, Hopkins, and Ickes to plan a public works program for 1935. The President seemed to be favoring an appropriation of $5 billion for that year, followed by decreasing amounts in the next two or three years. In one meeting funds for the Army and Navy were discussed, and it seemed that they would need about one billion for rehabilitation, replacements, and so on. "We discussed whether this would be included in the $5 billion or be additional thereto. I made the remark that there was no use going ahead with a seventy five per cent program; that the money for the Army and the Navy would not give work to the unemployed but would merely keep those now employed at work." The President "seemed to be inclined" to the view that the Army and Navy funds should be in addition to those for public works. However, three months later we find Ickes appearing before a special Senate committee investigating the munitions question. "I was questioned for better than an hour on allocations to the Army and Navy out of public works funds. The committee was particularly interested in the $238 million set aside for the Navy by the Executive Order of the President the day that the Public Works Bill was signed. I confined my replies to statements of fact. When my opinion was asked in order, if possible, to reflect upon the President, I declined to answer."[23]

In fact, the diversion of public works funds seems to have been largely brought about by the President. Secretary of War George Dern had recognized from the start that the public works program contained "a lot of camouflage." He told the very first meeting of the Special Board for Public Works that the original $3,300,000,000 was in large part just a transfer of funds from other departments: "We are trying to fool the American people with a program of $3,500,000,000 [*sic*] on public works when we haven't got it."[24] To what extent this was conscious politicking on Roosevelt's part and to what extent it was forced on him by the stringent restrictions imposed by Director of the Budget Douglas, cannot be determined. In this rare instance Ickes' concern for the disadvantaged did not cause him to take issue with Roosevelt. His devotion to FDR, flawed though it was by his jealousy over the President's relations with Hopkins and, to a lesser extent, Henry Wallace of Agriculture, and his reluctant suspicion that Roosevelt was deceiving him over Forestry, was too great for that. His later fierce competition with Hopkins over the apportioning and control of recovery funds does not appear so much a principled stand over the rightful employment of those funds, as a personal rivalry for power, prestige, and Roosevelt's confidence.

But for the first several months of the New Deal it was full steam ahead for Harold Ickes. There was little sign of the trepidation, the qualm that he may have bitten off too much, that would be understandable in a man on the verge of sixty, suddenly elevated to a position of power and authority that would have seemed impossible of achievement only weeks before. Not only did he confidently assume control of Interior, but he also had himself appointed Public Works Administrator and Oil Administrator. With just as great firmness and despatch did he seize control of his private life, where for so long he had been the bitter underdog.[25] For some months Anna stayed behind in Chicago, serving out her term in the state legislature. She would have been assured of reelection once more, but she was profoundly impressed by Ickes' sudden rise to national prominence and decided not to run again. In his personal memoirs he says that, to his surprise, she quickly lost interest in her own political career and came to believe that his career should be advanced. That is not to say that she became self-effacing. She and Raymond and Robert came to Washington with Ickes for the inauguration, and Anna seemed proud of their new status and enjoyed posing for the photographers. Harold was glad when she returned to the state leg-islature in Springfield immediately after the inauguration. He was glad also to leave Chicago and begin his new life. He felt a changed attitude toward him on the part of friends and acquaintances and the public in general, and indeed his new position at once presented an opportunity, which he was confident enough to seize without any trace of his long-ingrained suspiciousness, to enlarge his personal life.

During his first week in Washington, Ickes received a telephone call at his hotel from a woman whom he had known since she was a small girl, though in the intervening thirty or so years he had seen her only once, about ten years before, when she was a young wife. He says that as he greeted her on that occasion he sensed her strong sexuality and desired her. Now, having read of his appointment as Secretary of the Interior, she had called to tell him that she was di-vorced, living in Washington, and engaged to another man, and to ask whether he could find her fiancé a job. She promised to reward him with a kiss. He made an appointment for her to come to his hotel for the interview the next Sunday afternoon, hardly an ortho-dox time or venue for a businesslike encounter. In his personal memoirs Ickes muses about the strange effects that sex can have on a man. He may have been especially vulnerable because he had been emotionally starved so long. When she arrived there was no doubt that she had made herself attractive as possible, and as soon as he closed the door he embraced and kissed her passionately. She was rather taken aback, but he reminded her of her promise. (In these personal memoirs Ickes refers to this woman only as "X," although her identity can be deduced from other writings.)

On this first occasion, though X could not stay (her fiancé was waiting outside in a car), Ickes told her bluntly that he wanted her. She said she would have to consider his proposition, and he told her that he would have to survey the situation at his office concerning the man's employment. An appointment was made for the following Sunday, and this time the tentative deal for an exchange of favors reached a satisfactory conclusion. They entered upon a passionate involvement that endured for many months and perhaps brought about some amelioration of Ickes' almost pathologically distrustful attitude toward women. Certainly it restored his confidence in his sexual potency, which, for all his protestations, had been severely shaken by his tortured relationship with Anna. His new positive self-image in that important area of life could only have added to his newfound ability to exercise power in the political arena. Ickes describes his physical relationship with X as being perfectly fulfilling, so different from that with Anna who was never free from moral inhibitions. So great was his passion that he grew reckless, willing to risk even his job in order to continue the affair, he claims.[26]

If a man entrusted with such great power and responsibility could value his office below that of an illicit sexual relationship (which he admitted to be purely physical, since X had little depth of sensitivity or intellect), one would have to think that the air of propriety necessary for public confidence was a mere veneer, barely covering an unstable, impulse-ridden personality. If Harold Ickes had abdicated office over a sordid affair, the credibility of the whole New Deal would have been shaken. But his passion for his position was far stronger than that for X, and the foregoing declaration may have been just an overdramatizing of his feelings in retrospect or a way of rationalizing and concealing from himself the true nature of his treatment of Anna.

Ickes used his power as Secretary to send X's fiancé to a job in the Midwest, an arrangement with which she seemed perfectly satisfied, and they met very frequently, though not really with the degree of recklessness that he ascribes to himself. He took her driving at nights in his official car, but only out into the countryside. Whenever she came to his home—at first in a hotel, then, after a couple of months, a small rented house in Georgetown which had been occupied by the counsellor of the Danish Legation—precautions were taken so that she could approach and later slip away as discreetly as possible. Even so, during that summer of 1933, vindictive anonymous letters about their relationship began to appear, some addressed to X, some to Anna, who had gone to spend a couple of months in New Mexico after the adjournment of the Illinois legislature. It is difficult to tell from Ickes' journal how widely these letters were distributed; probably he did not know himself, but they found their way into many newspaper offices, though none stooped to print them, either on principle or because the letters were so scurrilous that an action for libel would have appeared certain. Anna wrote Harold that, although she found the letters disturbing, she realized that they had no basis in fact; she was warning him only so that he might be on guard. Ickes records that naturally he reassured her, though the ground for that "naturally" is obscure, considering his claim of reckless commitment to X.

Ickes' suspicion had been diverted from the most likely suspect, X's fiancé, by the fact that when the letters had begun appearing, with Washington postmarks, he was in the Midwest. After some months, X passed on a request from the fiancé that he be brought back to a post in Washington, and Ickes consented. The letters increased in frequency. Ickes saw the fiancé on a few occasions after his return and described him as ill-bred, devious, and unattractive. He could not understand how X could be attracted by such a man and felt that she must have been submitting to him in order to avert trouble. (What he did not discover until much later was that X now had resumed her sexual relationship with the man, and would even visit him directly after leaving Ickes.) The letters began to make Ickes edgy, though in his memoirs he maintains that he did not care what happened: his relationship with Anna was so desperate and his sexual fulfillment in X so great that the emotional gain outweighed the risk.

In August 1933 he talked to Louis Howe, Roosevelt's personal secretary, about the letters, giving him a general idea of their nature without making any admission. Mixed up with the allegations of impropriety with X, claims had been made to congressmen that PWA was a failure; that as Oil Administrator, Ickes had sold out to oil interests; and that as a lawyer in Chicago he had mismanaged the winding up of the estate of a person named Saunders.[27] Naturally enough, Ickes considered this a wide-ranging assault on the tenability of his position in Washington. Howe referred the matter to Captain Moran of the Secret Service, who assigned someone named Burns to the job. Burns turned out to be stupid, Ickes charges, and months went by without result. According to the *Secret Diary* entry for 21 March 1934, Ickes lunched with the President and told him that "in my judgment a well-conceived conspiracy was in process of being carried out in order to make my position in the Cabinet untenable." One of these pressures came from a Chicago lawyer, Lucius J. Malmin, who had been a judge in the Virgin Islands during the Wilson administration and now wanted to be Lieutenant Governor there—an appointment under Ickes' control as Secretary of the Interior. From the beginning Malmin had deviously threatened him that he would make public the accusations of a person

Ickes describes as "a drunken bum of a lawyer in Chicago," who claimed that Ickes had been guilty of fraud in settling the Saunders estate while he was still practicing law in Chicago. No evidence of malpractice was ever brought forward, and eventually Ickes had Malmin disbarred by the Supreme Court of Illinois; but at this time he was still a nuisance. Malmin was also charging Ickes with manipulating the value of some real estate he had bought in Skokie Valley.[28] Further, some of the Hearst papers, Ickes had been told, were working up a story concerning his relationship with X.

That same month Ickes had found occasion to speak to the President about his long-standing friendship with X and her family, explaining that they had merely renewed the friendship in Washington, as they would have in Chicago or Altoona. He says Roosevelt agreed that there was no reason why he should not continue to see her from time to time. Having thus disguised the true nature of that relationship, Ickes went on to say that if the right to see friends was inconsistent with holding office, he would retire from public life. In the context of this conversation, the latter proposal was not likely to be accepted.

Although each of these sources of irritation and anxiety was real enough, it is arguable whether they were a concerted "conspiracy." In his entry for 20 March, Ickes had written: "My theory is that Malmin is being financed by the same people who are undoubtedly bent on trying to make my position here untenable." No such organized plot was ever revealed, but the pressures on Ickes at this time were such that he may be forgiven a trace of paranoia. After unburdening himself to Roosevelt at the luncheon on 20 March, he wrote: "I am relieved to have had this talk with the President. He took the whole thing just as I thought he would. He was friendly and understanding and human, as always." This attachment to Roosevelt grew and was to be a major determinant of Ickes' career as long as FDR lived. However, on this occasion the President simply sent for the same Chief Moran of the Secret Service who had previously been contacted by Louis Howe and directed him to inquire into Ickes' problems.

Up to now Ickes had been reluctant to set his own manhunter, Louis Glavis, on the scent, because he wisely did not want him to know anything about his intimate personal affairs; but in April 1934 he did so, and within a short time Glavis announced that the fiancé was the author of the letters. Ickes sent the man away for a few days on a trumped-up job so as to give Glavis a chance to break into his apartment. Glavis returned triumphantly with samples from the fiancé's typewriter and some carbons used when the letters were typed, proving that they had been written on this machine. There was no doubt about his guilt.

Now X's loyalty was put to the test. At Ickes' request, she met her fiancé at the train on his return and persuaded him to go immediately to his bank, where he had some documents in a safe-deposit box that Ickes wanted her to check on. Just what the point of this was is not made clear, but Ickes writes that he had some doubts about her at this stage, imagining that she might betray him. However, she carried out her sensitive mission with complete loyalty. Perhaps that was the main point: she had proved her loyalty to Ickes by being disloyal to her fiancé. In unpublished portions of the *Secret Diary* Ickes boasts of his showdown with the fiancé. He called him to his office and demonstrated the evidence of his guilt. He hurled abuse, calling the man a despicable coward and every other epithet that came to mind; he was disgusted to find he lacked the manliness to fight back.[29] Of course Ickes fired him on the spot.

The affair with X did not now have long to run; she resigned two months later from the position in Interior to which Ickes had advanced her, because she had decided to marry her fiancé. But while it was at its height Ickes had used it to achieve a momentous and deeply wounding victory over Anna. In his memoirs he writes that he was deeply and recklessly involved in the affair with X when Anna returned from New Mexico in the summer of 1933. He claims it was a much deeper affair than those earlier occasions when he had simply sought casual physical relationships without emotional involvement. Because his emotions were so involved on this occasion he decided that it was only fair that Anna should be told. To keep her in ignorance yet continue to live with her would be an anomaly, and he loved X so passionately that he felt under an obligation to reveal the true situation.[30]

This seems to argue an extraordinarily refined moral sensibility on Ickes' part, since none of the practical reasons he vaguely includes have any force whatever. In what sense could he have felt himself under an obligation to tell Anna of their affair when, as he says explicitly and as events confirmed, he had not the smallest intention of divorcing Anna or even separating from her, and no intention of giving X the benefit of anything but a clandestine connection? In view of those intentions, the humane thing, one might think, would be for him to maintain as politely as possible the fiction that nothing out of the ordinary was going on. After all, as he insistently tells us, he had been scrupulous in abstaining from sexual relations within his marriage—that is, preserving his virtue—for a dozen years, so Anna would have no cause to expect anything from him and he have no cause to feel that he was behaving like a prostitute in going from one bed to another. This particular kind of self-righteous nice-mindedness is likely to conceal a vindictive intent toward the person who is, regrettably, to be its sacrifical victim. That Ickes acted from such a motive is clear from his own account.

Anna did not come to Washington until November, in time for the President's annual dinner to the members of the Cabinet, on the 16th. Ickes writes that she had long looked foward to the event and was greatly excited that evening. He says that Anna had come to see herself as being just as important with the public as Eleanor Roosevelt, and even more popular. He was reluctant to ruin the evening for Anna, but that night while they were undressing, and though he disliked doing it, he told her flatly that he was in love with another woman.

Because of the anonymous letters, Anna guessed at once who X was and wanted to know whether Ickes had been sleeping with her. He denied it because, he says, he had always believed that a man in such a situation owed this much to the woman. Anna's reaction suggests that she could not have believed this extraordinary and implausible denial. Without the connotation of physical relations, Ickes' announcement would have been overblown, even trivial. He loved another woman, but did not intend to leave Anna and in any case had not loved her for years. The actual import was far from trivial: she was devastated by the news.

Ickes says the hell that subsequently developed was the worst he had ever known. There were awful scenes, with Anna's hysteria reaching new heights. He felt some guilt over her distress, but recognized that what had happened had been inevitable. This is disingenuous. Ickes had deliberately inflicted the suffering on her. He contrives to suggest that he had unwittingly, even reluctantly, been caught up in a grand passion, an inexorable force whose logic he must obey; the truth was that he had consciously used his privilege of patronage to procure this woman as his mistress, and that while it may well have been an unusually fulfilling physical relationship, he did not ever see it as going on into the indefinite future as a life partnership, but rather as something essentially limited. Nothing caused him to profess this other "love" to Anna except his desire to humiliate her and establish his psychological independence of and indeed dominance over her, as someone he no longer needed. Ickes writes of telling Anna plainly that the long years of submission, of trying to adjust his life to hers, were over, that her hold over him was broken. Although there continued to be flare-ups between them, he knew he had defeated her, and she knew it too, notwithstanding the cruel way in which it had been done. There could be no clearer declaration of Ickes' motivation than that last sentence.

The final crisis for Anna came on Sunday, 25 March 1934, when they were having a particularly ferocious quarrel, and in her despair Anna called for some third party to be brought in, some woman she could talk to. She asked for Antoinette Funk of the General Land Office, whom they had known in Chicago. Anna hysterically heaped accusations and abuse on Harold and, as he recalled, showed such animal passion and hatred that Mrs. Funk was entirely alienated from her. Harold took Mrs. Funk home about midday, and when he returned found that Anna had taken an overdose of a drug prescribed by her physician. It was not a lethal overdose but the familiar "cry for help." She had immediately telephoned her doctor, who persuaded her to go to a nursing home for two or three weeks. During this enforced rest she became reconciled to their changed situation, Ickes writes, and came back believing that in the end she would win out over X, that if she allowed her husband free rein he would come back to her. In time they worked out a "modus operandi," as he says, under which they managed better than they had before X entered his life. A positive factor was that she liked being the wife of a Cabinet member; also, he says, she apparently realized that she had been failing him sexually. This seems an implausible attribution on his part, since he was the one who had taken the initiative in terminating their sexual relation. It was based on the fact that Anna now tried to seduce him, which he found very trying. He believed that it probably caused her great chagrin to realize that he was not impotent after all. Very occasionally he took pity on her and they did have intercourse, though with reluctance on his part. Not surprisingly, sexual congress under such conditions was not a success, and Ickes protests that the fault was not his. He records incredulously that Anna told her physician she was a passionate woman, a claim Ickes dismisses as ridiculous.

It is impossible not to feel a good deal of sympathy for Anna, despite the portrait of her that Ickes has left. When his affair with X drew to its unedifying conclusion, Anna, he asserts, was genuinely sympathetic, which argues a generosity of spirit not many wives or husbands could encompass in similar circumstances. That romance had begun to break up when Ickes discovered that X was intimate with her fiancé as well as with him, which caused him to display as much possessiveness as Anna had. There was a predictable sequence of estrangements and reconciliations and, for Ickes, one or two harrowing emotional crises. When he found that the fiancé had taken an apartment in X's building, his world almost fell apart and he had to call in a doctor since his nerves had pretty completely gone to pieces. Hard work, he says, saved the day for him: he consoled himself for the loss of one position of dominance by the exercise of another, and so regained his self-control.

When X stormed into his office one day in July 1934, threw his diamond ring on the desk, and told him she was leaving Washington to marry her fiancé, he retained his composure and told her to go ahead. He later discovered that she had hoped he would pursue her and bring her back, but he did not, and the marriage took place three or four days later. Ickes writes that he had a very bad time but pulled himself together and became reconciled to the situation. He reasoned that marriage with X was impossible unless he divorced Anna, which was unthinkable. But for X it was not a clean break. She telephoned him several months later, saying that the marriage had been unhappy from the beginning and pleading to see him. They did in fact resume their relationship, but in a planned and, on Ickes' side, rather cold-blooded manner. He rented an apartment for several months in a quiet lower-middle-class section of Washington, and they met there usually twice a week, but only briefly. He says that X realized that he was not now prepared to place his official position in jeopardy through an open scandal.

So, Ickes had chalked up two victories in his long, undeclared war against women. But although those victories had restored his confidence in his sexual powers, they had not yet dissolved his suspiciousness of women, his hypersensitivity to real or fancied attempts to dominate him. A ready-made focus for this touchiness was Eleanor Roosevelt, not only because she was herself energetic in public affairs of a welfare kind, potentially infringing on Ickes' concerns, but because she was also the wife of the President, about whose person some of Ickes' deepest if largely unacknowledged feelings were becoming organized. As the President's wife she aroused Ickes' jealousy, as did the two or three men who seemed to stand closest in Roosevelt's affections; but also as his wife she could not be the object of Ickes' open ire, which had to be suppressed, and received only guarded expression even in his private writings.

The matter of subsistence housing caused him the greatest turmoil. This part of the Public Works program had been undertaken too hastily and with too little groundwork, Ickes felt. The Subsistence Homesteads Corporation was organized on 2 December 1933, and in his *Secret Diary* entry for that day he expressed concern about the Reedsville, West Virginia, housing project. Colonel Louis Howe, FDR's private secretary, had rashly promised the President that they could start work within three weeks, and "in order to make good on this rash boast," Ickes says, "we have rushed about pell-mell" and were spending more money than necessary. He goes on: "Another thing that bothers me is that Colonel Howe, with I think the approval of Mrs. Roosevelt, wanted us to enter into a contract for some sixty or seventy-five knockdown houses. I understand these houses are only about 10 feet wide and I am afraid they will look a good deal like a joke."

If it had not been for Mrs. Roosevelt's backing, Howe, who had no official status in housing, could have been easily overruled by Ickes, especially in his highly charged state at that time. Two weeks before he had told Anna of his "love" for X, and he and Anna were locked in their final crucial battle. In the same 2 December entry he expresses dissatisfaction with the situation in Public Works, saying that he had allowed it to get out of hand and that he was going to strengthen the organization and make it more directly responsible to him. The entry two days later records that he worked "under a great deal of strain and stress today due to personal matters of a serious nature," and that he had his deputy, Colonel Waite, in "for a frank talk." He accused him of building up an organization that looked to Waite himself as the administrator, rather than to Ickes, and declared that he "could not get along any longer on the present basis." They talked things over "in the utmost friendliness," but Waite, not unnaturally, offered to resign. Ickes told him he ought not to think of doing that; however, after a series of veiled threats, "suggested that he think about the matter overnight and take it up again." Waite lasted a few months longer, then left, though the appearance of civilized dealing was maintained. Ickes says that during this discussion with Waite, both expressed a preference for a strong centralized organization headed by one man, rather than a series of independent bureaus (the point at issue being, of course, who that one man was to be). In his discussions and proposals for the organization of various bodies under the New Deal, Ickes is strikingly consistent in his preference for hierarchical, centralized lines of command, traditionally considered a typical authoritarian structure, rather than a more open, independent, cooperative (that is, democratic) system—an indication that his liberal convictions, though firmly held, were of an acquired, doctrinaire kind, grafted onto what was basically an authoritarian character structure originating in the introjection of his mother's puritanical standards. The fact that he restrained himself from overruling Louis Howe's proposals for the housing project is evidence of the influence of Eleanor Roosevelt's support for Howe.

With regard to the nature of the housing at Reedsville, Ickes' own personal desires were in conflict. We have contended that his pleasure in good building came at least in part from the timeless body-symbolism of dwelling-places, and in building the family home at Hubbard Woods the delight in those feelings had easily been allowed to override the proposed limitations on Anna's and his budget. Thus, Waite's proposal for cheap but ugly and inconvenient housing was deeply distasteful to Ickes; yet the project already under way at Reedsville was even now looking too expensive—always a sensitive point for the parsimonious Ickes—especially for a program supposed to make it possible for the poorest family to own its own home. Three months later, on 10 March 1934, he went to view an exhibit of the Reedsville Subsistence Homestead project, along with the President, two executives of the division concerned, and the architect, Eric Gugler, who had been selected by Eleanor Roosevelt. He writes that "the sketches and pictures were very attractive indeed but the cost of the thing is shocking to me." The

President defended the cost on the ground that it was a model for other homestead projects, but Ickes inquired with an edge of sarcasm what it was a model of, since it certainly was not one of low-cost housing.[31]

Months later, in his diary entry for 16 October 1934, he tells how Eleanor Roosevelt had come to see him after she had undertaken a weekend inspection of Reedsville. Everything was going very badly. The previous May, Ickes had authorized the immediate building of some seventy-five additional houses but "not a lick" had been done on any of them. Thirty barns were waiting to be built while the cows got along the best they could. "Mrs. Roosevelt was very ladylike about it all, but she certainly wasn't pleased. Nor was I." Director Wilson, who had gone back to Agriculture, had been replaced by Charles Pynchon. When Ickes called Pynchon in, it turned out, despite his dissembling, that he did not know who, if anybody, was in charge at Reedsville. Burlew and Slattery told Ickes that Pynchon's wife had social ambitions "and keeps the poor man running hither and yon every night, with the result that he is worn out and has no real pep to put into his work. I feel sorry for him." Ever ready to believe complaints against wives, Ickes, though he went on complaining about Pynchon's executive ability, did not get rid of him.

Apparently, at a lunchtime meeting with the President on 4 November 1934, Ickes actually made a guarded complaint about Mrs. Roosevelt. He had had to report to the President his problems with Subsistence Homesteads, and confided to readers of the *Secret Diary*, if not to Roosevelt, that Eleanor Roosevelt and Colonel Howe had "interfered altogether too much with its administration," with the result that they had an undefendable project at Reedsville. "Work down there has been extravagant and wasteful to a degree. Mrs. Roosevelt, especially, has interfered all along the line, of course with the best intentions. As the President remarked to me: 'My Missus, unlike most women, hasn't any sense about money at all.' He added with respect to Louie Howe, that Louie didn't know anything about money.

The tension and dissatisfaction that both Ickes and Eleanor Roosevelt felt because of the Reedsville Housing Project became one thread in a tangled skein of undeclared rivalry and ill-will. These emotions came close to public hostility at the beginning of 1935. In the *Secret Diary* entry for 5 January 1935 Ickes writes:

On Wednesday [2 January] hell began to pop and it has been pop-
ping ever since. *The New York Herald Tribune* carried a front-page
story by Lindley to the effect that the President had practically ordered me to discharge Glavis and Burlew. The story was a highly
sensational one. It charged Glavis with wire tapping, with espionage
of high Government officials, both inside and outside of the Department, and Burlew with disloyalty to the New Deal, with terrorizing
employees in the Department, and with building up a machine of his
own within the Department. There were other charges made against
Burlew, having to do with the Reedsville Subsistence Homestead
project and other matters.

At separate press conferences later on that day Roosevelt and
Ickes expressly denied that any such instruction had gone from the
President to his Secretary; and Ickes claimed he "left no doubt in the
mind of anyone that I intended to stand behind both men." Ernest
Lindley, who had written the story, came to his office that afternoon,
and Ickes spent some two hours explaining the duties of Ebert Burlew and Glavis and praising them as efficient and able men. It was
hard to make an impression on the journalist, so in the end Ickes
called Burlew in, and together they defended Burlew against the
charges that had been made against him. In particular, "There was
one patronage matter in which Mrs. Roosevelt has been perniciously active and on which Lindley had entirely the wrong slant."
The reporter was much impressed with both Ickes and Burlew, and
his follow-up story on the Thursday morning was more moderate.
But evidently Ickes thought he had begun to sniff out one of Lindley's sources. If he had got "the wrong slant" on a matter in which
Mrs. Roosevelt had been "perniciously active," then presumably the
misinformation had originated with her.

Ickes was always very ready to defend his subordinates against
unjust criticism. And in the case of Burlew and Glavis there was the
additional element that criticism of them in their official role
amounted also to criticism of Ickes' department, whose reputation
he was trying to restore, and of Ickes himself, which meant that his
competence and authority were under threat. Moreover, mixed in
with all this criticism was the notion that his department was working out of alignment with administration policies, and that was a
threat to his relationship with Roosevelt. Ickes was "thoroughly
persuaded" that the criticism was emanating from "an active cabal

working against him." Thus, "There has been a great deal of underground criticism going on and a lot of it has reached the White House. A good deal of this criticism is aimed at Burlew directly but really is meant for me, or at least so I believe. Glavis is also being criticized. The sum and substance of this criticism is that I am not really running the Interior Department but that Burlew is doing it, and he is being described as a standpat Republican who is out of harmony with this Administration."

Ickes had no doubt as to who was at the center of this cabal, but his relationship with Roosevelt prevented him doing much about it: "I have defended Burlew on two occasions to the President and on one to Mrs. Roosevelt. The latter is the most outspoken critic so far as I know. She has even gone so far, on at least two occasions at her own dinner table in the presence of Interior Department officials, to criticize the Interior Department, particularly Burlew. I think such criticism in such circumstances is in extremely bad taste, but I am at a distinct disadvantage in a matter of this kind with the wife of the President."

Yet Ickes felt that "a constant repetition of these groundless charges on her part is bound to have an effect sooner or later on the President." He says that he determined to bring matters out in the open, that he was "entirely willing to have a showdown," and went so far as to write to the President inviting him to have an investigation made of the Interior Department. However, because he did not name Mrs. Roosevelt as the author of the criticisms, there was no real threat of a head-on conflict. The President (putting his hand on his shoulder) said a few days later: "Harold, I wouldn't worry about the matter that you wrote me about if I were you; that matter is straightening itself out," and the immediate crisis was averted. But in the same 22 December *Diary* entry Ickes had expressed fear that Mrs. Roosevelt "can't make such statements as she has been making at her own dinner table without the thing spreading all through the official life of Washington and finally seeping into the newspapers." As we have seen, that is exactly what occurred on 2 January. Although the President officially denied at his press conference on that day that he had said anything to Ickes about firing Burlew and Glavis, Ickes got a rude shock the next day. On 3 January it was reported to his press bureau that Steve Early, Roosevelt's press secretary, had told the White House correspondents that, although the

President's denial on the Glavis-Burlew story still stood, they could say that a White House aide had suggested their dismissal to Ickes. "This report was a great shock to me," Ickes wrote, "because, if true, it indicated that the President was willing to have these men dismissed, but that he didn't want to appear to be asking for it directly." He telephoned Early, whom he considered to be friendly and straightforward, and was told vigorously that it was all a "damned lie"; that he had made no such announcement. Early practically admitted that he believed Mrs. Roosevelt responsible for the Glavis-Burlew story in the *Herald Tribune*, and that if she were asked a direct question at her press conference she might divulge it. Ickes remarked, and Early agreed, that this put Ickes on "a very hot spot indeed." All that he could do at his succeeding press conferences was to deny the President's involvement and say flatly that he was not contemplating dismissing either man.

Ickes' suspicions of Eleanor Roosevelt and other members of the administration simmered on and on. On 9 April 1935 Tom Corcoran, counsel for the Reconstruction Finance Corporation and by now a close friend, came to see him. One of the typescript passages omitted from the 10 April entry in the published diary tells how Corcoran began to list Ickes' enemies, people seeking to destroy him. Richberg, Morgenthau, McIntyre, Hopkins, and Moffett were mentioned. Ickes then suggested Mrs. Roosevelt, and Corcoran agreed that she should be added. In order to make Ickes' own position clearer, Corcoran advised him to tell the President what his wife and others were doing.

Years later, while gossiping about Roosevelt family affairs with Betsy Roosevelt, who had just broken up with the President's son James, it was borne in upon Ickes why he had really always disliked and distrusted Mrs. Roosevelt. As Betsy spoke, it dawned on Ickes how much Eleanor Roosevelt and Anna were alike. Both performed impressively in public; both were impossible in private, even to their own children.[32]

Though the particular involvement of Eleanor Roosevelt in the Glavis-Burlew matter, an involvement that had begun over her dissatisfaction with the way Interior was handling the Reedsville project, slowly receded, criticism continued from a number of quarters about the Department's intense security surveillance. Ickes' sensitivity about this issue surfaced in a submission that he made to

Senate confirmation hearings, in 1938, into the nomination of Bur-lew as First Assistant Secretary of the Interior. He sought to place the question of surveillance in its full historical perspective. When he had become Secretary, the Department's reputation had been unimpressive. Yet, not only had he been charged with the task of preserving the public domain from exploitation, but he had been called on to administer billions of dollars of PWA funds and even greater sums of private money through the Petroleum Administra-tion. The potential for graft had been vast, in the confusion of the change in administrations and because of the horde of adventurers who descended on Washington in search of plunder.[33]

Until organizations and procedures to perform these tasks could be established, and the integrity of departmental personnel guaran-teed (many of them had been appointed during Albert Fall's reign), Ickes considered it necessary to institute protective measures. He found Louis R. Glavis, the man who had uncovered the Ballinger scandal, seemingly ideal for the task and gave him, as head of the Division of Investigations, discretion to initiate proper investiga-tions. Some of the details of his methods make interesting read-ing—as does Ickes' justification of these authoritarian procedures as necessary for the pursuit of politically liberal aims. He says that during the first twenty-two months of his secretaryship Glavis had tapped certain telephones within the department. These phones, Ickes points out, should have been used only for official departmen-tal business and were really "his," as chief executive. So far as he knew, no telephones other than Interior Department ones had been tapped. Such listening-in as was done was not at his specific di-rection, but it certainly fell within the general ambit of his instruc-tion to Glavis to see that there was no fraud and that the public interest was protected. Ickes claimed that the wiretapping had ceased once the reliability of staff had been established and sound administrative routines instituted.

Under the circumstances prevailing at the time, Ickes was quite prepared to defend the use of such practices, arguing that it was jus-tified by the extremely good record of the agencies under his control in protecting the public purse from graft. During his administration Congress had appropriated a total of $6,147,248,472.61 for his three agencies, and of this a mere $13,311.80 had disappeared as the result of a minor embezzlement. If he had had to appear before a committee of Congress to defend against a misappropriation of funds, no one would excuse him if he had pleaded that, although he could have protected the public by a division of investigations, he had declined to take the necessary practical steps out of fear of ill-considered criticism. It was possible that Glavis had overstepped the mark in his determination to protect the administration and the public, but both Glavis and he deserved praise for the practical results that had been achieved.

After this disquisition on the theme that the end justified the means, Ickes proceeded to a logically suspect conclusion. If President Taft and President Harding had been prepared to use whatever means necessary to protect the public interest, the nation might have been spared the scandals associated with Ballinger and Fall. Taft actually had had Glavis at his disposal, but dismissed him. Harding did not want such a person at all. The vast sums Ickes had been given to administer were secure because the present administration saw things differently.

There were some revealing attributions of responsibility in that last paragraph. By implication, Ickes was linking President Roosevelt with himself as "the present administration," which properly employed watchdogs, though of course the responsibility for Glavis' methods was Ickes' own. Further, as we shall see, there was a Ballinger scandal precisely because Glavis was on the job, investigating Alaskan coal leases, and may have created the "Ballinger scandal" out of unjustified, insufficiently researched suspicions. In blaming Taft and Harding, Ickes seems by analogy to be trying, knowingly or not, to shift the blame for those scandals away from the Interior Department onto some higher power which had failed its responsibility. This desire to remove the stains from his Department's image always had been and always would remain an urgent one. Plainly he felt that Glavis' methods, unscrupulous though they may have been, were justified in serving that end—though he refers only to the goal of protecting the public purse.

Nevertheless, by April 1936, Ickes had grown very restive about Glavis and his activities—an echo of the feeling in his earlier guarded admission that Glavis' zeal may have driven him too far. This restiveness may have arisen in some measure from moral concern over Glavis' methods, but it related also to the directions in which those methods were employed. As we have seen, Ickes had turned Glavis' talents to his own personal service in the case of the slandering letters about Ickes and X and he may have regretted the necessity that permitted Glavis to discover an uncomfortable amount about his private life. In the *Secret Diary* for 4 April 1936 Ickes protests, with some lack of conviction, that he is not worried by the prospect of Glavis' damaging him, but then asserts that he intends greatly to restrict Glavis' investigatory powers, since "He has raised up a veritable Frankenstein's monster. These investigators have become persecutors, man hunters, and they are just as eager to drag down members of my staff as they are lobbyists and crooked contractors against whom we are trying to protect the Department and PWA."

The problem was how to find a way of easing Glavis out of the Department without making trouble. Glavis himself had become dissatisfied with his position, perhaps because of continuing criticism of his surveillance of the staff; the previous December, Ickes had talked to him about rumors of his resignation, telling him that he "was cordially hated by nearly everyone." Glavis tried to suggest that if both of them denied that difficulties had arisen between them the question of his resignation would be settled, but Ickes said that this would not put an end to the stories. He again instructed Glavis to stop "hounding members of the staff with investigations."[34]

In July 1936 Glavis finally resigned, to go into private practice as lawyer and investigator. This was to Ickes' "profound satisfaction" and, he believed, "to the equally keen delight of practically everyone in the Department and in Public Works." But this did not mean that the staff could relax. Ickes had always done a good deal of supervising—not to say hectoring—on his own account, concordant with his desire to restore Interior's reputation and to be its most competent manager. Department of Interior solicitor Warner W. Gardner, who believed Ickes to be one of the few Washington officials ever able "to overcome the jello-like consistency of the bureaucracy and make it do what the Secretary wanted," attributed his success in part to Ickes' "generally wholesome talents for terror." Suspecting his subordinates of failing to read lengthy documents before initialing them, on one occasion Ickes had his secretary copy a large part of *Alice in Wonderland*, disguise it as a PWA application, and circulate it. The bogus file returned with ten sets of initials. "If any of those ten had a real contribution to offer the Interior Department," Gardner surmised, "I'm sure he was forgiven. If he didn't, he may have been out hunting for another job." Gardner went on to note that "That sort of conduct repeated often enough brings even quite large departments into a sudden stage of intimidation."[35]

Laziness and inefficiency were not to be tolerated in his bureaucracies. Ickes himself set an example of sustained hard work, far beyond normal office hours, that could hardly be equaled; he made sure his employees were aware of his dedication. Interior Department order number 785 of 28 May 1934, gives an indication of his style:

> The Secretary of the Interior has come to the conclusion that he too would like to have some free time on Saturday afternoons. He does not recall that he has had a Saturday afternoon off since he became a member of the Cabinet. He has not only worked Saturday afternoons but generally Saturday nights and almost without exception at least half the day on Sundays. This pressure on him has been due in considerable mesure to lack of consideration on the part of some of the bureaus in the Department. In order to clear up their own desks and so have the weekends free from official cares, it has been all too customary to pile work on the desk of the Secretary on Saturdays. I think this has been thoughtlessness and not because of any additional pleasure arising out of the reflection that he was helping to keep the Secretary's nose to the grindstone over the week-end while he himself was having a little necessary relaxation. It must be said that a careful study of the dates on much of the correspondence that has been piled on the Secretary's desk on Saturday indicates that with a little diligence most of this correspondence could have gone forward one, two or even three or four days earlier than it in fact did go forward.[36]

In addition to supervising and nagging, Ickes performed a vast amount of his own constructive work. An impression of how he went about it, and of what the daily substance of his work as Secretary of Interior and administrator of PWA consisted, is found in a pen picture left by a *New York Times* reporter who interviewed Harold Ickes in March 1934. The article obviously has a favorable slant, but it is corroborated by many other reports. The reporter describes how Ickes interviewed callers at his desk, while half a dozen others were visibly waiting at the other end of his big, walnut paneled room; this encouraged people to get to the point. If anyone dropped his voice to a confidential tone and began tentatively hinting at a special consideration, he would be invited to speak up loud and clear: public business was public business.

Mr. Ickes has thin, sandy gray hair, kindly blue eyes behind gold spectacles, and a mild patient manner that on this particular morning is swiftly becoming flintlike. Chin in hand, he listens to a half-circle of important-looking persons seated before his desk as one by one they tell him that to doubt the eventual soundness of their great but defaulting city is unthinkable. At last, Mr. Secretary speaks.

"Gentlemen, how can I look myself in the face and say that these bonds of yours are good security? There isn't one of you that would take a different view if he were in my place."

He softens a little. "I don't say there may not be a way out for you. A special session of your Legislature might do something for you—it's being done elsewhere. Appoint a committee to sit down with our legal staff for two or three days and see if something can't be worked out."

Another delegation gets still briefer attention, representing as it does a city politically so corrupt as to be unable to meet the Federal Government even half way. "The American people," says the Secretary, "are not willing to pay graft for salvation. Go home and clean up your rackets, then come back."

Now an attorney for a power company, introduced by a statesman from the Capitol, draws from the Secretary a sharp "Please don't try to tell me what my duties are," and the attorney hastens to say, "Oh, but I didn't mean it that way, sir."

It is fast work at high pressure . . .

Enters a party of Osage Indians, including stout squaws in blankets of rainbow hues. The Secretary rises, shakes their hands, sits down again and listens gravely. Chief Lookout, hair in long braids, addresses him in a strange tongue, another Indian interprets and the Secretary in a kind voice responds:

"I have been interested in your people all my life. I selected as Indian Commissioner a man whom I knew to be sympathetic toward you and I have supported him in all that he has tried to do for you. I will talk to the President and try to get the administration behind your bill."

The Osages depart and a flock of newsfolk fills the room. "I'm all ready when you are," says the Secretary, smiling . . .

To handle the business that pours through his office he needs to be the "strong man" that the observers say he is . . .

Mr. Ickes knows all the rackets that infest the construction industry. He is a terror to collusive bidders and skimping contractors. He warns that the PWA fund is a sacred trust fund and that only traitors would graft on a project undertaken to save people from hunger. He insists on fidelity to specifications; cancels violated contracts mercilessly; sends inspectors to see that men in their eagerness for work are not robbed of pay by the "kickback" swindle.[37]

The description of Ickes' sympathetic attitude toward the delegation of Indians draws attention to another of the themes of his administrative career: concern for minorities. Blacks were not the only group to benefit directly from Ickes' policies. From the outset he had worked harmoniously with his Indian Commissioner, John Collier, not only to ensure that PWA projects and other New Deal benefits were extended to Indians but also to reverse the assimilationist policies of the past, which Ickes equated with oppression of the weak by the strong. The latter move was controversial. It was one thing to institute conservation programs on Indian reserves, to build schools and hospitals and irrigation systems with PWA funds, and to provide relief for the desperately poor; it was another to replace boarding schools, which separated children from their parents for long periods, with day schools, and to restrict the access of white missionaries to them. When the Indian Reorganization Act of 1934 extended these policies further by permitting tribes to govern themselves and by seeking to return lands, hitherto capable of being parceled out in individual allotments, to a system of communal ownership, it encountered much opposition, not only from white missionary and trader groups but also from large sections of the Indian population. None of this deflected Harold Ickes, who was confident that a great step forward had been made. The recently passed Reorganization Act, he assured the Blackfeet Indians, when they made him a chief of their tribe in August 1934, would give Indians an unprecedented freedom to control their own affairs. If white men attempted again "to steal from you your lands and rights, they will think of me not as 'Big Bear,' but as 'Big Bad Bear.' "[38]

On 31 August 1935 an event of enormous importance for Ickes' personal life occurred, one whose immediate consequences reveal a contrasting side to this man dedicated to protecting government funds in the interests of the weak. Anna, his wife, who had again spent the summer in New Mexico, was returning to Santa Fe by automobile with two friends after a visit to the Pueblo at Taos. As Ickes describes it: "With Allen [Anna's driver] apparently driving at a high rate of speed, estimated by some to be sixty miles per hour, the car struck some loose gravel on the shoulder of the road, turned over three or four times, and landed upright in the ditch. Anna and Frank Allen had broken through the top of the car with their heads. She never regained consciousness and within a short time she was dead."[39]

Extending the Empire: PWA and the Forests

TO HIS CREDIT, in view of their relationship, Ickes made no pretense of being devastated by Anna's death. He swung into action, telephoning the scattered members of the family so as to gather them in Winnetka, making arrangements to have Anna's body sent there from Santa Fe, planning the funeral, which was to be a large, formal one with many government repesentatives at the Hubbard Woods house that he and Anna had built. But in his memoirs he describes the funeral as stilted and unemotional, revealing to him how completely his own emotional involvement with Anna, and that of Wilmarth, Raymond, and Helen, had died. Robert alone seemed affected.

The family's major interest was in the contents of Anna's will. Ickes informed them the day after the funeral that, if he survived her by ten days, he would inherit everything. It is interesting that, during the troubled period in Washington, Anna had threatened to make a new will effectively dispossessing him. Harold stoutly declared that he did not give a damn; the notion that he had married her for her money was only one of her fancies. When she died, he did not know whether she had made such a new will and telephoned Anna's attorney, who was a friend of his, to inquire. He was told that Anna had in fact, in the summer of 1935, executed a codicil in which she had cut Harold down to his statutory share and named Wilmarth (her son by James Westfall Thompson) as executor in place of him. Was this codicil still in force? According to Ickes' account of what the lawyer told him on the telephone, the lawyer had subsequently met Anna on Michigan Avenue and remarked on her improved appearance. She attributed this to the better relationship between her and Harold and said that, since she no longer felt as she once had, the codicil should be removed. The attorney invited Anna to his office nearby so she could do this, but she declined and told him to destroy the codicil for her. But the lawyer had not done so; he now told Ickes that he was perplexed and asked for advice.

A lawyer who conducted his clients' affairs in such a haphazard, word-of-mouth, forgetful manner might well be perplexed, but that hardly justified his seeking advice from such an interested party. However, Ickes' principles were equal to the strain. He told his friend to make his own best judgment, in the light of all the circumstances. The following day the man telephoned to tell Ickes that he had felt it his duty to remove the codicil from the will, as Anna had instructed.

That was how Ickes acquired Anna's property. It is possible that all this account was true, that both men acted in good faith, and that justice was done—but one cannot say that it was *seen* to be done. Further, the inheritance was the end-product of quite a sequence of seemingly disinterested actions on Ickes' part. The main part of Anna's estate was a large property on State Street, Chicago, which her father had left to his children, of whom Anna was the sole survivor, during their lives, with the remainder going to their children. Mr. Wilmarth's will provided that no lease could be made on this property unless it included a five-year renewal clause. In his memoirs Ickes argues that this clause was a disincentive to prospective lessees and claims that for many years the property had been bringing in less than half ($18,000 net per annum) of what it might otherwise have earned. Just before their marriage, Anna asked Harold to assume the management of this property. He studied the language of the will closely and decided that the remainder mentioned in it was contingent, not vested. The distinction was important because, under Illinois law, contingent remainders could be removed. He engaged a lawyer who successfully undertook the necessary court proceedings, and Anna was given fee simple title, which allowed her to lease the property without specifying that it must be renewed every five years.[1] The result was that Ickes was able to negotiate a new lease, which increased Anna's rent for the State Street property from $18,000 to $40,000 a year net, a very substantial amount. What he does not mention here is that this legal move also annulled Mr.

Wilmarth's proviso that the property should pass on in turn to Anna's children.

This consequence was forcefully brought to Ickes' attention in the early 1920s by Wilmarth, his stepson. After Wilmarth returned from the war, he decided to attend Northwestern University. But he was more interested in playing than in studying. Ickes claims that the young man's allowance was well above average, but says that he began to demand more spending money and to act belligerently if denied. Ickes breaks off at this point to remind future readers of how close he and Wilmarth had always been; he had never doubted Wilmarth's affection and loyalty.[2]

Once when he asked for an increased allowance, Wilmarth shocked Ickes by accusing him bitterly of robbing him of his inheritance from his grandfather's will. Ickes expresses incredulity that Wilmarth could have believed that in some nefarious way he had harmed the young man's financial status. But the plain fact is that, whether it was done nefariously or not, Ickes had indeed damaged Wilmarth's financial status, and it seems disingenuous of him to express such astonishment. He went on to explain carefully how the legal move in question had made it possible to more than double the family income and pointed out that under his and Anna's wills Wilmarth would recover what his grandfather had given him. Until that time he would share the benefits of Anna's increased income. Wilmarth refused to be mollified.

For reasons we shall see, Wilmarth did not have the sticking power to outlive Harold and inherit the property. But for the time being matters were smoothed over.

Ill feeling with regard to family finances erupted again some years later because of dealings of Ickes that were strikingly at variance with his characteristic caution, not to say niggardliness, with money. He indulged in a long bout of speculative investment, or simply gambling, in the stock market and the grain market. It had begun, he says, soon after his return from France, when he was indifferent to life itself. He had never been at all interested in markets and speculation, believing speculation to be foolish, but a friend connected with the securities industry talked him into opening a small account just for a diversion. Ickes says that, in a marital situation such as his, some men resort to drink, or gambling, or women; he deliberately tried gambling, and in time found himself in its grip. He was already speculating pretty heavily when the mild depression of 1921 came along, but he managed to avoid serious losses. During the Coolidge prosperity boom he bought wildly, at once time accumulating more than a quarter of a million dollars in capital gains. With this he was able to complete the purchase of Hubbard Woods and buy a good deal of additional real estate. Through his stock-market winnings he was also able to acquire The General Printing Company and give Anna as much additional money as she desired.

Anna had been nagging him to close his law office, and at length he agreed to spend the summer with her and Raymond and Robert in New Mexico. This was in 1930, and while they were away, with Ickes rarely seeing a newspaper, the stock market crash came. By the time he reached Chicago the market was plummeting. He held on, hoping for recovery, but finally had to sell at disastrously low prices. His paper fortune vanished, though he escaped financial ruin. Ickes was badly shocked by this experience and says that he stopped gambling forever.

What unsuspected aspect of Harold Ickes' personality had broken through in this extraordinary way? Psychoanalysts propose that compulsive gambling may be an expression of a deep-lying, orally demanding mother-fixation. Fate is seen by such a person as a mother-image, and to gamble is to demand from her a magical supply of the goods of life; it is to challenge her to withhold them.[3] We have already considered the evidence that Ickes was powerfully fixated upon his mother, and the things which he associates with her memory tend to be oral pleasures and oral deprivations. For example, he refers to the ritual annual indulgence of the Sunday-school picnic. "I don't know how our mother stood up under the burden of our annual picnics, which were not picnics at all so much as they were gluttonous Bacchanalia. We really played a mean knife and fork in those days—or rather claws and fangs."[4]

Because of the church teachings for which his mother stood, he remarks that even as a young man he had never smoked tobacco, never tasted beer, never kissed a girl. Whether or not we insist on that literally oral interpretation of his needs, we know that his mother's construal of the church doctrines had impressed on him in his formative years the moral rectitude of self-denial and of thriftiness and responsibility in handling the good things provided by nature. Such moral requirements are understandably accompanied by a repressed desire to rebel against them from time to time. Although in adulthood Ickes rejected the established church, he retained the values of thrift and care throughout his life in his own affairs and those of the state—with the exception of this one outburst of gambling. What prompted it? There is little reason to doubt his declaration that it resulted from the privations he was suffering at home. We have speculated that unconsciously Ickes perceived Anna as a mother-figure, since in the early years of their relationship he was economically dependent on her, and because she was slightly older than he and was a mother. The suppressed resentment against his mother's moral dominance that he had felt as a boy had been transferred to Anna, who, he claims, was forever trying to improve his mind and character. He blamed her for denying him the warm, all-forgiving affection that he craved, perhaps unrealistically. In frustration and despair he sought a magical helper in the goddess of chance, only to be dealt another cruel blow, largely because, in a momentary return of sentimental weakness, he had allowed Anna to take him away, out of reach of financial news. It is not surprising that when, within two or three years, Roosevelt plucked him out of this spiritual wasteland and made him a virtual custodian of the nation's resources, a warm stream of something akin to devotion was turned toward the President. But it was devotion that could turn to bitterness if Roosevelt seemed to fail him.

Though Ickes says that he got out of the stock-market crash with his capital largely unimpaired, he may have been reluctant to admit the full extent of his losses. In fact it was really Anna's capital that was involved, for Ickes had little of his own, and Anna had given him control of her business affairs. When the crash came, Wilmarth, in angry scenes and with moral support from his mother, demanded that Harold turn the management of his mother's property over to him. Ickes managed to win this struggle by demanding payment of an overdue note Wilmarth had given him in return for money that Ickes had put into the General Printing Company, in which he had made Wilmarth a partner. He knew Wilmarth could not pay and threatened to take over the company, ousting Wilmarth and his partners. Wilmarth immediately capitulated, and the bid to unseat Harold was at an end.

Nevertheless, there is evidence that Ickes was left with financial problems. In 1933, after he had gone to Washington, correspondence between himself and the Honorable Mabel G. Reinecke, Secretary of the Board of Election Commissioners in Chicago, shows that he had left unpaid a substantial part of his taxes for 1930 and 1931.[5] He had disputed the valuation placed on the Hubbard Woods property for tax purposes, claiming that he was being penalized because of political animosity, but it is at least possible that this was a delaying tactic, because of the difficulty of finding the several thousands of dollars involved. Now he was anxious to get the matter cleared up and the taxes paid, partly because of the mounting interest and penalities on them but also because he was afraid that enemies of the administration in Washington might discover the circumstances and create a scandal, picturing the new Secretary of the Interior as a tax defaulter.

After the market crash Ickes was unable to keep up the payments on various parcels of land that he had bought on deposit during the boom and had to deed them back at a loss. He asked May Conley, his confidential secretary, to check the amounts of these transactions, so he could claim the losses as tax deductions. On 21 May 1934 he was impelled to write to President Roosevelt, setting out similar unsuccessful real estate investments in the Skokie Valley area near Chicago, and he concluded: "My excuse for burdening you with this unimportant detail is not only that Judge Malmin is making this unfounded charge but that certain other persons are circulating in Chicago a report that I had an interest in establishing the CCC camps in the Skokie Valley because of the beneficial effect they would have upon the real estate holdings of myself and my family."[6] To accuse him of manipulating real estate values for personal gain, when in fact he had had to sell at a loss, was adding insult to injury!

A further unpleasant consequence of the crash was that Ickes found himself in debt to his brokerage firm and could not pay. After some negotiation the firm, Slaughter, Anderson and Fox, agreed to let the matter rest for a while. But in 1933, with some of the Chicago partners replaced and New Yorkers in control, they were threatening to bring suit against Ickes. Their counsel, Oliver Max Gardner, former governor of North Carolina, professing reluctance to embarrass the administration, told Colonel McIntyre, one of Roosevelt's secretaries, of the impending lawsuit. It is difficult to think of any motivation for Gardner's act other than the belief that it would put pressure on Ickes to pay. Of course McIntyre reported it to the President, who sent him over to have a friendly chat with Ickes. Ickes tried to explain that he had got into trouble because of the brokers' inept advice and then by being away in New Mexico. The next afternoon Ickes tendered his resignation to the President, who refused it immediately and was uncensorious, saying, "All of us have been in trouble some time or other," and that powerful concealed interests were using material such as this to get at the administration. Ickes wrote: "I felt very much relieved at his altogether human and friendly attitude. Whatever may be the outcome, I can never forget his kindness and understanding. I have never been given to hero worship, but I have a feeling of loyalty and real affection for the President that I have never felt for any other man, although I have had very deep attachments for other men."[7]

Slaughter, Anderson, and Fox were claiming about $107,000, but Ickes says that the last time he had looked at the account, only a few months earlier, he had thought that the sum outstanding was about $54,000. Two months later his own auditors had the sum down to $11,000, and the brokers had dropped their demand first to $50,000 and then to $30,000. Ickes told the President about this, and Roosevelt supported his intention to pay only the $11,000. This apparently closed the matter as far as the brokerage firm was concerned, but in October 1934 the *Chicago Tribune* sent a reporter to ask Ickes to comment on a story that he had owed the firm $90,000, which he had settled for forty cents on the dollar; "that this money was raised for me by the Democratic National Committee; that payment was not with my own check but with a Democratic National Commitee check"; and that he had twice previously gotten into financial difficulties and had had to be rescued by Anna, "to the serious hurt of her private fortune." Ickes told the reporter that he hoped the *Tribune* would publish the story, for it would give him "excellent grounds for a suit of libel."[8] It was not published.

The further consequences of Wilmarth's unsuccessful struggle with his stepfather for his mother's money are in part pitiable and in part sordid. After Harold and Anna moved to Washington and were locked into their bitterest quarrels, they several times sent for Wilmarth to come from Chicago for consultations. Ickes claims that Wilmarth pronounced him to be in the right, thereby earning his mother's disfavor, but in his memoirs he writes that he subsequently decided that Wilmarth's true motive was to bring about a divorce between Harold and Anna, with a view to removing the main obstacle between himself and Anna's money. Apparently on several occasions Wilmarth did recommend divorce, but to speak out in Ickes' favor seems an unlikely way to insure that he would again become his mother's beneficiary. Undoubtedly there was bad blood between him and Harold. The latter, working on his memoirs about 1939, claims that he had recently been told that, during the affair of Ickes, X, and the poison-pen letters (in 1933), Wilmarth had taken some of the letters to the managing editor of the *Herald-Examiner,* asking him to publish them. The editor, a man named Black, wanted to do so, but the paper's publisher, Homer Guck, refused. Black insisted on their consulting William Randolph Hearst, who sustained Guck. The truth of this reminiscence could not be tested, but Ickes was ready to believe it, even though it gave him a great shock. At the time he had believed Wilmarth to be in full sympathy with him.

When, after Anna's death, Ickes disclosed the contents of her will to Wilmarth, the latter naturally was not surprised but seemed to accept its terms with good grace. Later, he learned that Wilmarth had telephoned Anna's attorney, to whom Ickes had already spoken, asking whether there was a codicil. The attorney told him what he had told Harold, about Anna's change of mind. Robert, the boy who had been raised by Anna and Harold Ickes but never adopted, eventually told Harold that Wilmarth had burst into the library where he was waiting for news, angrily exclaiming that they had lost out and that Harold would receive everything.

These bitter feelings were suppressed and good relations restored, on the surface. Harold persuaded Wilmarth and his wife Betty, Helen and her husband ReQua, and Raymond to sign quitclaims relinquishing any rights to Anna's property. As he worked on his memoirs, Ickes regretted not having had Robert do the same. He neglected to do so because Robert was only a foster child, without the automatic legal claim on the estate that a natural or adopted child might have. But now Ickes was subject to a long-drawn-out and worrying action by Robert, who claimed that his foster mother had intended him to inherit a substantial portion of her property.

Ever since his marriage in 1923 to Betty Dahlman of Milwaukee, Wilmarth had been steadily getting into financial difficulties. Ickes recounts that Betty, about twenty-one years old at this time, had two younger sisters: Anne, ten years younger than Betty, and Jane, who at eight or nine was of an age with Raymond, Harold and Anna's son. The piquancy of this is that little Jane was destined to become Harold's second wife. After Wilmarth left Northwestern University without graduating, he found a position with a well-established firm of haberdashers, through Ickes' unwanted and behind-the-scenes contrivance. He continued to work there for the first few years of the marriage, during which a boy and two little girls were born. But he lost his job, for unexplained reasons, and had difficulty in getting another. Ickes discovered that Wilmarth had been spending freely and living off what little capital he had. Eventually, Ickes, during this boom period with the stock market, purchased the General Printing Company and made Wilmarth a partner, on the understanding that Wilmarth would repay his share of the capital. Wilmarth, perhaps because he resented Harold, did not apply himself to business, preferring to spend the afternoons playing bridge at the University Club. He continued spending money freely and began to stay away from home nights, while Betty managed on a meager allowance, Ickes tells us. They were renting, with an option to buy, a house which Anna and Ickes had purchased, and Wilmarth fell seriously behind in his rent, as well as in the capital repayments for the printing firm. He became more and more of a playboy and had romantic affairs, which Betty put up with as best she could. This was the state of affairs when Anna died, so it is not difficult to imagine Wilmarth's rage and despair when it was confirmed that Harold had "got everything." Anna was killed on 31 August 1935. A year later, on the anniversary of her death, Wilmarth killed himself with a service revolver in his bedroom at Hubbard Woods, which Harold had been allowing him to use while Betty and the children were away for the summer.

The suicide of a relative would have been unwelcome publicity for the Secretary of the Interior in any case, but in his memoirs Ickes records that even as he took his own life, Wilmarth attempted to destroy him.[9] Ickes was referring to Wilmarth's suicide note. To the informed reader it does cast blame on him, but Ickes' reaction seems exaggerated, for the note, addressed to Betty, is barely coherent and refers to Ickes only in passing and only by the initials "H.L."— Harold Leclair. In the offending passage Wilmarth simply says that, although he realizes that he is letting Betty down, he is no longer prepared to stand "H.L.'s" treatment of him.[10]

There is no direct indication in the note of what that treatment was; however, since the sentence directly follows one about Betty's financial situation, the suggestion is conveyed that Wilmarth blames Harold for his desperate money troubles, and feels somehow in his grip. But that can be read into the note only by someone who knows a good deal of the family history, including material that was not public property. Harold's oversensitivity may be interpreted as a kind of acknowledgment that Wilmarth had grounds for resentment, despite the fact that some of his specific complaints were not founded on fact and indeed were hardly rational.

The policemen called to the scene of Wilmarth's suicide had given the note to Chief Peterson, a fast friend of Ickes' son, Raymond. After reading it, Peterson denied to the press that anything had been left in writing, declaring that a previous report to this effect by a junior officer had been in error. He showed the note to Ickes, who had hurried to Winnetka, and a smooth, professional work of collusion, involving the chief of police and the coroner, was effected.

Chief Peterson told Ickes that he would have to show the note to the coroner, but expressed the hope that it could be kept out of the inquest record. Ickes told Peterson that he knew Coroner Frank Walsh; he suggested that he might take temporary possession of the note and approach Walsh informally with it before the inquest. Peterson was agreeable. Ickes explains in his narrative that he was on friendly terms with Walsh, whom he had supported politically more than once. The two met clandestinely, and Walsh decided that, having seen the note, he could ignore it. Ickes assured him that Chief Peterson and his officers were prepared to swear that no note had been found.

The inquest took place as scheduled. "The Lieutenant ... who had found the note, was put on. Walsh ... asked him whether he had made a search for letters and notes. The Lieutenant, looking the Coroner straight in the eye, told him that he had searched carefully, but had found nothing. I think that Chief Peterson denied that anything had been found. They perjured themselves magnificently and I have always felt tremendously grateful to them. Nor has my conscience bothered me about this matter."[11]

When Ickes said that his conscience did not bother him, he did not mean that he had consciously performed an unscrupulous, self-interested act and shrugged off moral considerations. He meant that, despite mere legalities, he was in the right in defending himself against Wilmarth's groundless bitterness; consequently, it was right of him to suborn the coroner and the police, and right of the police to perjure themselves "magnificently" in support of this good man, himself.

Ickes' own testimony concentrated on Wilmarth's ill-health (he had recently been diagnosed as tubercular) and commented that his stepson was not the sort of person who could face the prospect of protracted suffering.[12] Right to the end Ickes had proved too tough a competitor for Wilmarth, even though we may accept that he never consciously intended to defeat and dispossess him.

The aggressive defensiveness that Ickes displayed, rationalized by an unswerving belief in his own rectitude, and a readiness to feel betrayed were very characteristic of his public career. They can be observed in his working relations with other men, even when, or perhaps especially when, he felt strongly attracted to them. By the middle of 1935 his rivalry with Harry Hopkins over control of work-relief funds was coming to the boil. Ickes' attitude was predictable. He seemed to be doing well, but felt insecure. In April of that year the President created a large Allotment Advisory Committee to receive and consider applications for projects. Ickes was appointed its chairman, although for weeks the press had been forecasting that Hopkins would have this position. Ickes did not like the idea of such a large committee, twenty or more, feeling that time would be wasted in useless debate; however, he thought that he might be able to handle it in the way he had handled the Public Works Board, a technique which he sketches in in the *Secret Diary* for 21 April 1935: "At the outset we took a good deal of time to consider projects but before long it was running very smoothly, which means that I was running it practically to suit myself."

He also felt that "Hopkins will find the new Administration an entirely different proposition from giving out money without regard as to whether or not it is being invested in permanent projects." His confidence, however, rested on a shaky foundation. From the first meeting of the committee, in May 1935, Ickes appeared to fall in with Hopkins' proposals for getting men off the rolls, but with the proviso that the projects undertaken should be solid and productive, not just make-believe. Arguing that otherwise the public would be disillusioned, he managed for the most part to get agreement from

Roosevelt and Frank Walker, director of the National Emergency Council. Hopkins, however, still had power as Emergency Relief Administrator and could withhold approval of PWA projects. His requirement that people on the relief rolls be given employment first was a major stumbling block to Ickes, because if Hopkins estimated there was insufficient unemployed labor in a community, its project would not be approved.

Ickes tried to persuade Roosevelt that Hopkins' lavish spending was politically unwise and could jeopardize the President's re-election the next year, 1936. He sought to establish a defined range of projects over which PWA would have sole control, urging that any community that could put up 55 percent of the funds for its project must turn to PWA and not be permitted to get funds from Hopkins' WPA. The President seemed to incline toward that view, but as was to happen so often, when it came to an issue he appeared to sit back and wait for events to take their course.

At a meeting of the Allotment Advisory Committee on 6 August 1935 Ickes balked at Hopkins' bringing in a long list of his projects and requesting blanket approval without any scrutiny as to whether any of them should have gone to PWA. "We had a long and tense discussion. The President sat quietly by without interrupting once."[13] In the end the motion to approve Hopkin's projects was carried, and still the President had said nothing. Ickes was "thoroughly disheartened." A day or so later Ickes had an audience with the President and advanced the cause of PWA; as a result Roosevelt told Hopkins that Ickes should have the right to search out PWA projects.

Ickes made further ground at a meeting of the Allotments Advisory Committee on 20 August, when the President supported him in having a motion passed to the effect that, if a community were able, even though unwilling, to finance its project as a PWA project, it could not get money for it from any other government source. Ickes was pleased to be able to point out that over a thousand applications for PWA projects were backed up, awaiting approval in Hopkins' office. But a rude shock was in store. On the 26th Ickes received from Roosevelt a letter dated 22 August, advising him that all future applications for allocations must be submitted to the Allotments Advisory Committee, "to be acted upon in the same manner and to the same extent as that committee acts with respect to allocations made under the Emergency Relief Appropriation Act of 1935." He took this as meaning that PWA no longer had its own separate allocation, that it had been merged with the work-relief program, and thus in effect had no separate identity. His fiefdom was under threat of invasion. He reacted volcanically: "When I read this I went right up into the air, and I didn't feel any better when I discovered that the noon edition of the *Washington Star* had carried a news release on this letter, the headline of which was: ICKES IS SHORN OF PWA POWER. This headline was sustained by the story itself and the story was a perfectly justified interpretation of the President's letter as practically doing away with the PWA."

His authority having been challenged and his powers "shorn," Ickes was very angry and hurt and determined to resign. He called his old friend Hiram Johnson, who persuaded him to talk to Roosevelt before he resigned but also commented on "the cunning way" in which the President had done this. Ickes said bitterly that it was customary for Roosevelt to deal with men on the basis of a fait accompli. But he did call the President, in order to thrash the matter out with him. Roosevelt pronounced the newspaper story unjustified and denied any intention to change Ickes' status as PWA Administrator. Unmollified, Ickes accused him of putting PWA "out of business." The President "said the newspapers were cockeyed and that I mustn't be childish. I told him I wasn't being childish and that I had good reason to take exception to learning first from a newspaper about a matter vitally affecting my administration. I was pretty angry and I showed it. I never thought I would talk to a President of the United States the way I talked to President Roosevelt last night."

It is an index of the strength of Ickes' concern for PWA, his special child, that the threat of losing it could make him speak to the revered Roosevelt in such a way. The President insisted, perhaps honestly, that his intentions had been misinterpreted and ordered the release of a press statement categorically denying that there was any intention to change Ickes' status as Public Works Administrator. The whole question of finance for PWA had been rendered uncertain and difficult for the President by the Supreme Court's recent decision that the National Recovery Act, which among other things had given PWA authority to advance money to municipalities, was unconstitutional. The very basis of the entire New Deal was shaken.

Nevertheless, Ickes wrote grumpily in the *Secret Diary* that he had been "sidetracked." He retaliated by being very aggressive and unbending at a conference on the following day, arguing among other things that Hopkins was trying to take over an Atlanta sewer project as a WPA one, whereas it came properly under PWA, and getting the President to agree. But after this exchange they went into the Cabinet room for a meeting of the Allotments Advisory Committee, where "millions upon millions" of dollars, as Ickes describes it, were voted "absolutely blind" to Hopkins, whereas his PWA projects were subjected to the closest possible scrutiny, "with Hopkins exercising what amounts to a veto power." Ickes angrily continued: "We vote him money by the carload and he spends it at his own sweet pleasure. It is apparent now that instead of allocating for specific projects from here he will give lump sums of money to his local administrators to spend as they see fit. I can see all sorts of scandals ahead."[14]

A few days later, on 9 September 1935, Ickes records that in conversations with his staff and his friends, all were agreed that the undermining of PWA and the growth of Hopkins' own program could mean political disaster for the President in the following year, because of "an increasing sentiment in the country" against Hopkins on both counts. He claims that Hopkins would turn down a worthwhile PWA project on the ground that the labor cost per man was too high, then undertake a similar project in the same community on the basis of a 100 percent federal grant; again, he would break up a big PWA-type project into a number of smaller ones, each costing less than the critical level of $25,000, and claim them as WPA works. "No one checks or supervises what he is doing. I am thoroughly convinced that he is a lawless individual." After talking with his friend Tom Corcoran, counsel for the Reconstruction Finance Corporation, and his Under-secretary, Charles West, Ickes wrote a letter to the President in which he "temperately and courteously, but firmly" pointed out the political implications of Hopkins' methods. "I told him that things were being done that could not be defended in the campaign next year and that the political repercussions might be serious to him and disastrous to the country."

It seems evident that Ickes was sincere in this belief, but what is also evident is his talent for rationalized political bitchery. His contest with Hopkins was presented not as a power struggle, but as a matter of high principle, with Ickes being disinterestedly in the service of the administration and, most specifically, of the President, whereas more personal, if dimly recognized factors were at work. The emotional, almost spiteful tone of his references to Hopkins is reminiscent of a jealous offspring resenting a parent's favors to a rival sibling. Not only was a part of Ickes' kingdom being filched away, but the traitor was the same father-figure who had first given it to him. This was the underlying script for any number of Ickes' feuds in the Cabinet.

Another of the titanic bureaucratic battles in which Ickes was then engaged was seen by him in similar terms, though perhaps with more justification. This was his attempt to transform his department into the conservationist arm of the federal government. By now Ickes' determination to conserve the nation's resources had run well beyond his obvious desire to put a stop to the corrupt expropriation of those resources by private interests, which some of his predecessors had been prepared to countenance. Increasingly he had become absorbed with the notion of gathering all federal conservation activities into his own hands and wisely administering the nation's natural wealth in the interests of all the people—just the kind of orderly, protective, maternal role that he had always longed to play.

Ickes publicly declared these aims at the opening of the new Interior Department building in April 1936. If Interior had previously functioned as "the sales agency of a government so rich in lands and natural resources that it was willing to sell them for only a fraction of their real value," if it had been "created . . . to exploit the resources of America," the time for such policies had passed. The reorientation of his department's functions that he had begun in 1933 must now be completed, and the seal set on that momentous and historic change. The Department of the Interior should be renamed the Department of Conservation, and the government should assign the responsibility for "an orderly and logical arrangement of conservation activities" to it alone.[15]

There were several more facets to Ickes' conservationism. One was aesthetic. From his youth he had loved the outdoors and responded to the beauty of flowers and trees. The plants and soil for the rockery that, as a boy, he had proudly created in Altoona had been collected during his wanderings through the surrounding hills, a recreation in which Ickes delighted. A love of gardens and flowers shines through his descriptions of the Hubbard Woods home that he and Anna had built and his account of the bucolic loveliness of the farm that he later bought at Olney, Maryland. At Hubbard Woods he had developed a new strain of dahlia, of which he was enormously proud. He always listed gardening (along with stamp-collecting) among his hobbies; when close friends fell ill, he invariably sent them a bouquet of his best flowers.

During his period of residence with Anna and her first husband, Ickes had sometimes taken Wilmarth, their son, to holiday ranches; on these and other vacations which he took as a young man he often trekked on horseback through wilderness areas. The wildness and beauty and freedom of this life was a counterpoint to his tortured existence in the Thompson home, just as his boyhood ramblings had come to symbolize an escape from his mother's exacting regime. In March 1934, in a radio address about national parks, he recalled a visit to Glacier National Park in 1916. For fifteen days he and a friend, with their guide, had ridden through the park on horseback on "as wonderful a trip as I have ever had." Ickes went on:

> I love nature. I love it in practically every form—flowers, birds, wild animals, running streams, gem-like lakes, and towering snow-clad mountains . . .
>
> Imagine a great valley literally massed with lovely flowers in full bloom. A riot of color. No formal garden this, meticulously planted with an iris here, a phlox there, and a peony yonder, but such a planting as only nature itself could plan or afford . . .
>
> And those lakes . . . All shades of blue, depending upon altitude, location, and proximity to glaciers. The mountains themselves were marvellous, beautifully wooded at their bases and gently sloping . . .
>
> But I have almost forgotten the point of my story.[16]

It is debatable whether aesthetic pleasure can be regarded as autonomous, or whether the pleasure derives from other biological drives.[17] According to one psychoanalytic interpetation, landscapes often function as symbols for the female body, which explains the pleasure of their beauty. On the other hand, the forest giants of which Ickes writes so lovingly are classic phallic symbols, and we have seen how concerned Ickes was with protecting his own genitality. Combining the body of mother earth and the towering forest rising from it we have the image of the phallic mother. Roosevelt had made Ickes the "mother" of PWA, with vast funds to nourish his country. But, unconsciously, becoming a mother entails for a man the trauma of castration. If this was true of Harold Ickes, then no wonder that the preservation of the nation's forests elicited an almost religious fervor in him, or that he pleaded endlessly for control of them with the man who had put him in this position of combined power and danger.[18]

Be that as it may, Ickes was very receptive to the arguments of Horace Albright, who was director of the National Parks when Ickes became Secretary, and who became his close confidant for some time thereafter. Albright's concept of conservation was aesthetic and preservationist rather than utilitarian. Ickes had always proudly identified himself with the conservationist policies of Theodore Roosevelt and was a close friend of Gifford Pinchot, who, as Roosevelt's Chief Forester, had been so influential in developing those policies. He had been a member of Pinchot's National Conservation League, and in the late 1920s had served on the National Conservation Committee. But in the early months of the New Deal, Albright helped to sway Ickes's ideas in the direction of the aesthetic, preservationist ideal, as against the more utilitarian notions of controlled exploitation espoused by Pinchot and his followers. Partly for this reason, throughout his term as Secretary, Ickes aggressively sought to extend the area of national parks in order that timberlands and areas of natural beauty might not be despoiled.[19] He also steadfastly opposed any scheme to divert water from national parks for irrigation or commercial uses or to permit the "selective logging" of their timber areas, policies that brought him into conflict not only with powerful private interests but with Henry Wallace's Department of Agriculture.

Along with this went a remarkably prescient and farsighted recognition that the resources of the United States—and the world—were finite, that the use of them was in many cases profligate, and that the time had passed when private and uncontrolled exploitation of diminishing reserves could be allowed. Although bureaucratic and personal motives sometimes lay behind Ickes' conservationist activities, there is no doubt that he accurately perceived the nature of the approaching crisis and, through public speeches and writings over many years, worked tirelessly to raise the consciousness of Americans on the subject of conservation and to convince them of the need to halt the headlong destruction of irreplaceable national wealth.

In a *Saturday Evening Post* article, which appeared in February 1935, Ickes observed caustically that "a nation that has complacently chewed its gum while our forests were being devastated; a people that has not evinced the slightest interest while the public range was being destroyed and turned into irreclaimable wilderness by cattlemen and sheep herders . . . are not to be diverted . . . by the . . . statement that we have suffered and are continuing to suffer losses in the exploitation of our oil resources running to billions of dollars." He went on to draw a picture of "burning oil wells, billions of feet of natural gas escaping into the air, insane competition . . . [and] wasteful methods of capture." "When they [our resources] are gone," he warned, "they are gone forever."[20] In a similar piece in *Survey Graphic* he ridiculed a perhaps imaginary acquaintance, who, when Ickes had criticized Americans' reckless use of land, had "laughingly" pointed out: "If the Chinese have farmed the land for two thousand years, I guess we can go on for a few centuries." The man had ignored the fact that Chinese soil was "an aerial deposit, accumulated through countless ages from 60 to several hundred feet thick and does not have hard-pan or rock within several feet as in our case." By contrast, soils in the United States were normally six to sixteen inches deep. Once squandered, such soil could "be restored only through nature's slow process to be measured by centuries, not seasons."[21] Though there was often an obvious political and, as we shall see, a personal dimension to such appeals, Ickes' keen perception of the seriousness of the problems and his commitment to solving them is unquestioned.

Bound up with such ideas was Ickes' typically Progressive hostility to "the interests," those selfish and generally corrupt groups that exploited the people for the sole aim of aggrandizement and profit. The antipathy was one that his campaigns in Chicago against utility magnates Yerkes and Insull had nurtured. "We know the exploiters are still on the job," he told the North American Wild Life Conference in February 1936, "men who would pollute our steams without regard to the effect on fish life; men who would cut down the forests without thought to the future. Their only interest is profit."[22]

There were, then, weighty and admirable reasons, as well as long-standing political imperatives, underlying Harold Ickes' determination to become the main champion of conservation in the Roosevelt administration. But there also seems to have been a strain of fanaticism in his concern for the conservation of the nation's natural resources, a fanaticism embodied most particularly in his persistent, hectoring demands and maneuvers to have the Forest Service transferred to his own department.

In his *Secret Diary* Ickes claims that in the early months after becoming Secretary of the Interior he cared more about National Parks than about Forestry. The entry for 18 April 1933 records that Henry Wallace, Secretary of Agriculture, came to discuss the possibility of placing the Forest Service and the National Parks in the same department. Wallace wanted both agencies in his Department of Agriculture; Ickes thought they should be in Interior. "I argued that it was time that the stigma under which this Department has been resting ever since the Ballinger days and down through Fall should be removed and the Department given a chance to function so as to merit a return of public confidence. I added that National Parks were particularly interesting to me and that fifty per cent of my interest in this Department would be gone if they were taken away. The National Forests used to be in the Interior Department but were removed to Agriculture when Hitchcock was Secretary of the Interior."

By "Ballinger days" Ickes is referring to the scandal beginning in 1909, in which Gifford Pinchot, then head of the Division of Forestry, accused Secretary of the Interior Richard A. Ballinger of helping corporation interests "to plunder the public domain" in connection with certain water power sites and coal lands. President Taft dismissed Pinchot for insubordination and a joint congressional committee sided with Ballinger. But the controversy continued to make front-page news and Ballinger resigned in March 1911 to save the administration further embarrassment. "Fall" was Secretary of the Interior Albert B. Fall, who was found in 1924 to have engineered the leasing of two great oil reserves to private interests (the "Teapot Dome" scandal), and who was eventually convicted of bribery, fined and jailed.

It is quite true that a considerable odium did attach to the Department of the Interior in the public mind, and a significant part of Ickes' motivation in the Forestry issue was the desire to remove this stigma from the Department with which he strongly identified himself, concordant with his vehemently held self-image of virtue and honesty. This result, he was coming to believe, could be achieved, if Forestry, which had been taken from Interior in 1905 because of maladministration, was restored. It is also true that Horace Albright specifically suggested to Ickes that the Forest Service should be brought back into Interior, since only in this way could the destructive rivalry between it and the National Park Service be eliminated.[23]

Shortly after this exchange between Wallace and Ickes, Pinchot wrote with obvious concern to Roosevelt, urging him not to make the transfer: ever since Forestry had been removed from Interior thirty years before, he had fought every move to return it. Interior had been organized not to preserve natural resources but to give them away, and that orientation could not easily be changed. Agriculture, on the other hand, with its knowledge of soils and plants, was ideally situated to supervise the growing of timber. Pinchot thought highly of Ickes, but he would not be Secretary of the Interior forever and could easily be followed by a man like Fall. Roosevelt replied that he had heard nothing of the proposal.[24]

Pinchot sent a copy of this letter to Ickes and asked him to postpone any decision on the transfer until they could discuss the matter. He assured Ickes of his complete confidence in him, but repeated his suggestion that Ickes might be followed by a man interested in plunder. It was a fatal mistake. The suggestion was bound to strengthen in Ickes' mind the connection between the return of Forestry and the integrity of the Department over which he had just assumed control and which he was determined to rehabilitate. Ickes' reply betrayed his irritation. Except for his talk with Wallace, he knew nothing of any proposal to transfer Forestry and had made no moves in this direction himself. But, he went on stiffly, in view of the stigma resting on his Department he wished to challenge the assumption that secretaries of the Interior would be corrupt, like Ballinger or Fall, and Secretaries of Agriculture invariably honest. Raising the possibility of the transfer at this time might damage Ickes' standing as a conservationist, and should the National Parks be taken from Interior, this would further reflect on his integrity. Agriculture, by contrast, could surrender Forestry without suffering any loss of integrity, and the morale of his Department would greatly be increased were Forestry to be returned. Clearly, battle lines were being drawn.[25]

The National Forest Service does not reappear in the *Secret Diary* until 7 March 1934. Ickes lunched with the President and took up with him the question of transferrring the NFS to Interior. Ickes claims he was able to persuade Roosevelt that the transfer should be made and that the President told him that if he "could bring it about, it would be quite all right so far as he was concerned."

This was the first of a long sequence of half-promises and seeming acquiescences by Roosevelt designed to keep Ickes quiet on this issue and avert head-on confrontations between members of the Cabinet. Roosevelt had not been convinced by Ickes' arguments that some impersonal, objective concept of efficiency dictated that Forestry should go to Interior; but he could see that Ickes was developing an *idée fixe,* which would have to be humored in order to keep this valuable public servant functioning.[26]

In June 1934 Pinchot received a series of letters from officials of the Forestry Service and the American Forestry Association, warning that an attempt was being made to add to the Taylor Grazing Bill an amendment that would have the effect of transferring Forestry to Interior. Ickes, the writers charged, was behind the amendment and was claiming that he had the President's support. (Interestingly, copies of these letters, together with Pinchot's replies, found their way into Ickes' papers.) Pinchot sought an interview with Roosevelt soon afterward and was assured that no transfer would take place during the current congressional session.[27]

In December 1934 Ickes was still trying to disclaim any interest in Forestry. "I do want it, but I have never raised my hand to get it, except to talk in a friendly way with Henry Wallace and Rex Tugwell, and jointly with them, with the President. As a matter of fact, there was a movement in Congress at the last session to transfer Forestry over here, but I discouraged it and succeeded in stopping it."[28] In view of the conversation between Ickes and Roosevelt just described, this disclaimer seems less than frank. In fact, writing to the President on 2 June, Ickes had displayed considerable interest in the Taylor Bill amendment that would have given him Forestry, advising that it could now pass the Senate and probably the House and that Roosevelt's support might insure the success of the bill itself.[29]

On 5 March 1935 Ickes had begun a move positively directed at taking over Forestry, although that goal was now incorporated and (as he may have hoped) partly concealed within a broader one: to have all conservation activities consolidated within the Department of the Interior. During a lunch with Ickes, the President began to talk about his ideas for new committees to control the disbursement of PWA funds. Ickes was to be chairman of the main new committee, but the arrangement still represented some possible restriction of his executive powers—a sensitive point, as Roosevelt knew. Ickes proposed a deal: he would relinquish public works, if Roosevelt would give him control of conservation. If this happened, he could help the President establish a record in conservation that would stand for all time. Roosevelt replied: " 'You know, Harold, that I want to do that, but how can I?' I then asked him whether he would let nature take its course if anything should happen up on the Hill. He said he would, which I regard as giving me carte blanche to try to put some legislation through bringing certain bureaus over here, such as Forestry, that I really want very much."

The proposal came up again a month later, when Ickes stormed in to protest about the loss of the Soil Erosion Service to Agriculture. He asked Roosevelt "whether he was still of the mind that I could go ahead with my bill. He queried me— 'Your Conservation Department Bill?'—and I answered in the affirmative. He said, 'All right, go ahead,' and then I asked him whether he would make it an Administration measure. He hesitated and then said that perhaps he might. I told him that I was having the bill drafted."[30]

Ickes felt that he had gained some ground in this conversation, but Roosevelt was temporizing. He found an excuse to refuse Ickes' later request that the bill be sent to Capitol Hill in Roosevelt's name. As drafted, the bill was to change the name of the Department of the Interior to the Department of Conservation and to give the President power for two years, subject to review by Congress, to take bureaus out of that department and bring others in—with Forestry of course as Ickes's main target. In his diary Ickes deceived himself in the way he hoped others would be deceived. On 16 May the Senate Committee on Expenditure in the Executive Departments discussed the bill, and in the diary Ickes expresses surprise that the Chief Forester and one or two other members of the Forest Service seemed to oppose it by "a metaphysical discussion of what conservation might mean." What they had in the back of their minds, he suspected, was the fear that the change might lead to the transfer of the Forest Service to Ickes' Department. This suspicion was entirely justified, but in his diary Ickes pooh-poohs it, simply because the bill did not actually mention Forestry. "I became impatient with the character of the opposition and expressed myself quite frankly on the subject. I resented the fact that Henry Wallace should permit members of his Department to oppose me on a matter that was not the slightest concern of his Department. Of course, if and when it is proposed to transfer Forestry to this Department, it will be well within the rights of Agriculture to object, but it did seem to me to be highly improper for his Department to object to a change in the name of this Department. A name after all is a matter of choice and taste."[31]

By this time other champions of the nation's forests had entered the field. Professor H. H. Chapman of Yale, President of the American Society of Foresters, attacked the proposed transfer in a provocatively worded press statement and received an answering volley from Ickes. Gifford Pinchot wrote hundreds of editors throughout the country in July 1935, warning that the forests were again endangered because of the name-changing ploy; he forwarded a copy of his letter to Ickes, who sent a sarcastic and insulting reply.[32]

While this public controversy raged, Ickes continued to press Roosevelt to lobby for the bill, telling him that "it would be a simple matter . . . if he would only crook his little finger." He was "shocked" when the bill failed to pass the House Committee on Expenditure in the Executive Departments, and came close to disillusionment with Roosevelt. "The cold fact is that I don't think the President had put any pressure behind this bill at all . . . In his heart I think the President does want it, but apparently he doesn't want it enough to help me get it."[33]

Ickes directed Harry Slattery, one of his Department assistants, to prepare to meet the anticipated attack by the Forest Service on "our Departmental bill" during the coming session of Congress. Ickes wanted to know the extent to which the functions of the Forest Service overlapped with those of the Park Service, how much the Forest Service spent, how extensive its lobbying activities had been. A complete case should be assembled, so that the Forest Service could be put "on the defensive."[34]

Yet after the further opposition Ickes was prepared to press on with only that part of the bill which sought to change the name of his Department to Conservation. He asked Roosevelt several times to notify Agriculture, and especially the Forest Service, that they were not to lobby against the bill; the President as often agreed. On

13 May 1936 the bill passed the Senate. Ickes urged FDR to allow him to "get a rule" in the House, that is, seek a recommendation from the Rules Committee that the bill be debated there; and he agreed. He told Ickes that he had sent this request to Speaker Joseph W. Byrns. It appeared later that Roosevelt really did send word to Byrns to give the bill a rule, but somehow (so Ickes heard) this did not ever reach the chairman of the Rules Committee, John O'Connor, who in fact got the impression that the White House did not want the bill passed. When Ickes spoke in person to the President, Roosevelt told him that he had heard from Henry Wallace that a political fight was brewing over the bill. Despite Ickes' claim that any trouble was only what Wallace had stirred up in the first place, Roosevelt kept repeating that he did not want a fight (the presidential election was approaching) and would not intervene. The bill was doomed. For Ickes, it was "a plain case of being 'sold down the river.' " At best he would try to believe that the President had told the opposition to cease lobbying, but if that were true then Roosevelt was being deliberately flouted. Even so, "I do know that once again he has broken faith with me. He did it with respect to soil erosion; he had done it on other occasions; and now he had done it in a manner that affects me very deeply."[35] Despite these reproaches, Ickes could never resist the President's charm and charisma.

But one of Harold Ickes' idols of former years had fallen. Gifford Pinchot, the hero of conservation of earlier years, by opposing Ickes' plans to take hold of the conservation activities of the government had thrown in his hand with the exploiters. Now, in the wake of the failure of Interior's conservation bill, Ickes publicly attacked Pinchot in an election speech in Altoona. He had returned to his birthplace, he told his audience, not only to explain what benefits the New Deal had brought to Pennsylvania but also to reveal why Pinchot, the state's former governor, had "run out on the New Deal" (a reference to Pinchot's decision to support Republican presidential candidate Alfred M. Landon). Ickes revealed that in 1934 Pinchot had put pressure on him to persuade Roosevelt to force Joseph Guffey to withdraw from the senatorial race so Pinchot could take his place. When Roosevelt refused, Pinchot had treacherously attacked both Democratic nominees, including the man with whom he had wanted to run. "It was a stinking thing for Harold Ickes to make the attack on me he did," Pinchot wrote to a friend; but he

would not respond, "because I regard his attack as unimportant; and
. . . because, in order to answer it, I would have to imitate him and
break confidence—and that I won't do."[36]

Thus matters stood as Roosevelt's first term drew to a close. The
strange mixture of farsightedness and irrationality, of altruism and
ambition, that marked Harold Ickes' career as a Cabinet officer had
driven him not only to restore the damaged reputation of his ailing
Department but to strengthen the nation through growth-sustaining
PWA projects and to stop the drain on its precious resources. But
the ambitous pursuit of those aims, as well as his bellicose style, had
brought him into conflict with other powerful members of the New
Deal team and raised the first doubts in his mind about the reliability of the President himself. Roosevelt remained the strong leader
beside whom he could continue to fight, but by now Ickes had at
least a presentiment that even Roosevelt, who had showed signs of
failing him on crucial issues, might lack the necessary fortitude and
firmness to meet some future national crisis. In the President's second term, Ickes' rivalries with Hopkins and Wallace, in particular,
would become more intense, his doubts about Roosevelt more insis-
tent. At the same time, important changes in Harold Ickes' private
life, following Anna's death, would begin to diminish his long-
standing lack of confidence in his own ability to lead from the front.
And in this, too, lay the seeds of future conflict with Franklin D.
Roosevelt.

SIX

Harold and the Men around Franklin Roosevelt

ICKES HAD returned to Washington from Anna's funeral declaring soberly to himself that he wanted no more women in his life. He had had his passionate fling with X, from which he could carry through life memories of a perfectly fulfilling physical relationship. He suspected that certain women in the capital would succumb easily to his power and position; in fact, with a tinge of smugness he goes into some detail about a couple of them. At a quiet social affair given by the Cordell Hulls, a personable widow prominent in official circles, with whom he was slightly acquainted, asked whether she might come to his office to request a favor. She scarcely had entered his office, when she told him that she loved him and asked him to visit her in her apartment. She said nothing about marriage, Ickes reports, but he knew he had to be on guard. To avoid giving offense, he did visit her a number of times, at infrequent intervals. He gave her no direct encouragement, but each time he was about to leave she would kiss him passionately. Ickes says that the woman was proud that her bosom was still firm, and drew his attention to the fact.[1]

Harold felt sufficiently worldly wise and battle-scarred to withstand the blandishments of women displaying their sexual charms. Shaw's play *Man and Superman* had crystallized his slowly developing suspicion that it was not really necessary for men to overcome women's reserve by ardent wooing; behind their pretense of passivity they were the pursuers and men had to be on guard. But his wariness proved not to apply to all women; it was selective.

A couple of months after Anna's death, in the fall of 1935, Ickes received a note from Jane Dahlman, the youngest sister of Wilmarth's wife, Betty, asking if she might come to Washington to get his advice on something important. She had written from Smith College in Massachusetts, from which she had recently graduated. He found the prospect rather boring and was not keen on playing host to the girl, but the family connection was such that he could not refuse. Jane wired that she was coming on a certain morning train, and Harold felt it his duty to meet her and offer the hospitality of his home. It is not surprising that in retrospect his memory set the date of this meeting later than it was; in his diary entry for 15 May 1938 he gives the date as the fall of 1936, and in the still later personal memoirs as the spring of 1936, but contemporary entries in the *Secret Diary* unequivocally fix the actual time as fall 1935.[2] Certainly his confident intention to have no more women in his life, even the intention to observe a decorous period of mourning, did not endure long. In his memoirs he describes how he went to the station to meet Jane and saw her, a striking young woman with lovely red hair, struggling along the platform toward him. Before they had even met, he says, he knew that he loved her.[3]

Even in the generally more sober diary he confesses that, literally, he loved Jane at first sight. He knew his age made him ineligible, but says he was swept along by emotions too strong to control. Perhaps, he speculates, this sudden gust of feeling occurred because he had been denied love for so long.[4] This explanation does not square with other things he had said about his personal life. He had been seeing X up until only a few months before this dramatic meeting, and that hectic affair was supposed to have provided memories to carry him throughout the rest of his life. It seems that even Harold felt that his sudden new passion called for some explanation. It could not have been based on an instantaneous revelation of the worth of Jane's character and so must have been, at this stage, a purely erotic response. He is at some pains to explain how casual and disinterested his only previous contact with her since she had emerged from childhood had been. That had been during the period in 1934 when Anna was in the convalescent home, recovering from the effects of her overdose of poison. Jane and her next older sister, Ann, had spent two or three days in Washington as Ickes' guests. Ickes admits that Jane had grown into a tall, slender, good-looking young lady, with the most beautiful red hair he had seen, but she had other people to see in Washington and Harold had only a few glimpses of her. She had been escorted by Raymond, his son, and had one or two other beaux. After Jane and Ann left, they passed out of his thoughts almost completely, he says.

Actually, he had always found her attractive. When Wilmarth had married Betty in 1923, Jane, then a freckle-faced ten-year-old, had attended the wedding. Afterward she would often visit Betty and spend time playing with Raymond and the other children. Ickes says that he was fond of her and would kiss her as she came into the house, just as he would have his own daughter. But one day Anna told him to stop—yet another manifestation of her all-consuming jealousy.[5]

We have seen, in the case of his adopted daughter Helen during World War I, something of what Harold considered a natural degree of closeness between father and daughter, a degree which, however innocent it may have been, could lend itself to a different interpretation. It is possible that Anna was irrationally suspicious and jealous; it is also possible that she understood Harold better than he understood himself. A man who is uneasy about his own potency may well find young, dependent, and thus defenseless females sexually provocative, precisely because they cannot challenge him to come up to some sexual standard. Mature, sexually aggressive women, however, such as the one who drew his attention to her good body, would scare him off, if deep down he felt that he might not be able to meet their challenge. X, with whom he had first achieved physical fulfillment, had been a sexually experienced woman, but she was also about thirty years his junior and had come to him suing for favors, a suppliant to his political power. Now, this beautiful twenty-two-year-old, who had given him preadolescent kisses and whom he must have suspected of coming to seek his help, appears in the depths of the railway station, struggling in her feminine way to cope with luggage and porters until he arrives with his masculine strength—it is as if a slow-burning fuse, lighted a dozen years ago, had reached the powder keg. To suggest that he fell in love with Jane in an instant because she could satisfy, in one person, his wishes for a loving daughter and a compliant sexual partner is not for a moment to decry her intrinsic worth or to say that their later happy marriage was based on nothing but an illusion. Ickes was lucky indeed that his infatuation seized on a woman of admirable sense and character, and that this first flood of passion developed into an enduring relationship of real substance.

Jane's reason for her visit to Washington was that, having graduated with honors from Smith, she could not face the thought of returning to her home in Milwaukee, because her mother's disturbed psychological condition made life intolerable there for her. She wanted Harold to find her a job, which he was able to do, assigning her to the Park Service for historical research work, which, he says, she did very well.[6] For the first few days she stayed in his house—Hayes, an old colonial house he rented—then found a small apartment. Harold writes that immediately he began to court Jane with all that was in him. That New Year's Eve they went to a dinner party given by his friend Ruth Hampton, an officer in Interior; Ickes reported, "Ruth is enthusiastic about Jane."[7] On 27 January he gave a birthday dinner party for her at Hayes, remarking in his diary, "Curiously enough her birthday is January 27, which was Anna's birthday date." This coincidence, which surely must have been remarked on in earlier years, could well have helped enmesh Jane in Harold's unconscious fantasies, though just how we can only speculate. Present on this occasion was Edward H. Foley, then legal counsel for PWA, whom Ickes had invited because he was single and of an appropriate age for Jane. Jane and Foley in fact saw a good deal of each other in the next few months, while Harold, with principled self-control, stood aside. He felt he owed Jane the opportunity to form an attachment for this younger, eligible man; eventually however, on the eve of his marriage to Jane, Harold wrote that her relationship with Foley had never amounted to much and was definintely over. He had matured a good deal since the days when he agonized over Anna's relations with her first husband. His memoirs convey the impression that deep down he was always fairly confident of winning Jane.

The day after the birthday party Harold went with Jane to a musicale at the White House, having persuaded Mrs. Roosevelt's social secretary to include Jane's name on the invitation list. He was proud of the impression she made on the gathering, especially on Roosevelt, who told Ickes the following day that he thought Jane was not only very good-looking but also sweet and attractive.

Throughout the winter, spring, and summer of 1935–36 Harold kept pressing Jane to marry him, while she held him at arm's length.

Her feelings about him were mixed. Hindsight shows that she had formed a strong and lasting attachment to Harold, yet the pressure of conventional notions of eligibility was such that it seemed beyond the bounds of reason to marry someone almost forty years her senior. To have time to clarify her feelings, she resolved to go away to Europe, to Germany which she had long wanted to visit, in June 1936. Harold pressed her two sisters to persuade Mr. Dahlman to finance the trip, which he reluctantly did with the sum of $1000. Harold thought this was so little as to expose Jane to danger, and made her take his letter of credit for $1000, to be drawn on if necessary. She did use $300 of it but was careful to repay the sum later, he says. It distressed him greatly to say goodbye to her in Washington, but he could not bring himself to go to New York, and so she was seen off by Ed Foley, another friend Lawrence Morris, and her sister Ann. She was away until September, and Harold spent a miserable summer, both spiritually and physically.[8]

Ickes' reluctance to leave Washington to bid Jane farewell may have been a result of the fact that he had been passing through a turbulent period in his relationship with Roosevelt, over the competition between Hopkins' WPA and his own PWA. President Roosevelt had been preparing an appropriations bill for Congress, and was inclining heavily toward Hopkins. Ickes had a conversation with the President on 9 May 1936, and the *Secret Diary* records that until then he "really did not realize the extraordinary powers granted to Hopkins under this bill." "The huge sum of almost $1.5 billion is granted outright to the Works Progress Administrator, which means Hopkins ... in effect it gives Hopkins blanket authority to spend this huge sum of money as, when, and where he pleases, without check or hindrance from anyone, not even the President himself."[9]

What incensed Ickes was that under the bill as it stood, neither the President nor Hopkins could grant money to PWA or any other federal agency even if he wanted to; all of it had to be expended under the personal direction of the Works Progress Administrator. At his press conference a few days before Roosevelt had stated that whatever PWA projects might qualify under the new program could be carried on by WPA, and Ickes interpreted this to mean that the President "was prepared to help Harry Hopkins carry out the desire he had had at heart for the last two years to scuttle PWA and salvage from it whatever he can for the benefit of his own administration." Ickes bitterly discussed with James M. Farley the question of how Hopkins had attained his influence over the President. Ickes said that he had heard that "it was through cultivation by Hopkins of Mrs. Roosevelt and the President's mother," and Farley agreed that Hopkins was very close to Eleanor Roosevelt, though he did not know anything about the relation with the President's mother.

A strong move developed in the Senate to earmark $700 million of the appropriation for PWA. Ickes believed that PWA stood well with Congress and that many people shared his belief that in this campaign year it was politically suicidal for Roosevelt to align himself with the money-squandering WPA. The trouble came to a head at the Cabinet meeting of 14 May 1936. Roosevelt had discovered that Ickes was scheduled to appear before the Senate Appropriations Committee and that his staff was preparing a statement of what PWA had done and could do. Evidently the President suspected that the statement would employ figures comparing PWA's cost/benefit ratio favorably with that of WPA, and he began to direct Ickes as to what he could say to the Committee. He was not to give any figures on the stimulation of indirect employment, which Ickes regarded as one of the main virtues of PWA. "We hammered back and forth at each other on this subject and it was plain to see that the President was not in the best of tempers. Neither was I, if the truth be told, although I kept good control of myself ... The President said that I must not criticize the program of WPA and that it would be a criticism of that program if I should show to the subcommittee what PWA had done."

If Ickes' memory of that conversation was accurate, it does indeed seem discriminatory that he should be ordered not to list the achievements of his own organization for fear that it might reflect on that of Harry Hopkins. Not only that, but the President said flatly that if the Congress should earmark any of the money for PWA, he would veto the bill. Not unnaturally, Ickes found this too much to accept. "I was pretty angry by this time. It was clear as day that the President was spanking me hard before the full Cabinet and I resented that too. All the other members appeared to be embarrassed, but I could see Henry Morgenthau stealing a covert glance at me from time to time. Doubtless he enjoyed the spanking very much."

Ickes tried to confront the President at the end of the meeting, but Secretary of Labor Frances Perkins deliberately got in ahead of him and monopolized the President's attention until Ickes angrily stalked out. As she explained to Ickes on the telephone soon afterward, she wanted to prevent things "crystallizing" between him and the President before they had both recovered their equanimity. But Ickes told her "that so far as I was concerned, matters had crystallized and that even the President couldn't spank me publicly."

Even before Miss Perkins had called him, Ickes, miserable over Jane's impending departure and angry at the President's rebuke, had begun dictating his resignation both as Secretary of the Interior and as Public Works Administrator. He was assisted in this by Burlew and Slattery, his loyal aides in Interior. And, he says, "wishing an outside newspaper man's point of view, I called up James Waldo Fawcett at the *Evening Star* office and asked him to come over." Presumably if it came about, Ickes wanted to make sure that the newspapers understood the reasons for his resignation. The four men stayed up late that night drafting the letter, but Tom Corcoran arrived and some of the things he said about what the President might be persuaded to do for PWA caused Ickes to delay for twenty-four hours. The following night, Thursday, 14 May, however, Ickes and his three advisers prepared a document which "would state my case to the public." Ickes protests a number of times in the *Secret Diary* that this was not a threat to resign, it was a resignation; but by the time he arrived at the office Friday morning he had begun to feel that it was a mistake to send that particular letter to the President. "It was simply a knockout and left him no recourse"—that is, no recourse but to accept it. Accordingly, he dictated a short, moderate, and dignified letter in which he reproached the President for "statements made by you at recent press conferences by which, in effect, you repudiated PWA and indicated a lack of confidence in me as Administrator." The President's attitude had been confirmed at the Cabinet meeting when his orders "made it impossible for me to respond to the request of the Senate Appropriations Committee to present a statement of what PWA has accomplished up to date." In the circumstances he had no option but to tender his resignation, but he thanked Roosevelt for having given him the opportunity to serve his country.

It happened that morning that, in response to an earlier request,

Colonel McIntyre had given Ickes a luncheon appointment with the President that day. When he went in,

> the President looked at me with an expression of mock reproach and then, without saying a word, he handed to me a memorandum in his own handwriting as follows:
>
> The White House
Washington
>
> Dear Harold—
> 1. P.W.A. is not "repudiated."
> 2. P.W.A. is not "ended."
> 3. I did not "make it impossible to for you to go before the committee."
> 4. I have not indicated lack of confidence.
> 5. I have *full* confidence in you.
> 6. You and I have the same big objectives.
> 7. You are needed, to carry on a big common task.
> 8. Resignation *not* accepted!
>
> Your affectionate friend,
(Signed) Franklin D. Roosevelt

Ickes says that he read this communication and was "quite touched by its undoubted generosity and its evident sincerity of tone," but really all that he got from his letter of resignation was this point-by-point denial (without explanation) of his complaints, the expression "your affectionate friend," and a subsequent half-hour or so of conversation in which the President demonstrated his ability to make everyone believe he inclined toward their viewpoint. The resentments that Roosevelt had managed to soothe had more to do with his failing in personal loyalty and warmth, as Ickes saw it, than with the objective grievances that Ickes had mentioned. Roosevelt listened to a series of complaints to the effect that he had taken relevant decisions without informing Ickes or had received messages from inferiors which had bypassed Ickes; the President made sympathetic noises. Concerning the appropriation, he confided that someone had already suggested to him that the $1.5 billion should go to Ickes rather than to Hopkins. He said he might move in that direction because it would enable him to act on two or three plans he had in mind for keeping PWA going—specifically, by widening the powers of the Reconstruction Finance Corporation and by getting some contributions from the WPA funds as grants for PWA projects. These moves had already been in his mind before Ickes sent his resignation, but Ickes felt that "this talk with the President undoubtedly cleared the air." A couple of days later Ickes was allowed to go before the Senate Appropriations Committee and read a sanitized statement, cleared by the President, of what PWA had already done, but without mentioning WPA. A few days later still he heard that Jesse Jones, Director of the Reconstruction Finance Corporation and a subcommittee of the Appropriations Committee, had worked out an amendment that would allow funds to be made available for PWA through the RFC. Though it seemed that this was satisfactory to the President, Ickes told Senator Carl Hayden, who had been working on a rival amendment, that he was "Goddamned" if he would be "a tail to either Jones's kite or to Hopkins' kite."

But eventually the complex processes of government worked in Ickes' favor. Roosevelt "kept faith" and endorsed Senator Hayden's amendment to the Deficiency Appropriation Bill (an amendment drafted by Ed Foley), giving PWA the respectable sum of $300 million and directing the large appropriation of $1.5 billion not to Harry Hopkins but to the President. In this form the bill passed the Senate on 1 June 1936, later passed the House with further endorsement by Roosevelt, and was signed into law by him on 19 June. Ickes writes: "In the law as finally passed Hopkins is not even mentioned . . . All told, I am quite satisfied with the way this matter has worked out. Instead of being kicked out of bed, PWA has been formally recognized, and the fight developed the fact that PWA has a good many friends on the Hill."

This change of fortunes must have made Ickes better able to support Jane's departure for Germany. Though he was anxious about the safety of her person (secured only by a series of unreliable rendezvous with Smith friends) and the security of her affections for him, the developing presidential campaign soon commanded a large share of his attention and energy. His unqualified confidence in his own ability as a campaign manager made him barely able to tolerate the lack of organization in the Democratic program, led too casually, as Ickes saw it, by Roosevelt himself. On 18 July he wrote that the President had the absurd idea that Landon was the weakest candidate who could be nominated by the Republicans, and so had not wanted anyone to attack him in any way that might have prevented that nomination. Roosevelt, who should have been acting boldy and decisively, instead had allowed the build-up for Landon to continue. Meanwhile, "the President smiles and sails and fishes and the rest of us worry and fume."

A few days later Ickes confided to the *Secret Diary* that election prospects were so bad that he wished he had taken up the proposal, put to him a year ago, that he resign from the Cabinet since there was a good chance that he could be nominated for President on the Republican ticket—a surprising admission in the light of his frequent assertion that the principles of the New Deal were vitally important. It was only loyalty to Roosevelt, he says, which had prevented his taking the suggestion seriously, though he also felt that he would not have been willing to make the political deals necessary to secure the nomination. "But as I see the thing now, if I had been nominated, in all probability I could have won in November with the situation standing as it does today. I am not shedding any tears, because . . . I have not now and never have had any ambition to be President."

This is the inhibition on which we have commented before: Ickes' feeling that he should not openly seek electoral office but must ally himself with a powerful leader. It would have been closer to the truth for him to say that he had never actually committed himself to the attempt than that he had never had (nor would have in future) the ambition to be President.

Part of Ickes' disillusionment with Roosevelt's leadership was caused by the President's apparently turning once again against PWA. On 6 August he complains that Roosevelt "has not come to time on public works funds' and the the newspapers were beginning to criticize him on his public works program. "He has laid down harder terms for us than he has ever laid down for Hopkins' outfit." Ickes was not blaming Hopkins, however; it was the President's fault entirely. "Apparently, he doesn't want to go ahead with the public works program and no one can make him. Well, he is the candidate and I am not, but I do hate to see a man play such poor politics as he seems to me to be playing right now."

Four days later, "the President has . . . come off his high horse on Public Works and relief." He had relaxed some of his stringent conditions on the percentage of relief labor to be employed, and it seemed PWA would be able to go ahead with a satisfactory program. Perhaps an effective electioneering speech by Ickes in the meantime had caused the President to change course. He was being very friendly to his old campaigner, who since coming to Washington had blossomed into a confident, forthright, and aggressively witty speaker. Roosevelt told him that "they needed four Harold Ickeses and I was only one"; and in fact it was hard to find another good campaign speaker in the administration apart from Roosevelt himself. But PWA was still a pawn in campaign tactics. By 18 August, Ickes was "compelled" to reveal at his press conference that "not a single project has been approved by the President under the bill adopted by the last session of Congress and that under the rules and regulations laid down by him there is little prospect of any being approved." Ickes' private feeling was that for two months "the President has dillydallied, apparently trying to find a way to strangle the child as quietly as possible." This was not the first, and would not be the last, time that Ickes used that imagery about PWA, a beloved infant given to him by a President who now seemed prepared to sacrifice it on the altar of political convenience. On 25 August, Ickes was allowed to know something of Roosevelt's motivation in all this "pulling and hauling." The President wanted to be able to keep saying right up to election day that his budgetary deficit was decreasing year by year, but he was operating on such a slender margin that he must not overreach himself on public works. "If he had only explained this to me in the first instance, I would have been understanding and sympathetic." Pressured by Ickes-inspired newspaper stories, the President began approving $5 million worth of public works projects a week. On 8 September, at lunch with Ickes, the President spoke enthusiastically about PWA projects, especially a Negro housing scheme, that he had seen on his recent electioneering tour through Illinois. He also announced his support for several other housing projects, which would be to his advantage politically, a suggestion which on this occasion was not objectionable to Ickes, who told Roosevelt that "Hard-boiled Harold understands."

Within days after Roosevelt's crushing victory in the presidential election, Ickes was telling him that they should make further allocations for public works, "because otherwise the impression might get out that we had made PWA allotments merely for political purposes, since we were making a good many just prior to the campaign and none since." Roosevelt expressed agreement, but by and large the history of PWA right up to its demise in June 1939 was a repetition of old themes, with Ickes competing with Hopkins both for funds and for Roosevelt's favor, and with Roosevelt continually expressing admiration for PWA, yet often delaying approval of new projects until he felt that the time was economically and politically ripe. He would then expansively present Ickes with an armful of projects and send him away happy.

There were some new variations on this basic structure. For the first few months of 1937 Ickes seemed to have risen above any anxious concern over the continuance of PWA. In January, in a speech to the Mayors' Conference, he took the position that PWA had done its job as a recovery agency and that it ought to wind up its affairs, except as a continuing organization ready to jump into action if another depression struck. On 15 May 1937 he wrote:

> There isn't any doubt that Hopkins has done his best to shove PWA off the map and he has pretty well succeeded. It makes me smile when I reflect that at my instance in 1935 the President issued an order, concurred in by Hopkins at the time, that any project costing more than $25,000 was to be regarded as a PWA project. Hopkins has totally ignored this order. He has competed with PWA for labor; he has bid against PWA for municipal projects; and there has been no limit to the amount of money spent by him on a single project. I am thinking seriously, when I next see the President, of suggesting that he transfer all of PWA to Hopkins since he has imposed on me rules under which I cannot operate, while Hopkins has an entirely free hand.[10]

The notion of giving PWA to Hopkins was not just an angry, sour-grapes gesture, because Ickes referred back to it the following November, when Tom Corcoran suggested to him that he trade Public Works to Hopkins in return for Hopkins' support for Ickes' Department of Conservation plan. He writes that he "can't win any more credit out of it [PWA] than I already have; on the contrary, something unexpected might happen which would blur the fine record that we have made."[11]

Perhaps the promising state of his relationship with Jane made Harold capable of such equanimity over the prospect of renouncing

PWA; made him "smile" rather than fume at Hopkins' maneuvers. During the previous summer, 1936, he had had a wretched time while she was away in Europe, trying to shake off her attachment to him. He wrote her long, impassioned letters almost every day. Jane also wrote him generously and, toward the end of her trip, about early September, she began to say how much she wanted to see him and how much she was looking forward to meeting him at the pier. But it was certainly not an immediate surrender. After learning that she would not tell anyone else the date of her return because she wanted to meet him alone, on a Sunday late in September, Harold went to the pier to greet her arrival on the *Bremen*. He had to search for her in the crowd, and when he did come upon her he was thunderstruck to find her with Ed Foley and Lawrence Morris. Harold made little attempt to hide his fury and repulsed her attempts to explain the presence of the others. But in the end Jane was able to get free of them, and she and Harold traveled together by train to Washington.[12]

Jane remained in his house less than a week before she suddenly decided to go home to Milwaukee. She loved him but, because of the age difference, could not face the possibility of marrying him. However, almost as soon as she arrived home, she began to feel desperately that she wanted to get back to Harold and began telephoning him two or three times a day. He pretended to be cool and self-possessed and, he says, called her only because she insisted on it. Her father and sisters pressed her to break off with Harold, saying anything to prejudice her against him. Mr. Dahlman demanded to know whether she was aware of Harold's reputation as a roué, having been put up to this, Harold believed, by Wilmarth, who was Mr. Dahlman's son-in-law, as Harold hoped to be. But Harold had already given Jane an account, in outline, of his relations with other women, of which in any case she preferred to know no more. She realized that chastity was more difficult for men than for women. Jane became subject to severe bouts of asthma and was almost isolated in her room. Finally she could stand it no longer and called Harold to say she was returning to Washington. When she arrived, she agreed to do whatever he thought best.

Harold had accumulated enough experience by now to be able to retain his psychological advantage. He pointed out that he had not tried to hold her back when she had gone to Europe, nor again when unexpectedly she went off to Milwaukee. He told her that he had already begged her over and over to marry him, using all the arguments he could muster. He understood her inhibition and so would not plead with her any longer. She could stay as long as she liked; they would remain friends; but he would not again ask her to marry him.[13]

He says that it took him some time to realize that if he had deliberately tried to find the best way of breaking her down he could not have discovered a better one. Before long Jane was artfully trying to elicit a proposal, which Harold now refused to repeat.[14] The strain soon became too great. Ickes says that, whether it was a gradual understanding or whether Jane declared that she wanted to marry him, their intention to wed became a settled matter sometime in the winter of 1936–37. From that time on Harold's personal life became stable and serene as it had not been for a quarter of a century.

In May 1937, at the period when he was calmly contemplating giving PWA to Hopkins, Ickes purchased as his and Jane's future home a country estate near Olney, Maryland, called Headwaters Farm. It consisted of a ten-room house with a lodge for the servants and a modern dwelling for the farmer, set in farmlands of some 230 acres together with 50 acres of second-growth woods. He loved it from the start. The conveyance, for $85,000, was signed on 25 May. Two days later, perhaps in part because he was still anxious over a tangle of financial commitments arising from inheritance taxes relating to Anna's estate, he suffered a coronary thrombosis. On 31 May 1937 he was taken by ambulance to the Naval Hospital at Bethesda, Maryland, and confined to bed until the end of June, though he was still able to carry on some of his responsibilities as Secretary of the Interior. On 2 July he was transferred to his private suite in the new Interior Department building, where the third office had been fitted up as an emergency bedroom, and here he began to regain his strength. By 15 July he was well enough to be installed, with Jane's help, in his new home on the farm and to dispense with the constant care of doctor and nurse. Harold and Jane were not to be married until 24 May 1938, some ten months later.

Jane's support would be invaluable to Harold during the long period of estrangement that followed the loss to Ickes of PWA, metamorphosed into the new Federal Works Agency in June 1939. This was one outcome of the Reorganization Act of 1939, which, though conceived at the beginning of the second Roosevelt administration, had been subject to innumerable amendments before its final stormy passage through Congress. Ickes had been a strong supporter of the Reorganization bill right from its inception, if only because it envisaged changing the name of his Department to that of Department of Conservation, which was easily his greatest ambition. In addition, he thoroughly approved of its intention to increase the President's administrative power by authorizing him to transfer bureaus and agencies from one department to another, subject to disapproval by Congress within a reasonable period of time. Ickes always inclined to the view that the effective functioning of democratic government called for a considerable degree of centralized executive power, so that the mandate given to such a government could not be frustrated by self-interested departments or a reactionary public service.

The prospect of getting a Department of Conservation had helped to reconcile Ickes to the phasing out of PWA. In November 1937 he had lunch at Harry Hopkins' house in Georgetown and offered him what was left of PWA if Harry would help him "put over my Department of Conservation, with Forestry included." Hopkins agreed; but all the time Henry Wallace of Agriculture was pressing the President fiercely to leave Forestry where it was, in Agriculture. As the months went by, the signs began to look black for Ickes. In the *Secret Diary* entry for 29 January 1938 he wrote: "As to the present reorganization bill, I fully believe that the President is getting ready again to let me down. I have talked to him. So has Henry Wallace, and I know that Wallace has been carrying word up to the Hill that the President doesn't care anything about a Department of Conservation. The President admitted that he had said to Henry that the name did not matter after all."[15]

Early in February the President told Ickes that he was going to leave it to Congress to decide upon the name of his Department, and Ickes grudgingly and bitterly began to resign himself to backing off from that issue lest it imperil the whole bill. On 12 February the Senate Committee on Reorganization revised its bill so as to leave the name of Interior unchanged. With the fight for Conservation apparently lost for the time being, Ickes' need for a continuing PWA revived. At lunch on 8 April the President told him he had a new public works program in mind but had not decided how it was to be administered. He would want to use the present PWA organization but was thinking of turning it into a corporation. Ickes had taken with him a list of 222 PWA projects "to force the President's hand," and, although Roosevelt agreed that it would be a good thing to announce them now, he pointed out that they would have to go to Budget "for some kind of bookkeeping arrangement." Ickes wrote grimly that he intended to fight hard for his new PWA program. With the prospect that he could head a new Department of Conservation receding, he could see "no reason why I should give up PWA without a struggle."[16]

Harold Ickes' need to do everything he could to ensure the passage of an appropriation bill for public works kept him in Washington and caused a readjustment of his elaborate plans for his wedding to Jane. This elaborateness was caused by their wish to keep the wedding secret from the press until it was over. Ickes was sensitive about the great discrepancy between their ages and felt sure that the press would have made a Roman holiday of the occasion. He says in *The Autobiography of a Curmudgeon,* written some five years later, that he and Jane concluded that, despite the legitimate public interest, "our marriage was primarily a matter personal to ourselves."[17]

Because they did not wish "to have to jump off with newspaper sharks and cameramen in swift pursuit," it was arranged that Jane should go to Dublin, Ireland, ostensibly to visit her uncle John Cudahy, who was American Minister there, but also to make arrangements for the most unobtrusive wedding possible. Harold was to follow. After completing his evidence before the appropriations committee he told the President about his plans. Roosevelt was kindness itself, waving aside the age difference, saying that there was a comparable gap between his own parents' ages, and arranging with Cordell Hull to smooth Harold's departure abroad on a confidential mission. Under-Secretary Harry Slattery, through a connection in the State Department, arranged for Ickes to travel incognito on the *Normandie.* With the purser's connivance, he boarded the ship through the kitchen. His meals were served in a private dining room at unconventional hours so he could exercise on deck while the other passengers were eating. He escaped recognition at Southampton, was hustled onto a boat train for Liverpool, and reached

Dublin at six o'clock the next morning. He and Jane were married at ten by Dr. R. K. Hanna, minister of the Presbyterian Church, who did not know their identity until the press descended on him later that afternoon. John Cudahy, a Catholic, who had tried to dissuade Jane, refused to attend the ceremony; nor did he call on Harold while he was in Dublin. Harold made this recoil on Cudahy's head a week later in London, by letting him know that he had brought a message from Roosevelt for Eamon De Valera, Prime Minister of Ireland, but had not been able to deliver it because of Cudahy's avoidance.

After the ceremony Ickes cabled Mike Straus to give out a press release. Reporters soon caught up with Harold and Jane, first in Cork and then in London, but on the whole they seem to have treated them considerately. Nor did the newlyweds get a cruel press in the United States, but quite a favorable one. They spent a week in London, where Ambassador Joseph P. Kennedy was hospitable, introducing Ickes to Lord Halifax, then Foreign Minister, to Winston Churchill, Neville Chamberlain, and other high officials. After a state dinner at the Embassy, Ickes was sought out by Lord Stanley, who wanted to know the American attitude toward three atolls in the Pacific—Howland, Baker, and Jarvis—which had just been taken over by the United States and placed under the administration of the Department of the Interior. Roosevelt had told Ickes that he could say unofficially that there would be no difficulty if the British wanted to work out an agreement for a free joint use of the islands, which "greatly reassured" Lord Stanley. Perhaps it was these encounters in London that gave Ickes the taste for amateur international statesmanship that was to cause further friction between himself and Roosevelt. London was followed by a delightful week of sightseeing and socializing in Paris. Then Ickes felt the newly appropriated funds for public works calling him. The couple returned by the *Paris* and established residence at Headwaters Farm.

Ickes' determination to preserve the independent life of PWA was in vain. The reorganization bill squeezed through the Senate in March 1939, and Ickes made desperate last-minute attempts to persuade the President to use his new powers to transfer Forestry to Interior or, in default of that, to maintain Ickes as administrator of the revised PWA program by appointing him to the new post of Federal Works Administrator.

Roosevelt had written to him routinely, asking for suggestions as to what changes might be made under these new powers. Ickes was inclined not to reply, saying petulantly that if he could not have Forestry he did not want anything; but then he composed a long impassioned letter, expressing "the hope that it goes to you as my friend as well as my President." His "most cherished hope" had been "that under your Administration and while I could help you do it, you would build up a Department of Conservation." That goal had become paramount; Ickes had even "been willing at all times to give up Public Works if instead I were to have a Department of Conservation, of which Forestry ... would be the keystone." He continued, with pathos but some lack of elegance: "I know myself pretty well. I know that my work is my life; I know that although I will never consciously sulk in disloyalty, the fine edge of enthusiasm which has made me so much want to achieve for you, cannot help but be dulled if you pluck out for others all the plums of the pudding of my dreams and leave me only the mess of uninteresting dough."[18] He went on to say that if Interior were not to become a Department of Conservation, "then I respectfully suggest that you might well consider appointing me additionally as Administrator of this new agency"—the Federal Works Agency.

Neither of these plums fell to Ickes. John M. Carmody was appointed to Federal Works, and Ickes was crushed and humiliated. In the *Secret Diary* for 25 June he noted that he felt "very bad" because his administration of public works had never seriously been criticized, because Carmody was mediocre, and because of the way Roosevelt had handled the matter from the outset. That last thought contains the key to the matter. Ickes felt that the man he loved had deceived and betrayed him. On the afternoon of the announcement he stayed away from the Cabinet to begin drafting a long valedictory statement to the President. In it he reiterated yet again the virtues of PWA in bringing out millions in private capital for public works without the United States Treasury's having to disgorge a cent for several months from the beginning of the projects. The letter continues: "From an early date I have been conscious that PWA has not been a favorite at the White House. This has both puzzled and distressed me, not only on my own account but because of the thousands of sincere, devoted and hard-working members of the PWA staff who have been conscious as I have been that, while not literally in the doghouse, PWA was just outside. This failure of PWA to be rated at its true worth has undoubtedly been my personal failure, because I have been the contact between PWA and the White House. Apparently I lack the ability to 'sell' myself." Inevitably, he resorted to the image he found most apt: "For six years I have been Administrator of PWA. A newly born child was laid on my doorstep and I have taken care of and loved that child as if it were my own."

There follows a catalog of grievances to substantiate his complaint that Roosevelt had "cut more deeply into my jurisdiction than that of any other member of your official family." Not only had he lost PWA, one of the most important agencies in the government, but also the National Resources Committee, the Office of Education, the United States Housing Administration, and the Management of the Federal Buildings in Washington. In return he got only Fisheries and the Biological Survey, which he had in fact wanted, together with the Bituminous Coal Commission and the Bureau of Insular Affairs, neither of which he had sought. Most grievously, Roosevelt had not given him Forestry. Ickes concluded by heaping coals of fire on the President's head: "But instead of complaining, I ought to be thanking you for allowing me to be Public Works Administrator during the past six years . . . And I do thank you, Mr. President, with all my heart, for the opportunity that you gave me to perform a unique, and what I firmly believe will be regarded in the future as an outstanding, public job."[19]

Roosevelt's reply, dated three days later, is forthright, sincere, and friendly, but in places it gives the impression that he can only just contain his impatience with Ickes' tragic posturing. He freely admits the value of PWA's role and Ickes' administration of it, but bursts out: "My dear Harold, I wish you would not make assumptions which have absolutely no basis in fact. If, as you say, you have been conscious that PWA has not been a favorite at the White House, you are just utterly and 100% wrong. If you have been puzzled and distressed it is your own fault for imagining things that do not exist." And: "My dear Harold, will you ever grow up? Don't you realize that I am thinking in terms of the Government of the United States, not only during this Administration, but during many Administrations to come." Ickes, he says, was the kind of person who could at the same time run both the Interior Department, "which is slowly becoming the Conservation Department," and Public Works as well, but there were "mighty few" who could. Roosevelt could not rely on personalities and was trying "to leave behind an orderly and logical set-up."[20]

The President signed himself "Affectionately," but Ickes needed a great deal more affection than that from him and was bitter at Roosevelt's failing him. His long struggle with Harry Hopkins over funds for PWA rather than WPA was not just the proper zeal of an administrator to ensure that his agency could function successfully, though it was that in sufficient measure. Deeper down it was a struggle for Roosevelt's heart and mind and for public demonstrations of his confidence, affection, and trust—demonstrations that Ickes would always critically need.

This was very much in evidence in Ickes' jealous rivalry with Henry Wallace, a recurring theme throughout the whole Forestry dispute. For example, on 1 February 1938 Roosevelt had telephoned Ickes to talk about the proposed change of name to the Department of Conservation and complained that Wallace had been in to see him after hearing that he had expressed a preference for such a department. "According to Henry this meant that the President was taking sides against him." After this conversation Ickes determined to have a "showdown" with Roosevelt. He saw him by appointment and accused him of having decided against a Department of Conservation. The President replied that "my complaints were precisely those of Henry Wallace"—that is, of showing preference. "After the President had blown off steam, I began to blow off some on my own account. I told him that . . . in deciding to keep hands off he was really weighting the scales in Henry Wallace's favor . . . I told him that in every issue between Henry Wallace and me from the beginning he had decided in favor of Wallace. At this point he interjected; 'That is just what Henry says.' "

One can only sympathize with Roosevelt in having to cope with these outbursts of sibling rivalry between two grown men. But cope with them he could:

> The President said that he couldn't take any sides as between Henry and me; that he loved us both. I insisted that he was taking sides and then I told him that I would not be interested if there was not to be a Department of Conservation. At this point he cried out, in an agi-

tated voice: "You mustn't say such things, Harold. You and I have a lot of things to do together yet. You have been with me a thousand per cent. I haven't been able to accomplish everything that I set out to do, but we have done some things, haven't we, and we must go on and try to do some more things . . ."

At some point during this remark he reached over and put his hand on my right arm . . .[21]

Even after PWA was lost to Ickes forever and Hopkins had no official position to constitute him an administrative rival, Ickes could often barely restrain his jealousy; yet when Roosevelt's attitude to them was not a bone of contention, Ickes positively like Hopkins. He responded to Hopkins' "old shoe" charm, to his human warmth and immediacy, as much as anyone did, and perhaps it was his awareness of how attractive Hopkins could be that provoked even keener jealousy over Roosevelt. Hopkins and Ickes were on quite intimate terms, discussed their careers and personal affairs, even sometimes went on vacations together. In April 1937, when Ickes was feeing contentedly disengaged from PWA, Roosevelt pressed him, as he often did, to take a holiday and told Henry Morgenthau to make available to Ickes a revenue cutter, so he could go cruising in the Gulf of Mexico. Harold telephoned Harry, who found he would be able to go. "I am delighted at this," Ickes wrote, "because Harry and I have always gotten along very well personally and he will make the best kind of companion"; and indeed they had an excellent time, fishing and sightseeing. In response to a joking ship-to-shore radio message the President replied, expressing "the pious hope that we would bury ourselves in the Everglades with a month's rations so that the budget might be balanced."[22]

That may have been a good joke as long as he was treating the pair as a team, but more often they were competing against one another for funds, and then they squabbled almost like children and reacted to Roosevelt's decisions as if he were distributing not just money but love. Thus, in one of his *Saturday Evening Post* articles, Ickes, recalling events back in 1935 concerning the competition between PWA and WPA, says: "At this time I was having hard sledding with the President. I had come to know that while in a contest with Harry I might win over the President's mind, his heart would remain with Harry."[23]

Years later, after PWA had ceased to exist as a cause of rivalry and Hopkins, following major surgery for stomach cancer, was prevented by ill-health from holding any office, Ickes could still feel almost vindictively jealous of him and his closeness to Roosevelt, as remarks in the *Secret Diary* show. In November 1940:

> Hopkins has the field [entrée to the White House] entirely to himself.
> The Hopkins intimacy disturbs me. I cannot believe that it bodes well for the President . . . I hear that, when Mrs. Roosevelt gets back, she will put Harry in his place, and that she is still "off of Harry." I hope that this is true, but the fact is that Harry continues to live at the White House, and it is still a matter of mystery what he is living on. I do not believe that he has yet been appointed Librarian at Hyde Park and if he has been, he is doing his work *in absentia*.

Again, in May 1941: "in the end he always agrees with the President. He is not going to run any risk of offending the President and lose his place under the President's bed."[24]

The last phrase recalls Ickes' somewhat malicious pleasure in June 1936, when the Deficiency Appropriation Bill did not even mention Hopkins and formally recognized PWA instead of its "being kicked out of bed."[25] The feline tone of the comments just quoted, speaking of Hopkins as if he were the President's mistress, with no visible means of supporting himself, cannot be missed. As we have seen, there had always been a strong unacknowledged feminine element in Ickes' personal relationships. Throughout his adult life he had found a succession of heroes to worship and serve, and he admired their physical aggressiveness, masculine presence, and thrilling oratorical powers as much as their moral splendor—John Harlan, Theodore Roosevelt, and Hiram Johnson are examples. He showed a sneaking admiration and affection for the three Democratic Party bosses in Chicago—George E. Brennan, John P. Hopkins, and Roger C. Sullivan—despite his disapproval of their consciously cynical attitude to power-broking. These men "had so sentimental a feeling for each other that they felt called upon to shout insulting names and swear like pirates, in the belief that they could thus dissimulate their warm mutual affection."[26] Franklin D. Roosevelt was much more sophisticated and complex than those provincial bosses, yet he too inspired a feminine attachment in

Ickes, and he knew how to exploit it. Consider his often-quoted reply to one of Ickes' many resignations:

> the President handed me an envelope which contained the following, written by hand, in lead pencil:
>
>
>
> The White House
>
> Washington   (Feb'y 7, 1940)
>
>
>
> We—you & I, were married "for better, for worse" —and it's too late to get a divorce & too late for you to walk out of the home—anyway. I need you! Nuff said. Affec. FDR.

Ickes comments: "It is pretty difficult to do anything with a man who can write such a letter."[27] What he did do was send this reply: "You are a hard man to deal with, especially when anyone admires and loves you as I do. Your letter quite touched me. I am yours to command . . . of my devotion there can be no doubt."[28]

It would be too literal-minded to speculate about who was husband and who wife in this "marriage." There were elements of masculine and femine role-playing on both sides, but, as in actual marriages, the important question is whether, and in what ways, one partner acts as a parent substitute for the other. The record suggests that Roosevelt elicited and provided scope for the strong moral convictions Ickes had acquired from his mother. We have proposed that Ickes identified with his mother and unconsciously wanted to embrace the maternal role as creator of life, sustenance, and growth. When, quite suddenly and unexpectedly, in the autumn of his life, Roosevelt made him, as Public Works Administrator, custodian of a vast store of wealth to pour forth as a life-giving stream into the body of the country, he had delegated to Ickes an administrative version of the maternal functions he had always wanted to perform. It is no wonder that Ickes saw PWA funds as something not to be squandered on insubstantial, non-growth-producing projects. The same set of attitudes was attached to his larger role as Secretary of the Interior, in which he had assumed the responsibility for conserving the irreplaceable natural resources of the country. For the unconscious reasons we have sketched in, the country's magnificent forest areas, or what remained of them, became the focal point of Ickes's concern, as if they represented everything that was most primal, most fecund, and yet most vulnerable in Nature. This concern was expressed in his unceasing campaign to have the Forest Service restored to Interior, which, as far as Ickes' involvement was concerned, came to a bitter climax in 1940.

Early in 1940 Ickes uncovered new evidence that he believed greatly strengthened his hand in the Forestry dispute. While on vacation he read Henry Pringle's *Life and Times of William Howard Taft,* which dealt in considerable detail with the Ballinger-Pinchot controversy, sparked off by Louis R. Glavis, Ickes' own Frankenstein's monster, then a zealous twenty-four-year-old special investigator in Interior. It is impossible here to give an adequate account of this fascinating story, but Pringle does make out a very persuasive case, apparently well-researched and documented, that the Ballinger "scandal" arose out of the oversuspicious construction Glavis had placed upon a connection between Ballinger, as commissioner of the General Land Office and later as Secretary of the Interior, and a group of small investors in Alaskan coal leases, led by prospector Clarence Cunningham of Wallace, Idaho. Pringle introduces his account by saying that from the early fall of 1910 the nation had been told of a "larcenous conspiracy," to which Ballinger was a party, involving valuable Alaskan coal lands. But, Pringle wrote, "The charge was as direct and specific as it was untrue. Certain of the editors of the United States had examined the evidence with gross carelessness."[29]

Pinchot's direct involvement in the case came about as the result of Glavis's appeal to the law officer of the Forest Service, of which Pinchot was head, in July 1909. Glavis, for no good reason that Pringle could see, felt himself under great pressure by officials of Interior, about whose honesty he had become extremely suspicious, to withdraw his allegations against Ballinger. Because the disputed coal claims lay within the boundaries of the Chugach forest reserve, Glavis turned to the great forester and archconservationist for help. Taft inquired into the matter, exonerated Ballinger (as did a later congressional inquiry), and dismissed Glavis (on Ballinger's suggestion), "for disloyalty to his superior officers in making a false charge against them." But Ballinger had been tried and convicted by the nation's press.

In Pringle's view, Pinchot was the chief orchestrator of this campaign. He had been prejudiced against Ballinger from the time of Ballinger's appointment to Interior, believing without foundation that he was opposed to Theodore Roosevelt's conservation policies.

Pinchot now had come to believe the same about Taft. Pringle attributes this to the fact that Roosevelt and Pinchot would do whatever the law would let them get away with in the service of conservation, whereas Taft and Ballinger insisted on restricting action to the powers explicitly given them by law. Be that as it may, Pinchot was intent on making trouble for the President as well as his Secretary of the Interior. Pringle quotes a letter of 6 September 1909 from Taft to his brother Horace: "I am convinced that Pinchot with his fanaticism and his disappointment at my decision in the Ballinger case plans a coup by which I shall be compelled to dismiss him and he will be able to make out a martyrdom and try to raise opposition to me on Ballinger's account. I am afraid that he has a good deal of the guile attributed to the Jesuits in his nature . . . His trouble is that . . . he seizes shreds of evidence as conviction stronger than the Holy Writ."

Taft's suspicions were well founded. In January 1910 Pinchot wrote to Senator Jonathan P. Dolliver of Iowa concerning Glavis' dismissal and, after implied criticism of the President, concluded: "rules of official decorum exist in the interest of efficient administration and of that alone. When they are used to prevent an honest and vigilant public officer from saving property of the public, their purpose is violated and they have become worse than useless."[30] Pinchot saw to it that this letter was made public, and, reluctantly, Taft had to act. He dismissed Pinchot on 7 January 1910, clearly signaling his break with Roosevelt.

It is not difficult to imagine the effect Pringle's exposé had on Ickes' mind. Everything inclined him to see his position vis-à-vis Pinchot as being exactly that of Ballinger, as Pringle described it. A dedicated but rule-following conservationist, vilified by an egoistic fanatic, even having been persecuted by the same power-crazed investigator—no wonder he took Ballinger's cause to heart, as a weapon against Pinchot. When he returned from vacation he called a meeting of his top staff, suggested that they might read the pertinent chapters of Pringle's book, and instituted a departmental investigation to see whether the author's charges against Pinchot could be sustained. If this were found to be the case, he would issue a public statement correcting the historical record. He, too, had had his "own unpleasant experiences with Glavis," and knew "what a zealot Pinchot is."[31]

Evidently there was some skepticism among members of Ickes'

staff concerning the project; as the investigation proceeded, however, his confidence grew. Eventually Ickes' charges against Pinchot were spelled out in an article in the *Saturday Evening Post* in May 1940, and in much greater detail in a fifty-eight-page Interior Department publication entitled *Not Guilty: An Official Inquiry Into the Charges Made by Glavis and Pinchot Against Richard A. Ballinger, Secretary of the Interior, 1909–1911.* Within the Interior Department building, Ickes had Ballinger's portrait shifted from its former position and hung outside his own door.[32]

In the meanwhile, Roosevelt continued to beguile Ickes with vague promises for future success. In January 1940 he was still intimating that he would transfer Forestry to Interior. In the background Pinchot was still fomenting opposition. Ickes again pressed the President to settle the issue, to send Congress an order making the transfer, as he still had the power to do. Roosevelt began again to temporize; influential Senator George Norris had told him that "to send the order up now would split his real friends in two factions." Ickes' diary for 27 January 1940 expresses desperation at what he has come to feel a mortal threat: "If Forestry is not transferred, I will feel that I am bankrupt intellectually and emotionally, and I undoubtedly will resign." On 4 February he writes that he "came home Thursday night with my mind made up to send in my resignation to the President if the order does not go up to Congress on Tuesday." Jane let him rage on, but he finally told her that unless the Forestry transfer went though, he "could not stay on and save my own self-respect any more than I could continue to serve under a man who had not carried out his promise to me."[33]

He did in fact send his letter of resignation on Tuesday, 7 February 1940. It pointed out that, although the transfer could have been made easily during the last session of Congress or even at the beginning of the present one, now that feeling had been whipped up it could not be done without a fight, and this might harm Roosevelt's chances of reelection. Ickes would not ask him to do anything that would risk that. The extravagant phrasing of the remainder shows how deeply the issue had worked its way into Ickes' mind.

> However, unfortunately, Forestry has become a symbol to me. I have had one consistent ambition since I have been Secretary of the Interior and that has been to be the head of a Department of Con-

servation, of which, necessarily, Forestry would be the keystone. I have not wanted merely to be *a* Secretary of the Interior; I have wanted to leave office with the satisfaction that I had accomplished something real and fundamental. I have told you frankly that, as this Department is now set up, it does not interest me.

So I have come to the reluctant conclusion that, as matters now stand, I cannot be true to myself nor measure up to the high standards that you have a right to expect of a man whom you have honored by making him a member of your Cabinet. Accordingly, I am resigning as Secretary of the Interior . . .

Although I now feel that I cannot go on, I want you to know how much I appreciate the many expressions of regard and confidence that I have had from you.[34]

These last phrases obviously were intended to wound Roosevelt's conscience: to say that the "expressions of regard and confidence" were insincere; that Roosevelt, the seductive parent to whose service Ickes had dedicated himself, had not valued him highly enough to give him Forestry, which had become such a symbol. This ultimately was his major grievance.

Franklin D. Roosevelt's redistribution of agencies under the 1939 reorganization bill caused a lengthy estrangement between himself and Ickes, cool on the President's side and sullen on Ickes'. The latter found his interest and involvement in his official duties declining. No longer was work the only thing that gave meaning to his life; the marriage with Jane was prospering, and with the birth of a son, Harold, that year, his need for parenthood was finding renewed satisfaction in family rather than career. Yet even now, an unpleasant survival from an earlier, more tortuous family life could surface to disturb this domestic serenity.

In November 1939 Ickes received a letter form Henry S. Blum, a Chicago lawyer, stating that Robert, Harold's and Anna's foster son, had consulted him about his rights under Anna's will. Apparently Blum had been unable to find any legal claim, for he proposed that Robert might be entitled to consideration on moral grounds. Ickes promptly replied with a long letter pointing out that Robert had no legal right whatever, since none had been conferred on him by Anna's will, which made Ickes sole legatee, and since Robert was not the natural child of either Anna or Harold and had never been adopted by either of them. As for "moral" obligations, not only had Robert been taken from an orphanage into a good home, been educated, and had jobs found for him, but he had to such an extent failed in his own reciprocal moral obligation that, according to Ickes' recent information, he had been spreading malicious gossip about Ickes in Pittsburgh. If Robert thought he could induce Ickes to buy him off with money to which his foster son had no legal claim, he was mistaken.[35]

Ickes had already been alerted to some such threat. In the unpublished manuscript diary for 4 November 1937 he describes an interview with Robert, who had come to ask for financial aid only to meet with a refusal and a stern lecture about the need to stand on one's own feet. If Robert were waiting for Harold to die, expecting to inherit a substantial mount, he was living in a fool's paradise. In a September 1939 entry Ickes discussed a letter that he had received from Raymond, who told him that Robert had somehow got hold of some letters that Anna had written to Wilmarth. These letters charged that Harold had cheated Robert out of one million dollars, as well as losing much of Anna's fortune through bad management.

Blum's letter was the first shot in a protracted legal campaign against which Ickes fought like a tiger, using every resource, overt and covert, of his official position. If Robert, assisted by Blum, was to attack him on moral grounds and threaten bad publicity, Ickes would be ready with similar threats against them. He retrieved from his files a half-forgotten letter from a woman complaining about Robert's behavior, and Ickes began to wonder whether he could construe any of Robert's actions as criminal, as contravening the Mann Act. He needed something with which to threaten Blum, so, he put J. Edgar Hoover and the FBI on his trail. On 24 March 1940 the manuscript diary records that on Ickes' return from a trip to California, Hoover had come in to report that an operative had bugged Blum's telephone in Chicago, and heard a conversation which was very likely with someone in the law firm of former Republican Senator from Illinois, Otis Glenn. Ickes thought that this information (really only a guess) that the Glenn firm was interested in the matter explained Blum's muted suggestions that prominent Illinois Republicans were involved. When a controversy in the Senate forced Solicitor-General Bob Jackson to ban wiretapping, Ickes contacted Tom Courtney, State's Attorney of Cook County, Illinois, and had another listening device put on Blum's line.

On 30 March Ickes writes that he had received a letter from Blum saying that he had found out something that horrified him and for which he believed Ickes responsible. Ickes, leaping to the guilty conclusion that the wiretapping was referred to, dashed off a sharp letter saying he was tired of Blum's threats. In his diary he protested that he had never requested the tapping of Blum's telephone and knew nothing about it until Hoover reported that all wiretapping had to stop.

Nathan Margold, solicitor for the Department of the Interior, who was working on the case, helped Ickes draft letters to Blum offering to arbitrate the legal aspects of Anna's will, but refusing to consider the moral points, and openly accusing Blum of aiding in blackmail. By April 1940 Margold, in a highly nervous state because of these negotiations, was not being much help to Ickes. But Ickes forebore to complain because Margold was performing this private legal work in addition to his official tasks and, Ickes felt, with admirable loyalty. Presumably Ickes felt that anything that protected the reputation of the Secretary of the Interior, whether in a public or private matter, was legitimate business for the Department's employees. Margold had made an extensive study of the law of blackmail as it applied to this case, and one can imagine that he felt a good deal of pressure to come to a favorable opinion.

In the long run, this background muckraking proved unnecessary. In February 1941 Robert finally sought to have Anna's will arbitrated by the Cook County Superior Court in an attempt to find a beneficial interest in it for himself. In his diary Ickes expressed confidence that Margold's brief would prevail before the arbitrators. However, the matter dragged on for a very long period, until, early in 1943, the issue was decided in Ickes' favor. Soon after this Robert formally filed suit in Cook County, Illinois, claiming that Ickes had disinherited him. His case turned partly on the interpretation of a clause in Anna's highly complex will, by which, if Harold were still living ten days after her death, the trustees of the estate were to "convey, make over and deliver to him" the entire estate of approximately $800,000. Through his attorney, Robert now claimed that this clause amounted not to a bequest, but to the designation of Harold as a sort of guardian of the estate, charged with carrying out the deceased's intentions. Robert pointed out that his foster mother's intention could not have been to disinherit him, since her will provided that, if Harold were not alive ten days after her death, "the trustees" should first maintain and educate Robert, then pay him up to $5,000 a year until he was thirty, $7,500 a year until he was thirty-five, and $10,000 a year thereafter, with discretion to pay him a sum not exceeding $200,000. Ickes, who had been paying Robert a meager allowance, offered to settle Robert's claim for $1,500; Robert wanted $200,000.[36] Eventually, almost a year later, the Illinois Supreme Court found unanimously in Ickes' favor, and then dismissed Robert's appeal for a rehearing.[37]

The most troublesome shadow cast by Ickes' first marriage over his second had finally been cleared away. But the closing scenes in that domestic drama had been played against the overpowering backdrop of World War II, which had given new scope to Harold Ickes' ambition and embroiled him in his final test of wills with President Roosevelt.

SEVEN

Warfare–Bureaucratic and Foreign

As THE PROSPECT of American involvement in the European conflict increased, Harold Ickes became consumed with the desire to play an active, even a dominant role in the coming struggle. He longed to replace the ineffectual Harry H. Woodring as Secretary of War, and in November 1939 Tom Corcoran encouraged him to believe that President Roosevelt intended to award him that prize. His hopes were kept high into the early months of 1940 by Corcoran, Henry Morgenthau, and Ben Cohen, but finally the President told Ickes that, although he favored him for the position, he could think of no adequate replacement for Interior. Ickes quickly assured Roosevelt that, "Not with reference to that possibility, but just in case I should fall dead at any time, you could safely make Wirtz [the present Under Secretary] Secretary of the Interior." Wirtz was "strong and able and he has our point of view."[1]

Ickes realized that the President was telling him "in a friendly way" that he would not make him Secretary of War, and there is little doubt that he was disappointed and resentful, not only of Harry Hopkins, who as usual had the President's ear and sought to block Ickes' plans, but of FDR himself. In the preceding entry in the *Secret Diary* he had written: "I frankly admit that I would like to have it [this appointment] myself now"—rather than La Guardia, whom the President was considering   and now, after this polite rebuff, he allows himself to express new doubts about the President's decisiveness and strength.

During the last two or three days I have begun to worry more and more about the situation. Although I believe that the President would be overwhelmingly elected today, I am not so sure that the country could not be turned against him by November . . .

My own belief is that the Administration, and this particularly means the President, is at a definite crossroads. In time of war, or threatened war, the people want a strong man who will give them affirmative action.

Could it be, in this gravest of looming crises, that Franklin Delano Roosevelt would fail to measure up?

It slowly begins to appear that it was himself, rather than the President, that Ickes was seeing as that strong man of affirmative action. From the very beginning of Hitler's despoliation of Europe, Ickes had been publicly bellicose toward Germany and Italy and scathing of all whom he considered "appeasers." At this period and for many months the State Department, under Secretary Cordell Hull, was the object of his contemptuous criticism, on the grounds that it was responsible for the Neutrality Act, which had prevented the United States from aiding the Loyalists in Spain and still hindered efforts to help "desperate England fighting with its back to the wall." State had gone along weakly with Chamberlain's conciliation of Hitler, where a more aggressive policy might have saved Austria and Czechoslovakia.

But Harold Ickes had been prepared to speak out. He scorned Under Secretary of State Sumner Welles, who recently had asked him to delete a certain phrase from a forthcoming speech because it might hinder Chamberlain's negotiations with Mussolini—another instance of the State Department's lack of moral fiber. He had been the first prominent American to denounce fascism; so persistent had been his criticism of Nazi Germany that Hermann Göring's Essen newspaper accused him of being the leading American agitator against the Reich (a compliment Ickes accepted with satisfaction). He had opposed the sale of oil to Italy after the invasion of Ethiopia. His suggestion that the aggressor nations be "quarantined" provided the keynote of the President's famous 1937 speech. The following year Ickes had defied both Roosevelt and Secretary of State Hull by refusing to sign a contract to sell helium to Germany, thereby effectively grounding that nation's zeppelin fleet. Given his assessment of the State Department, he was dismayed in the months leading up to the 1940 presidential election and for many months thereafter to see

Roosevelt giving it unqualified support and unfailingly siding with it in opposition to his own warlike stance.

Ickes had been vociferous in his support of Roosevelt for a third term, but as the time for the Democratic convention drew closer he was assailed by doubts. For one thing, the President seemed to have "gone into reverse" on the New Deal program. He seemed to be "throwing away everything that we have gained during the past seven years" and "doing it almost contemptuously so far as those people are concerned who have been his staunchest supporters through thick and thin."

These gloomy reflections were prompted by Roosevelt's having set up, in May 1940, an Advisory Commission to the Council of National Defense, which, though it included some labor representatives and administration experts, also called in representatives of big business, notably William S. Knudsen, an executive of General Motors, and Edward R. Stettinius, president of U.S. Steel. Ickes was depressed by the President's manner as he introduced this commission. He had been "conciliatory and persuasive and plausible, and yet, it seemed to me, ineffective." He had not given, Ickes remarked characteristically, "such an impression of strength as I think this situation calls for." Moreover, "the plans that he outlined for the members of the commission were nebulous and inchoate." The commission would be coordinating rather than executive, "yet it appeared to be given certain executive powers." Ickes was sure that it "would soon be in the hands of its strongest man—probably Knudsen—and would be functioning independently of the regular establishments and, perhaps, even extralegally." This commission was the object of Ickes' hostile suspicions for months; though in the long run it seemed not to find a significant role and most of its members were absorbed into more orthodox branches of the wartime establishment, it epitomized what Ickes, with considerable justification, saw as the great domestic danger of the war, that big business would take over the war effort and run it to its own advantage, producing another crop of war millionaires, capitalizing, as he says, on their patriotism. He agreed with Justice Hugo Black that, "unless we beat back the economic royalists, we may find ourselves with a fascist crisis of our own on our hands," and he wondered whether Franklin D. Roosevelt would be equal to the task.

Ickes' efforts to protect the gains made by the New Deal in defending the mass of the people against exploitation by powerful private interests, while still adopting a determined military posture, were sincere and unflagging. His vast experience as head of PWA and of Interior had made him aware of the persistence, guile, and self-interest of large elements of the business establishment of the day, as well as of the need for constant vigilance against them. Yet back in 1915, when he had written encouraging Theodore Roosevelt to take a vigorous stand against German imperialism, he had projected onto "our people" the feeling that they were "stale on questions of industrial justice and social betterment" and more concerned with the honor and dignity of their country in the international scene. At that time the young Progressive Party's socially advanced doctrines might be allowed to slip into the background for the duration of the crisis. That was not the case in 1940. Industrial justice must go hand in hand with war preparations. What had caused this firming up of his commitment to progressive aspirations?

One possible explanation both of Ickes' acute dissatisfaction with and desire to replace Roosevelt, and of his own more liberal attitude toward social questions lies in the great alteration in his domestic life. In 1915 he was in black despair over his marriage to Anna; now he was married to a young, beautiful, and noncensorious woman, who unfailingly supported his every decision, and who in September 1939 had presented him with a son, the beginning, he felt, of a new and altogether happier family life, of which he was in undisputed command. It was a situation to encourage a more optimistic view of the worthwhileness of ordinary humankind than he had had before, and to allay the deep-seated doubts about his own capacities, which had inhibited an aggressive, open display of ambition for so long. A decent self-respecting life seemed both possible and deserved for the ordinary run of American families. With the purchase of the farm to which he brought Jane as his new wife, Harold Ickes had in effect reverted to the role of small independent farmer, characteristic of the pioneering stock from which he had sprung—the life which he had so loved as a boy on his relatives' farms near Altoona. It seems that, despite his upward social mobility by way of education, professional training, and political involvement, Ickes always deep down identified with his social class of origin. Despite manifold opportunities to do so, he had never really felt tempted to merge himself with the wealthy and powerful elite. As a class they remained alien and inimical, even though he could maintain friendships with individuals such as Bernard Baruch, and he considered it now as his natural role to protect the public against the threat of exploitation.

But to Ickes it seemed that the President was playing into the hands of big business by his indecisiveness and his weakness in the face of demands for competent industrialists to be brought into the preparedness program. The press would be vocal in support of this new Advisory Commission, and the President would be boxed in. He felt his loyalty to Roosevelt weakening: "Considering what we are doing and apparently proposing to do, should the President be at the head of the country during the next four years?" Republican candidate Wendell Willkie was away and running and the President had not yet even declared himself a candidate. Not only did this show him as lacking in strength—strength being always a cardinal virtue for Ickes and just what the country was demanding now—but also he was letting down Ickes, who had been the first Cabinet member to support publicly the third term. This betrayal was compounded when Ickes arrived at Chicago for the Democratic Convention of July 1940 and found Harry Hopkins "fully established in supreme command of the Roosevelt strategy." Ickes remarks bitterly in his *Secret Diary* that "here he was sitting at the throttle and directing the movement that I had started and had kept hammering away at until it swept through the country like a cyclone."

This remark highlights a theme that was developing more and more strongly in Ickes' self-concept: of his own political effectiveness as rivaling, in fact though not in formal title, that of the President. He had seen himself as the unacknowledged kingmaker, running Roosevelt for office as he had run Anna and the others. It was gall and wormwood to find Roosevelt's favorite, Harry Hopkins, managing the convention. He visited Hopkins at his headquarters in a city hotel, where he "spent an hour or two listening to the political wisdom that dripped from the lips of a lank figure slouching in a dressing gown and bedroom slippers." Everyone flocked to ask Harry "what was on," because they knew he was "sleeping at the foot of the President's bed."[2]

For Ickes personally there was an even more important matter than the question of who was to stage-manage the "reluctant" Roosevelt's nomination. He believed Roosevelt to be ailing and weakening, and could see himself as the strong man looking over the President's shoulder, ready to step forward into his place if he should fall while in office. This image gained in substance at the convention when several Connecticut delegates came to talk to Ickes and said that they favored him for Vice-President; then Oscar Chapman, his Assistant Secretary, proposed starting up such a movement—he could deliver the Colorado delegates. Ickes had heard suggestions that he would be a strong vice-presidential candidate, and considered it possible that Roosevelt might want him as his running mate.

Jane, filled with youthful enthusiasm, got hold of their friends Helen Gahagan and Melvyn Douglas, delegates from California, and after a good deal of politicking they managed to get Governor Olson of California ready to nominate Ickes, with practically the whole delegation prepared to vote for him—a wonderful start. But Ickes' experienced eye began to see that some of these declarations of support were just talk, and that Roosevelt's choice would be decisive. In the first few days the convention seemed to be going badly, to be lifeless and indecisive, and on 16 July, Ickes sent a wordy, overdramatized telegram telling Roosevelt that the convention was "bleeding to death" and perhaps Roosevelt's reputation and prestige with it. "Prompt and heart stirring action" was needed to prevent this. Ickes advised Roosevelt to "insist upon a candidate for Vice-President who sees eye to eye with you on both domestic and foreign questions," someone who would be "generally considered to have sufficient stature to be the head of the nation."

This telegram was never acknowledged, but two days later, after the convention had come alight and nominated Roosevelt, Ickes sent him a congratulatory telegram and revealed that it was himself that he had in mind as vice-presidential candidate. First he suggested Robert M. Hutchins, president of the University of Chicago, then went on: "May I say also that if Hutchins does not appeal to you, I would feel honored to be considered as your running mate. I believe that the candidate should come from the West. I know that I have considerable strength in the West. I have the confidence of liberals generally and I believe that I have particular standing among such groups as the Jews and the Negroes."

Ickes' skepticism, however, was too long-standing to be easily dispelled by a wave of optimism. He was disillusioned with Roosevelt and felt Roosevelt was jaundiced toward him; he claims that he sent this telegram only so that Roosevelt could not plead that he had no idea Ickes was interested: "I was not averse to taking this defense away from him and, to that extent, to putting him in the hole."[3]

The qualifications Ickes claimed for himself were real. He came from the Midwest and well knew the political situation there. Just a year before he had been closely associated with the New Deal's most dramatic statement against racial intolerance: the Marian Anderson concert at the Lincoln Memorial. Two months later he emphatically rejected a request from the National Gentile League (whose slogan was "Vote gentile, buy gentile") to hold a rally at the Sylvan Theater on the grounds of the Washington Monument, with the ringing declaration that the theater "belongs to all the people of the United States regardless of race, color or creed," and should not be used by "an organization . . . designed to foster . . . race prejudice."[4] He had spoken out boldly against the treatment of Jews in Nazi Germany and proposed their resettlement in Alaska. No one in Franklin D. Roosevelt's Cabinet defended these and other minority groups with anything like the vigor and consistency of Harold Ickes, and their political allegiance was something on which he very probably could have counted.

As usual, he could not see any element of personal aggrandizement in putting his own name forward. He was fitted for the position, he implies, because almost alone among his Cabinet colleagues his judgment was unclouded by personal ambition. He was willing to become Roosevelt's running mate because the idea was greatly appealing to his wife; he would entertain the notion if his appointment would give Jane enjoyment—a disclaimer reminiscent, though in a different key, of the reasons he gave for seeking to enter the administration in 1933.[5] But in the following months and years of the war it became increasingly difficult to distinguish self-aggrandizement from public service in his efforts to challenge Roosevelt and in his unceasing attempts to extend his control over the nation's resources.

Harold Ickes' bitter expectation that Roosevelt would pass him over was fulfilled. "Pa" Watson, Roosevelt's secretary, telephoned him the morning of 19 July to say that, considering the farm vote, the labor vote, and the foreign situation, the President had decided that Henry Wallace, Ickes' old rival over Forestry, would be the strongest candidate. After a few sarcastic remarks from Ickes to the effect that Wallace was not nearly as strong with labor as he, and was a poor campaigner who could not meet Willkie on the stump, "Pa" went on to repeat the President's message that because Henry's nomination would mean that there would be a new Secretary of Agriculture, "that conservation matter" could be worked out to Ickes' satisfaction. Nor surprisingly, having "the Forestry bait" dangled in front of him once again angered Ickes: "I could not help wondering how many times the President thought he could bring me to the surface on the bait that he has been using since 1934."

This outright disbelief in the President's sincerity is a new note, followed in the *Secret Diary* by a couple of pages of sharp remarks about Roosevelt's deceptive and clumsy approach to the whole business of nomination. Wallace, as a former Republican, was a most unwelcome candidate to the convention and secured the nomination only after hours of confusion and wrangling and great political pressure, including a message from Roosevelt that he would refuse his own nomination if Wallace were not accepted. At the end, Ickes claimed to be glad to be out of it all. The Democratic ticket was in deep trouble, and, as running mate, he would have had to share the blame.

After Ickes returned to Washington the President was at some pains to conciliate him, explaining his problems in selecting a politically viable vice-presidential candidate, and as the campaign progressed Ickes had no doubt that Roosevelt's goals were infinitely preferable to Willkie's and became eager to get into the fight, though he still had reservations about the President's tactics. For example at a Cabinet meeting in August there was discussion of a proposed excess-profits tax to stop war profiteers, something Ickes had sought for a long time. Roosevelt's notion was that in the beginning they should just accept the best bill that Congress was willing to pass without too much pressure, whereas Ickes felt that "we ought to tell the country now that the big interests are insisting on a bill that will mean a new crop of war millionaires." The administration should announce that it would not allow this, "even if it means new factories of our own and taking over old ones and running them ourselves."

Over and above this disagreement about tactics, Ickes and the President shared a concern to oppose the growing demand for appeasement coming from big business. To Ickes it was a "foregone conclusion" that Willkie would be supported by such interests and that, if elected, "he will stand for appeasement and an American brand of fascism."

Yet Ickes professed himself almost in despair over the presidential campaign. Roosevelt believed he should stay close to Washington in case war should come, rather than be seen politicking about the country. Ickes saw the point of that, but by mid-October he was really thinking that Willkie would win unless Roosevelt joined in with a major political speech. Eventually he was able to persuade Roosevelt that Willkie's misrepresentations of the administration's policies had given him ample justification to do so. Ickes himself made a number of speaking tours throughout the country, once taking Jane along with him. Even at the end, waiting for the results to come in, he felt that he had never witnessed "such incompetent and inept management—if it deserves the designation 'management' at all . . . [or] so many good opportunities to score hits against the opposition absolutely ignored"—familiar themes with Ickes, whenever he was not in control.

Despite this mismanagement and Ickes' forebodings, Roosevelt scored another resounding victory, and, after the customary formal resignation, Ickes found himself back in business at the old stand, though not quite with the same good will as before. He describes the President's refusal of his resignation as "graceful and gracious," but a certain phrase in it must have stuck in his craw. Roosevelt wrote: "That is mighty sweet of you and if I were a Frenchman I would kiss you on both cheeks. As an American, all I can say is 'you are a very good boy.' Keep up the good work. And give my love to Jane."[6]

That expression "a good boy" may well have seemed too patronizing, too belittling to fit Ickes' enlarged perception of his own stature. Two years later, during which period he was rarely admitted to the President's presence, and consequently became very estranged, Ickes found the President again making overtures of friendship, inviting him to lunch and so on. Steve Early reported that Roosevelt felt that he, Ickes, had been more pleasant lately, but Ickes snapped back that the President could hardly have formed such a judgment since he had not seen him in two years. Roosevelt would soon be shown that he had not "changed into a good boy."[7]

During the 1940 campaign another of Ickes' idols revealed feet of clay. Hiram Johnson, his revered "Chief," the man he had urged to run for the presidency in 1924 and 1932, had come out publicly in support of Wendell Willkie. Ickes cast his mind back to the old days, to the California campaigns in which Johnson had fought against the railroad corporations and for public power. Now he was backing Willkie, "slicker, private utilities man, political corruptionist," and "on the specious plea that he is saving our country from a threatened dictatorship that would be implicit in a third term."[8] Ickes was inclined to blame Roosevelt for refusing Johnson certain legitimate political favors, but he could see no justification for Johnson's supporting of Willkie.

A major immediate cause of Ickes' disaffection with Roosevelt was his persistent ignoring of Ickes' claims to be included in the inner circle of the "War Cabinet." Following as it did on the refusal to appoint him Secretary of War, this was bemusing and aggravating. If he was not to be given official status as a war administrator, he would make every political ploy he could to extend his control over the sinews of war: oil, hard fuels, and electric power. He had been Oil Administrator under the NRA; the Geological Survey and Bureau of Mines, part of his empire in Interior, had conducted surveys of the nation's oil resources; and he was in a fair way to achieving control over bituminous coal. But for years power had been an overriding concern, almost an *idée fixe,* and with United States involvement in World War II fast approaching, he made a bold bid to become the administration's "power czar."

Ickes' determination to control power stemmed in part from his belief that the New Deal's public power program was in jeopardy. He had played a major role in the development of that program, using PWA to construct TVA facilities and policing private utilities by threatening government competition if rates were not kept low. Such activities had involved him in countless lawsuits, with utility lawyers such as Wendell Willkie charging collusion between PWA and TVA. The resulting litigation had not only retarded the public power program, it had also deepened Ickes' long-standing hostility to the private utilities. Yet with war threatening and with government surveys showing clearly that the nation's power resources would be inadequate to sustain a major conflict, cooperation between public and private utilities was a pressing need. It must not be achieved, Harold Ickes was determined to see, in such a way as to give private power any long-term advantage.

As with conservation, Ickes was able, by identifying his aim with the public interest, to absolve himself from any suggestion that personal ambition may have played a part in his efforts to achieve control over power and also to screen out from his consciousness any recollection of the deliberate and sometimes devious steps that he had taken toward that end. Thus, when columnist Marquis Childs wrote in May 1945 that TVA had long been an object of bureaucratic envy, and that Ickes, in particular, wished to add it to Interior and had worked tirelessly to bring this about, Ickes not only angrily denied the charge but claimed that when Roosevelt had tried to make the change, he had advised against it.[9]

Ickes' diary makes nonsense of these disclaimers. The entry for 13 May 1939, for example, reports a conversation with Roosevelt as a result of which Ickes believed that he had "won him pretty far over to my theory that all the agencies having to do with public power, including TVA, ought to be set up in one strong organization in Interior." According to the entry for 25 June 1939, the President had told him that he would send up an executive order giving Interior supervisory control over TVA and creating in Interior a "Power and Conservation Division," thus giving Ickes' department control of most of the government's power activities. Ickes then asked about the future of Forestry, and the President replied that he would give him Forestry "at the same time I give you TVA and on the same principle." It would have been interesting to hear what Ickes' irony might have made of the phrase "on the same principle" years later, when he still had not been given either of those prizes.

But in August 1939 Ickes, even more confident of success, had informed Roosevelt that he was "having a draft made of an Executive Order that would in effect bring TVA into the Department of the Interior." To this Roosevelt replied that he was sending the order to Congress with the one which would change the name of Interior to Conservation—and "you needn't kiss me on the cheek for that either." Ickes replied that he "felt like it but would forbear."[10]

Another of Ickes' moves was to try to bypass the National Defense Power Committee, set up by Roosevelt in 1939 to coordinate public and private power and to find ways to increase overall capacity. The Committee's intention to provide money for private utility expansion, rather than to construct a network itself and use it to control private electricity rates, had confirmed Ickes' worst fears. He therefore persuaded Roosevelt that the main responsibility for power policy should pass from the National Defense Power Committee to the National Power Policy Committee, a body that had not operated since 1936, but of which Ickes had been chairman. FDR revived this group, renaming it, significantly, the National Power Policy and Defense Committee. But these maneuverings brought Ickes into sharp conflict with, among others, Leland Olds, chairman of the Federal Power Commission, David Lilienthal, chairman of TVA, and Julius Krug, head of the Office of Production Management, who, though well aware of the threat to the public power program, nevertheless believed the issue of national defense to be a more immediate priority.[11]

Another tactic in this struggle was that, as each new public power authority was set up, Lilienthal would campaign for it to be an independent authority under a three-man board responsible directly to the President, whereas Ickes wanted a single administrator, who would, if Ickes could manage it, be appointed by Ickes himself and be responsible to him as Interior Secretary. For example, in December 1940 an Interior Department lawyer who had been in the Northwest looking after Bonneville affairs, told Ickes that Lilienthal had been in those parts spreading his idea of three-man boards for the Northwest and the Central Valley of California, and that George Norris was supporting him. Ickes did not want to fight Norris, who was the father of the public power movement, but he felt that Norris did not know anything about administration and had failed to realize that democracy was in peril from "divided councils, which necessarily result in waste and inefficiency." Angered by Lilienthal's activities, he contemplated anew the use of his ultimate weapon: resignation. "I have dictated a memorandum to the President on this matter ... if the President should permit Bonneville and Grand Coulee and Central Valley and perhaps even Boulder Dam to be taken away from me, I would resign immediately."[12]

Ickes' desire to be power coordinator locked in with his long-term struggle against the depradations of private enterprise. He wanted to see that the use of public power was not monopolized, or exploited at favorable rates, by private industry. For example, in February 1941 he recorded that the Aluminum Company of America (Alcoa) wanted to expand its plant at Bonneville. Certainly the country needed augmented supplies of aluminum for the war effort, but Ickes felt that this presented "a grave issue." Granting Alcoa all the power that it wanted would leave the government open to criticism because the company would then enjoy a monopoly of the power going to the Northwest. "The situation is all the more embarrassing," Ickes noted, "because only a day or two ago the Federal Government indicted the Aluminum Company and its principal officers . . . for conspiracy in restraint of trade."

When Ickes reported this to the Cabinet, the President set up a Cabinet committee, with Ickes as a member, to study the whole aluminum question. Roosevelt stated that he "did not want Stettinius or any of the Council of Defense people to sit in with us," which, to Ickes, was "the first tangible sign that all is not going well so far as the Defense Commission is concerned." This pleased Ickes, who had been suspicious of Stettinius and the Defense Commission from the beginning. He found his suspicions confirmed a little later. A dark picture of Alcoa was painted by the Attorney General's department, convincing Ickes that "this is one of the worst monopolies that has ever been able to fasten itself on American life." Alcoa was "practically a hundred per cent monopoly and its profits seem to run from seventy-five to one hundred per cent."

Ickes was even more determined to resist the company's request for an increase in its Bonneville power quota up to 42 percent; with the help of Frank Knox, Secretary of the Navy, he held out against Under Secretary of War Robert Patterson's "hysterical" support for Alcoa. Ickes found a small rival for Alcoa in the Reynolds Aluminum Company, and told it to go ahead drawing up a contract for Bonneville power, which it wanted. But this was held up because Averell Harriman, who had also pressed Ickes for more power for Alcoa, telephoned Reynolds and asked him "not to throw a monkey wrench into the machinery." Ickes writes: "This is confirmation that the Defense Commission is doing all that it can to favor its big business friends." However, a few days later a still bigger potential competitor for Alcoa appeared. Henry J. Kaiser wanted government help to build a magnesium plant, and Ickes asked him whether he would be willing to operate the projected government-owned aluminum fabricating plant. Kaiser was interested, and soon contracts were being negotiated for both an aluminum fabricating plant and a pig iron mill at Bonneville. Ickes preferred to deal with Kaiser because "he is not afraid of the Aluminum Company of America and will stand up to that concern."

In opposing these giant corporations Ickes was not necessarily tilting at windmills; the trouble was that all this increasingly confirmed his belief that no one but himself could be entrusted with the control of public power, and indeed of the nation's resources in general. If such men as Hiram Johnson, Pinchot, Robert Patterson, Harriman, Olds, and Lilienthal could, wittingly or not, lend themselves to the interests of big business, who could be relied upon to stand firm—if not Harold Ickes?

In February 1941 Ickes managed to obtain an invitation to lunch with the President, who told him that Congressman Rankin of Mississippi had been pressing him for a three-man board for the Arkansas Valley Authority, a public power body, and Congressman Voorhis of California for a similar arrangement in Cental Valley. The President, however, favored single administrators or "general managers." Ickes agreed, saying, "in my judgment it would be better if they were appointed by the Secretary of the Interior rather than the President." He also observed that "there would be more cohesion and a much better administration if the appointing power lay with the Secretary of the Interior rather than the President." There may be some substance to Ickes' line that single administrators made for greater efficiency and less waste than administration by group, even though it is an argument that has often been used by genuine enemies of democracy; however, one cannot overlook once again the strain of grandiosity developing in Ickes' conception of himself and his role. The President had told Rankin and Voorhis that all of these power authorities should be set up in Interior and should clear through Ickes directly to him.

> I observed that we had to be pretty careful in our definitions and understand what we meant by "clear." If the Secretary of the Interior is to have responsibilities without authority, the thing won't

work, and I told the President that the responsibilities and duties ought to be so clearly defined that the general managers would not try to run around the Secretary of the Interior to the President on the theory that the Secretary of the Interior was merely a means of passing on information and was without power or authority.

In April of that year Ickes set up within his Department a Division of Power, with Abe Fortas as its director, to coordinate all the power activities falling within Interior, which by now constituted a considerable empire. But this was not enough for Ickes. He was in essence controlling power authorities that had been initiated by higher policy-forming agencies, but with entry into the war looming, he wanted to be at the very heart of policy formation himself, coordinating and controlling both public and private contributions to the vast power output that would be consumed by war preparations.

In May 1941 the President, while still holding off on power, had appointed Ickes petroleum coordinator. Within a matter of weeks Ickes had celebrated his expanded authority by interfering with oil exports to Japan, an act which brought him into head-on confrontation with the President as to whether he had not exceeded his authority in an indiscreet and dangerous manner. Nothing abashed, Ickes sought an audience with the President only a few days after the rift had been papered over. He began by complaining about a report that Olds had made as chairman of the Federal Power Commission, recommending that a sum of a billion dollars be turned over to Jesse Jones, Secretary of Commerce, to finance additions to existing private and public power plants and to build new ones. Ickes writes that the President "made a gesture of disgust," and that it was unnecessary to add, though he did so, that Jesse Jones was scarcely friendly to public power. He told Roosevelt, as he had already told Olds, that "if the private power companies had been asked to report, they could not have done better for themselves than Olds had done on their behalf."

Olds and Lilienthal had managed to get Julius Krug appointed power coordinator for the Office of Production Management—an imminent threat to Ickes' ambition. Ickes addressed a final desperate plea to the President, saying: "I have been with you for over eight years through thick and thin and I have never once made a personal appeal to you. Now I am making one. If Krug ... continues as OPM Coordinator without the appointment of an over-all coordinator, my position will be untenable. I haven't asked you for anything in connection with the defense program, although I have made it known to you that I would like to have something to do with defense, but I am asking you to appoint me Power Coordinator."

The President seemed to entertain this as a real possibility, especially when Ickes put the proposal that he be appointed power coordinator in virtue of his position as chairman of the National Power Policy Committee, rather than as Secretary of the Interior. The latter would have caused an uproar in TVA, which would have seen itself as being taken over by the Interior. Nothing came of it, presumably because the President could foresee too much trouble from other officials, theatened by Ickes' expansionism. A month later Ickes poured out his bitterness in a letter to Ben Cohen. He realized now that Roosevelt would never appoint him power coordinator, that one of his enemies, probably Hopkins, had sabotaged the plan. He would therefore force a showdown with the President, tell him how tired he was of half-truths and broken undertakings, and either resign or behave so as to force Roosevelt to request his resignation.[13]

Roosevelt may not have been so much taken aback as Ickes imagined, by his threat to resign over control of petroleum, because of the incident affecting oil shipments to Japan. On 16 June 1941 Ickes, as petroleum coordinator, had received a telegram from the manager of a Philadelphia plant, complaining that over two thousand barrels of lubricating oil were standing on a wharf in South Philadelphia about to be shipped to Japan, while his own factory, engaged largely on defense orders, did not know where to find enough oil to keep operating. The entire Atlantic Coast was short of oil and gasoline, because normally 95 percent of its petroleum was brought in by tanker, and fifty of these tankers had recently been lent to embattled Britain, leaving a serious deficiency. Ickes was working hard to overcome this, but he was aware that considerable adverse public sentiment had built up about the continued shipment of petroleum to Japan. He at once got the Treasury Department to advise the shippers of this particular consignment not to load it until they obtained clearance from Washington. Later the same day he held up a much smaller shipment to Australia. He took the line that no Far

Eastern country that could just as easily get its supplies from the Pacific Coast or the Gulf of Mexico should be permitted to take any petroleum products from the Atlantic Coast, and he asked General Russell L. Maxwell, head of Export Control, to prepare an order, to be sent to the President through the State Department, that no oil of any sort could be shipped from the Atlantic Coast without an export license.

The following day, with Ickes sitting beside Steve Early's desk, there was a three-way telephone conversation with the President, relayed through Early. In answer to a query, Ickes said emphatically that he had not cleared the stoppage through the State Department; the oil would have been in Japan before he received an answer. Roosevelt said that the Japanese situation was a very touchy one, that there was a danger of war, and that he might have to appoint a "Coordinator of Coordinators"—a remark that Ickes thought was "probably semifacetious." But on the Thursday, 19 June, he received a letter from the President, which he described as "the most peremptory and ungracious communication that I have ever received from him." To an impartial observer, the letter, although cool and direct, would not merit such an outraged response, considering the gravity of the situation. Addressed "Dear Harold," it continued:

> Lest there be any confusion whatsoever, please do not issue any directions, as Petroleum Coordinator, forbidding any export or import of oil from or to the United States.
>
> This can be qualified only if you obtain my approval or that of the Secretary of State.
>
> The reason for this is that exports of oil at this time are so much a part of our current foreign policy that this policy must not be affected in any shape, manner or form by anyone except the Secretary of State or the President.
>
> I am sending a copy of this letter to the Secretary of State and to Brigadier General Maxwell.
>
> Always sincerely,
Franklin D. Roosevelt

By contrast, Ickes' unrepentant reply, several pages long, sounds heavy-handed and truculent. He took the line that he had merely suggested to the State Department that an order be prepared for the

President's signature stating that an export licence be required for shipment of oil. "It will thus be seen that I did not order that this oil be withheld from shipment to Japan. I merely asked for a breathing spell during which, through regular channels, an order could be presented to you, as a result of which this oil might be withheld, in line with the determined policy of the Administration." This disclaimer was disingenuous. Ickes must have known perfectly well that his action would be interpreted as preventing the sale of oil to Japan, and that the press would so present it. Even the responsible *New York Times* carried, on 17 June 1941, a story headed "Oil for Japanese Is Halted by Ickes," though it did go on to say that the action was basically one of coordinating supplies on the East Coast.

Ickes went on to suggest that Roosevelt should be grateful to him, and he sneered at the State Department. "You may know to what a degree public opinion has been inflamed along the Atlantic Coast by the very thought of shipping oil from any port in the United States to Japan while rationing is a very real prospect of that entire area for months to come. Of course, I did not expect the State Department to know this or to pay any attention to it." The conclusion reveals one cause of his pique. Since World War I, Ickes had believed that he could see through temporizing "ifs" and "buts" and pierce straight to the bedrock of international affairs. This talent, he felt, was not receiving adequate recognition, because he was not one of "the esoteric brotherhood of international statesmen."[14]

Ickes declared in the *Secret Diary* and in letters to his old friend Raymond Robins that he did not care what Roosevelt thought about what he had done. He told Robins that the President's letter had not bothered him at all, since the public supported him, and had he been forced into line there would have been an angry outcry.[15] In the *Diary* he went so far as to say that Roosevelt "would not dare to move against me publicly." His stoppage of the oil had been "too popular . . . for the President to run the risk of the popular flareup" that would occur were he dismissed.

A couple of days later Ickes felt that he had scored a great victory. Dean Acheson of the State Department came to see him. Ickes was expecting a showdown, but to his surprise Acheson "brought in a program which he wanted me to see and then submit to the President if I approved of it." Ickes says that the program was precisely that which he had been advocating regarding shipments of oil. He went on: "The country does not realize the victory that I have won in this matter and of course I will do no boasting. I am satisfied with the result. In spite of the President's ill temper and his open and covert threats, in the end he adopted the very policy that I was striving for."

One cannot miss the implication that he was just as powerful a figure with "the public" and "the country" as Roosevelt was. For months Ickes had been giving vent to the opinion that Roosevelt was slipping, that he was dangerously inactive in a time of absolute crisis. In the context of concern over the impending destruction of Britain by Germany and Italy, and the immediate ensuing threat to the United States, he professed to see "in every direction ... a growing discontent with the President's lack of leadership." The country was still behind Roosevelt, but would not be so much longer unless bold action were forthcoming. "People are beginning to say: 'I am tired of words; I want action.' " Unless the United States quickly did something drastic, England would fall, and "we would be left alone on this continent to face a hostile world with not a single ally in sight." He told John McCloy, Assistant Secretary of War, "if I could have looked this far ahead and seen an inactive and uninspiring President, I would not have supported Roosevelt for a third term."

After his "victory" over shipping oil to Japan, Ickes could not leave well alone. On 23 June 1941 he wrote to the President, telling him that there would never be a more propitious time to stop the flow of oil to Japan, since that nation was so concerned by developments in Russia that it would not move aggressively against the Dutch East Indies. To this analysis of international affairs the President only made a brief, sarcastic reply: "I have yours of June 23rd recommending the immediate stopping of shipments of oil to Japan. Please let me know if this would continue to be your judgment if this were to tip the delicate scales and cause Japan either to attack Russia or to attack the Dutch East Indies." Two days later, provoked by a smug note in which Ickes claimed that the new policy on oil shipping was exactly what he had been proposing, Roosevelt pointed out that the circumstances surrounding the whole situation were "peculiarly delicate and peculiarly confidential" and "could not be fully known to you or to anyone but the two persons charged with the responsibility ... the President and the Secretary of State."

In the middle of this furor Ickes forwarded the President a telegram from California oil man Edwin Pauley, urging drastic action with regard to Japan. Still trying to contain his impatience, Roosevelt told Ickes that, although the telegram was interesting, "I know that you realize that that kind of snap judgment foreign policy determination is something we get a lot of every day." If Roosevelt were able to brief Pauley for a week, "he might be beginning to graduate from the ranks of amateurs."

Ickes was perceptive enough to realize that this was "clearly intended for me and not for Pauley." After considering the rights and wrongs of the matter for a couple of days, on 30 June 1941 he sent the President a cool and magisterial letter of resignation as petroleum coordinator, explaining how all his actions with regard to oil for Japan were strictly within the terms of his letter of appointment. That could not be denied, even though the public impact of his action was appropriate to a much more drastic interpretation. Roosevelt turned the resignation aside, choosing not to be provoked by Ickes' theatrical gesture, and half-promising an additional prize which he knew to be close to Ickes' heart.

> There you go again! There ain't nothing unfriendly about me, and I guess it was the hot weather that made you think there was a lack of a friendly tone!
>
> As a matter of fact, I think the whole business of exports to Japan was made difficult by the press and the press only . . .
>
> You are doing a grand job as Petroleum Coordinator—so much so that it looks to me as if you will have to take unto your manly bosom the coordination of the whole power situation if things get any worse.

Roosevelt went on to say in a straightforward, friendly manner that he thought it would interest Ickes to know that the Japanese had been having a "real drag-down and knock-out fight" among themselves for a week as to whether they should attack Russia, attack the South Seas, or sit on the fence. This was the context in which Ickes' action had occurred, although the President did not belabor the point. Ickes considered the President's letter "more than a little disingenuous," but he was prepared to disregard that, feeling that the air had been cleared. With unconscious irony, in the next sentence he reveals how disingenuous his own letter had been, writing that he "never had any doubt that he would decline to accept my resignation as Petroleum Coordinator," since "I had him in such a bad spot that he could not have done this even if he had wanted to."

Throughout this period Ickes' estimate of his own stature relative to that of the President, in terms of personal force, perceptiveness, and decisiveness and in terms of appeal to the mass of the people, was so high that it wavered between healthy self-confidence and near pathological conceit. One can distinguish two factors in his personal life promoting that kind of self-image, one of which was on the side of mental health and the other decidedly against it. The first was his marriage to Jane. It must have been a tremendous boost to the ego of a man in his sixties to have won this beautiful girl of twenty, and in addition to her physical desirability Jane was a considerate, loyal, energetic, and unfailingly supportive wife. As she wrote to their friend Margaret Robins, she had hitched her wagon to his star, and though she did not see him through a romantic haze, she had determined to be a dedicated, admiring helpmate to him for their years together. All this was eminently good for his self-esteem, helped to free him from his emotional dependency on Roosevelt, and greatly increased his confidence in his own powers.

The second, malign, factor was pharmacological. For many years Ickes had suffered sleep disturbances and other symptoms reminiscent of anxiety neurosis, such as feelings of exhaustion and chronic and acute headaches. To get to sleep he relied on various sleeping pills and stiff drinks of whiskey. Since at least 1937 his sleeping medicine had been nembutal, as we know from his complaint in the *Secret Diary* entry for 7 October 1939 that it seemed to have stopped working for him after two years. But everything else gave him bad hangovers, so he continued with nembutal for years more, along with copious shots of whiskey. The effects of this combination, taken in sufficient quantities and if continued for a long period, can reveal themselves, in certain individuals, in regressive attitudes such as an inflated self-regard, a readiness to be injured, and a general failing in self-criticism. If that were Ickes' reaction, it would help explain his growing tendency to develop an unrealistic conception of his importance and sometimes to charge ahead with little regard for delicate contingencies. This, however, can only be speculation.

Only five or six weeks after the oil for Japan controversy, Ickes revealed at his press conference that a tanker was on its way from the United States to Vladivostok, loaded with gasoline for the Russians. This was a sensitive matter, since it had to pass so close to Japan. A day or so later, on 15 August 1941, he and Jane went to the Northwest on vacation, returning in mid-September. Ickes lunched with Roosevelt on 15 September and complained that the President had not given him any "war work." The point of that was that during Ickes' absence Roosevelt had set up a supreme war board of seven members, with Henry Wallace as chairman, while the envied Harry Hopkins had been made Special Assistant to the President, with general supervisory powers. Not only was Ickes not included, but he also heard that Roosevelt had declined to appoint him Coordinator of Hard Fuels. At their luncheon Roosevelt could only expostulate that "everybody was doing war work." This did not satisfy Ickes, who hinted that his enemies were coming between Roosevelt and him, to make sure that Ickes did not get his "nose above water." The President vehemently denied this, but admitted that sometimes Ickes did arouse opposition, instancing his announcement about the tanker of gasoline to Vladivostok. Roosevelt told him that "Hull had hit the ceiling when this was printed." Ickes replied that the statement had been released during his absence, but he declared that he had certainly made it. Not only was Ickes unrepentant, but he dared to presume that the President was grateful to him. "I remarked that this had effectively called the bluff of Japan and I supposed that he was glad that the thing had happened." Roosevelt said emphatically that this was not so, pointing out that what had angered the Japanese and made things difficult for him was not the shipment itself but its announcement by a high government official.

In view of this sequence of actions, considered indiscreet by Roosevelt and others, it is not surprising that there were people in government inner circles ready to urge the President not to include Ickes in the War Cabinet or give him the coordinatorship over still more resources, and it is not surprising that Roosevelt was predisposed to listen to them.

Ickes' reaction to the attack on Pearl Harbor, as recorded in the *Secret Diary,* was serious and objective, as befits such a momentous event. But in a letter to Margaret Robins the following day Jane expressed an opinion that must have been shared by them both.

Where now were those so-called experts of the State Department who had boasted of their ability to understand the Japanese? Was not Harold proved to have been correct in the prophecies he had made over the past three years?[17]

Yet this vindication of Ickes' forebodings seemed to bring not recognition and added responsibility but further frustration. Not only did the Bureau of the Budget, as part of its plan to concentrate war-related activities in Washington, move Indian Affairs, the Fish and Wildlife Service, and the National Park Service to Chicago (it exempted the Office of Education because of Eleanor Roosevelt's intervention—another intolerable example, to Ickes, of feminine influence), but the President himself seemed bent on undermining Ickes' legitimate authority. How else could Ickes interpret Roosevelt's decision in January 1942 to give Henry Wallace's Economic Warfare Board control over the export of petroleum products? Wallace's new powers, Ickes protested to the President, cut right across his own as petroleum coordinator. He had not been consulted or even given the chance to persuade Roosevelt that his peformance as coordinator had not been sufficiently poor as to merit the public dressing-down which the removal of some of his most important responsibilities so obviously implied.[18]

Ickes retaliated by giving journalist Raymond Clapper the inside story of the petroleum fiasco, showing him letters from Roosevelt and Wallace. The next day Clapper used the material to attack the problem of divided authority within the administration. But when a letter from Roosevelt arrived, bluntly instructing him to cooperate with Wallace, Ickes reached the limit of his tolerance. He was close to a breakdown, he says, and really felt that he must resign. He boiled over at Wallace's statement a short time later that the Economic Warfare Board would maintain adequate supplies of oil and gasoline for the United States and its allies. The information would have been interesting, Ickes told him sarcastically, had it not implied some inadequacy before Wallace masterfully assumed control.[19]

At a Cabinet meeting two days later there was discussion of a proposal by Mrs. Morgenthau that artists be commissioned to paint pictures of war events. Roosevelt suggested that there might also be paintings of war events within the administration, including one of Harold Ickes, stripped to his underwear and bearing a caption stating that everything else had been taken from him. Ickes replied testily that the jest was too close to the truth to be amusing.[20]

Ickes' outrage at his treatment by Roosevelt was intensified by the fact that he had been warmly complimented by leading British authorities for maintaining oil supplies to the Allies, accolades which accorded with his own view that he was doing the best war job in Washington. It is true that his success as petroleum coordinator had surprised contemporaries. As NRA oil administrator during Roosevelt's first term, he had had to grapple with problems of overproduction and chaotic marketing, and his hostility to an industry which he described as "ruthless, arrogant and haughty" had been plain. (He had once publicly demanded that an oil dictator be appointed and threatened to turn the industry into a public utility.) But the problem was no longer one of reducing production but of increasing it to satisfy the demands of war, and "it took only a little time to discover that we [the industry leaders and Ickes] could trust one another and work together for the good of the country." So popular did Ickes become with oil men that they took to announcing rationing restrictions themselves to save him from public embarrassment.[21] Justly proud of the way in which the East Coast had been kept supplied with oil after tankers normally used for that purpose had been lent to Britain, and his success in vastly increasing the output of 100-octane gasoline ("that superlative fuel that contains within it the molecules of speed, power and maneuverability that have contributed so important a part to . . . our brilliant victories"), Ickes found Roosevelt's ingratitude and apparent attempts to humiliate him all but intolerable.[22]

As these struggles proceeded, Ickes' personal relations with Franklin D. Roosevelt reached their nadir. The President contrived to be unavailable whenever Ickes sought an appointment and denied his Secretary of the Interior any special signs of affection or approval. Unable to see the substantial and objective reasons why FDR might have been angered by his behavior, Ickes blamed his archrival Harry Hopkins for his difficulties. Hopkins had thwarted his ambition to be Secretary of War and, still living at the White House, continued to poison the President's mind against him. In February 1942 Ickes discussed with Stephen Early an article that he planned to send to *Collier's,* critical of the State Department. (He can hardly have expected the White House to clear it for publication.) Early suggested that he take the matter up with Roosevelt, which gave Ickes an opportunity to point out that that would be difficult since he could not get in to see the President any more. He says that Early agreed with him that he had been out of favor for a lengthy period and that someone close to the President was stabbing him in the back. Although Hopkins was not mentioned directly, Ickes was sure that Early had him in mind.

Ickes was very depressed after one Cabinet meeting in March, feeling that the President's attitude had hardened into active dislike. The chance discovery that he was no longer being invited to Roosevelt's private poker-playing evenings pushed him closer to quitting. He discussed the possibility of resigning with Abe Fortas, his Under Secretary, and then with Jane. Some weeks earlier he had received a generous offer from William L. Chenery of *Collier's* to write a weekly page for that magazine. For this, he could earn $500 an article or $25,000 a year (though Ickes was not sure that he could command this sum if he ceased to be a Cabinet officer). He would contact Chenery again to see whether the offer still held good.

In May 1942 Roosevelt made two overtures of friendship to his neglected and aggrieved Cabinet officer. He invited Ickes to lunch and suggested that he might come out to Harold's farm for an evening of poker. On both occasions Ickes had (legitimately) to plead prior engagements; but he was not sorry. Roosevelt, who so long had neglected him, would learn that he could not see him whenever he pleased.[23]

Suddenly, against this background of alienation and resentment, in November 1942 Roosevelt offered Ickes an important new responsibility. Would he become Secretary of Labor with responsibility for war manpower, replacing Frances Perkins, and allow Paul V. McNutt to become Secretary of the Interior? The proposal, Ickes readily admitted, was just the kind of offer that he had been seeking, but it threw him into a quandary. He thought of many reasons why he should not accept. He was reluctant to abandon Interior, of which he was deeply fond; he doubted whether his physical strength would be equal to the manpower job. Yet if Roosevelt should issue the command, he must obey. He talked the matter over with Jane and several of this close friends. Jane, too, was concerned that his health might give way under the additional strain. Tom Corcoran,

Ben Cohen, Abe Fortas, and Bernard Baruch advised him not to accept. Oil industry leaders urged him to remain where he was. In the end, Roosevelt came to Ickes' rescue by telling him that he had decided, after all, not to load these new responsibilies onto him; he was too fond of Jane to worry her in this way. Ickes was so relieved, he says, that he did something he had never done: clasped Roosevelt's hand in both of his in a most affectionate way and thanked him profusely.[24]

If Roosevelt, who understood Ickes well, offered him this appointment in the belief that, even though it might be refused, it would soothe Ickes' damaged pride, the ploy succeeded. Ickes knew that Roosevelt had paid him a great compliment, of a kind he had not anticipated receiving again.[25] But because it was such a compliment, and because Ickes had such a record of dedicated empire-building, why was he genuinely afraid to accept and genuinely relieved when he was let off? We must assume that he could no longer realistically deny the irreversible weakening of his physical fabric. He was now sixty-eight years old, had suffered heart damage from a coronary in 1937, had problems with whiskey and barbiturates, complained increasingly of exhaustion, and had seen one after another of his colleagues die, victims, he believed, of the killing pressure of their responsibilities.

Moreover, Ickes had found domestic contentment after the long years of turmoil and bitterness. His and Jane's first child, Harold Jr., had been born in September 1939 and, Ickes told Raymond Robins some time later, had been totally lovable from the start. To William Allen White, Ickes wrote in April 1941 that his busy official life, admirable wife, and adorable child made him very happy. A month after this letter a second child, Elizabeth, was born. Significantly, in the light of still painful memories of Anna's attitudes, Ickes wrote in his diary that, on discovering that she was pregnant, Jane had been uncomplaining and sweet, without any of the regrets that others might have expressed even though they wished for another child.[26] Of course his personal life could not be entirely insulated against external sniping, and some was hurtful. For instance, when he introduced gasoline restrictions in August 1940, he had been savagely criticized by the press, and he and Jane were spied on by newsmen who wrote stories claiming that Ickes was running several cars. Sensitive to such charges, and in order to conserve gasoline and rubber,

Ickes had arranged for his official chauffeur to stay overnight at the farm and to bring in to Washington each morning the daily output of Headwaters Farm eggs. In doing so, he gave an opening to sections of the Washington press, especially Cissy Patterson's *Times-Herald*, to attack him for misusing a government vehicle. There was some ill-concealed satisfaction both inside and outside the administration when photographs appeared in the newspapers of Ickes being driven to work in a car that carried eggs on the back seat and chickens on the roof, and Jane confessed to Anna Boettiger that she was greatly distressed by such publicity.[27] But, as many entries in his diary make clear, Ickes' love for Jane and essential happiness in his family situation are unquestioned. With such domestic contentment and his life as a gentleman farmer still to be enjoyed, he had no desire to hurry the death which could not be many years away.

His unwillingness to accept Roosevelt's offer marked a turning of the tide for Harold Ickes. For years he had been clamoring for more wartime responsibility and a more exalted role; now, actually put to the test by the President, he had had to admit that he could not measure up. Henceforth a note of realism undercut Ickes' inflated conception of his own role and powers. His challenge was at an end, and the abandonment of his grandiose ideas of pitting his strength against that of Roosevelt allowed his affection and allegiance to the President to reassert themselves, though it would be some time before Roosevelt would permit those emotions to be expressed. Characteristically, Ickes eased the pain of having failed Roosevelt's test by attributing the outcome to Harry Hopkins' machinations. Hopkins, he now asserted, had persuaded the President to change his mind about giving him Labor and War Manpower. But this time Harry had done him a great favor, since the job would almost certainly have killed him.[28]

With the final abandonment of his attempts to challenge Roosevelt's authority, there is a slackening of Harold Ickes' interest in public life. The diary entries lose some of their buoyancy and verve; there is a sense of lassitude, a certain detachment from events of the day, and an increasing preoccupation with his physical and mental state. Financial worries intrude more often. Though the property inherited from Anna had been worth $800,000, it was not unencumbered; Ickes periodically had to meet large interest payments on it. Federal and state estate taxes had been heavy at the time of Anna's death, and the mortgage on Headwaters Farm had to be paid. Consequently, Ickes always felt the need to maintain a flow of current income over and above his salary as a Cabinet officer. He accomplished this by turning out a steady stream of books and magazine articles, often ghosted by members of his staff. But the farm, too, was expected to prosper and it never did, a situation which worsened during the war because of a critical labor shortage.

A letter from Jane to Eleanor Roosevelt in March 1943 shows clearly enough the difficulties she faced. With just one maid to help her, she had to run the house and the two farms (another had been purchased in 1941), on which production had been increased in response to government appeals. She had responsibility for several thousand chickens and the ninety dozen eggs they produced each day. About this time Jane told Margaret Robins that she had been working a fifteen-hour day for ten days, but that nevertheless Harold and she had decided to persevere with full-scale farming operations for at least one year more.[29]

Ickes' concern for Jane is expressed freely in his diary, but he seemed unable to lighten her load. Perhaps, having found his way back to his farming origins, he unreflectingly saw these long hours as a natural consequence of commitment to the soil, and as being recompensed by the basic long-term security of land ownership—something Jane would need when he was gone. In any event, Ickes' private need influenced in some measure his attitude to an important public question: the treatment of Japanese Americans.

Mingled with his repugnance at the spectacle of this blameless minority being cruelly driven from their homes and farms was an immediate practical concern to obtain labor for his farms. As a result, in Cabinet meetings Ickes pressed Roosevelt to release Japanese Americans from internment camps to work on the nation's farms, and (to deflect criticism) to issue a public proclamation that this was in the national interest. In April 1943, after long negotiations with the War Relocation Authority, Ickes obtained three such laborers. But the experiment was not a success, in part because the Washington press stirred up hostility against them, and before long the Japanese departed.[30] Even so, Ickes continued to campaign for the rights of this minority group. Of all the Cabinet, he, in 1944, took the most forthright and compassionate stand toward the internees and, with the War Relocation Authority now transferred to his own department, did what he could to help them.

In public life Ickes' main concern had become the nation's present and future oil needs. By 1942 the rapid depletion of American reserves had begun to worry him. He confided to his long-time friend Stacy Mosser that it appeared that the United States might have to supply the bulk of the Allies' oil requirements, and that he doubted whether this would be possible.[31] As the fearful drain on oil continued, even while the military struggle gradually swung in the Allies' favor, Ickes became convinced that American reserves would be inadequate to support another war, or even to meet peacetime demand for very much longer. By December 1943 he was warning that the nation was about to lose it supremacy as an oil-producing state. The oil empire's capital would move to the Middle East after the war, and if the nation's gasoline civilization were to endure, the United States must be prepared to go where that oil could be located.[32]

In pursuit of this objective Ickes first attempted to use the Petroleum Reserves Corporation, set up by Roosevelt in June 1943 to look into the possibility of acquiring foreign oil, and of which Ickes was president, to purchase the leading U.S. owned oil company in the Middle East. When that failed, he tried to organize the construction by the corporation of a pipeline from Saudi Arabia and Kuwait to the eastern end of the Mediterranean. The latter scheme in particular was severely criticized, largely on the ground that it portended socialistic government control of the oil industry, but Ickes defended his "new child" in terms recalling the image of PWA as a baby left on his doorstep. Hardly a year before, the Petroleum Reserves Corporation had been "no more than a twinkle in a bureaucrat's eye," yet "already it has been accused of . . . slyly leaving banana peels where its Uncle Samuel would step unwarily upon them." An even greater shock "to me, its nursemaid, [came] when I actually heard the whisper that it wasn't even legitimate." Under Ickes' proposal, the government would meet the cost of the pipeline and, in return, the oil companies would repay the cost over twenty-five years, set aside part of their output for defense needs, and refuse sales to any buyer of whom the State Department disapproved. Ickes also saw the pipeline as a means of putting pressure on other oil powers to conclude agreements regulating rights of access to the region's oil. Already American and British interests were clashing in the Middle East, and Russia had shown interest. It seemed to him that the future peace of the world might depend on the negotiation of such agreements.[33]

Despite State Department obstruction, Ickes continued to urge on Roosevelt the importance of such schemes. He claims that his persistence led to the successful negotiation of an Anglo-American Oil Treaty in 1944, a treaty that Ickes helped to negotiate and which he considered the first of a series of bilateral arrangements which might peacefully resolve the competing claims for the world's oil. The treaty failed to pass the Senate because of opposition from oil interests, which feared an extension of federal government control, and from those state governments which suspected that an increased importation of foreign oil would reduce their own revenues from oil. Ickes managed to renegotiate the treaty in 1945 in a way that satisfied some of its domestic critics. It was still under consideration by the Senate when he resigned.

Although Ickes earned the President's gratitude for his successful handling of the coal crisis in 1943, throughout 1943 and 1944 he was still socially and politically excluded from the inner circles of the White House. The friendly lunches and occasional jolly evening poker games were things of the past, and he had no access to the President's ear to influence government policy. His morale was badly affected, and the declining energy of advancing age further eroded his career motivation. He began seriously to consider leaving the administration and earning his living as a newspaper columnist, a field in which he could now command substantial fees, and, at least as important, one in which he might be able to influence affairs more than he seemed able to do in office.

But as the 1944 presidential campaign gained momentum, the sounds of approaching battle again stirred the blood of this old warhorse. The more he heard about Thomas E. Dewey, the more he felt the great importance of reelecting Roosevelt. Entirely on his own initiative, Ickes began stumping the country once more. He tried to obtain guidance from Roosevelt, but was told to do it his own way.[34]

Just after election day he won a reward that warmed his heart. On

8 November the President cabled: "You did a great job all the way through and I am sure you know that I appreciate it from the bottom of my heart." Ickes' gratification at this indication that the ice had melted, that the close relationship of earlier times might be renewed, is obvious in his reply. He had "never worked so happily in any campaign ... because the cause was just and the candidate superlative." He would begin soon to "nag" presidential secretary "Pa" Watson "until he manages to arrange for some real time with you."[35] Along with other Cabinet members he, and Jane, went to meet the Roosevelts' train when it returned from Hyde Park. As they entered the presidential car, Mrs. Roosevelt greeted them warmly, praising Ickes for making the most effective speeches in the campaign. Roosevelt, too, was unusually friendly to Harold and Jane, and when they went on to the White House he thanked Ickes for his marvellous effort and kissed Jane affectionately, as he had done in the past.

An even greater mark of personal esteem came a couple of days later, while the Ickes were at home on the farm. That Sunday the President telephoned Jane and invited himself out for tea. He was unable to stay long, but he was kind to the children and very friendly to Harold and Jane. Jane had the additional pleasure of having had to cancel an invitation to the "pretty snobbish" Dean Achesons, on the ground that she was entertaining the President of the United States.[36]

Roosevelt having been elected for the fourth time, Ickes, as was his custom, tendered his resignation. Again it was refused, with a more than usually affectionate reply in which the President warned the Secretary of the Interior that if he said anything more on the subject he would send a Marine guard to keep him at his post. Of course he wanted Harold to remain. They must see the war out together.[37]

Ickes was gratified by the tone of Roosevelt's response, but this time there had been something rather more to his resignation than a polite formality. In 1944 he was seventy years of age and his health had begun to break down after years of unremitting strain. The long-term combination of nembutal and whiskey for soporifics was having cumulative effects. Several times under their influence he had fallen at night, on one occasion breaking his collarbone, on another gashing his head. From February 1944 he rested once or twice each day on a bed in his Interior Department suite. In April 1944 he had to break off reading a statement to a meeting of coal owners and miners after the first page and ask Abe Fortas to continue, because he was short of breath and concerned about his heart.[38] He was aware that his wife had suffered much from the sometimes malicious press attacks on the family and often longed for the obscurity of private life. Interior was practically running itself. He could not go on forever, and there appeared to be few reasons why he should go on at all. Certainly he wished to play a part in the peace, but that might best be done by leaving the government. So it was not just a wish for some further expression of affection and esteem from the man about whom his life had revolved for twelve years that prompted Ickes to write to Roosevelt again, though even now he could not forebear to seek a final prize.

Roosevelt's letter had touched him more deeply that he could say. It came as a generous accolade after his dedicated career. Of course he had wished, having been among the first to see the war coming, for a more active role in its prosecution, but he was grateful that Roosevelt had given him responsibility for petroleum and hard fuels, and he had peformed these duties as well as he could. The demoralized department that he had inherited in 1933 had become one of the successes of the administration. He had always wanted to make things, to create, which was why he had enjoyed Interior, and loved public works—his finest achievement, he believed. Roosevelt now had before him the task of making peace, one of the greatest adventures in history. A Secretary of the Interior could have no part to play in this great event, so he was thinking of becoming a journalist, which would at least allow him to report what was happening. (That of course was Ickes' invitation to Roosevelt to include him in the planning for the postwar world, but he could not have been surprised when the President later turned it gently aside.) In view of all these considerations, Ickes concluded, he wanted a little more time to consider whether he should continue in the administration. He hoped that Roosevelt would be patient and would realize that he was not just being coy.[39]

When Franklin Delano Roosevelt died suddenly, a few months later, Harold Ickes was among those who traveled to Hyde Park for the funeral service. As she stood beside him that day, Frances Perkins was surprised to see tears rolling down his cheeks. He was "very, very moved by the whole situation" and, as they walked away, said brokenly: "Oh God, if this could only have been prevented!" It was, she said, as if he were thinking "how dreadful it is to have to lay him away."[40]

Ickes' career in the Truman administration was short and its end predictable. The foundations of his liberalism had always rested less on his faith in the democratic instincts of the people than on his hope that a strong leader could beat back their oppressors and guide them in the direction of greater liberty and social justice. Though he may have faltered at times, Franklin D. Roosevelt had provided that kind of leadership. Harry S Truman never could. Even on the train that carried the official mourners from FDR's funeral back to Washington, Truman recalled, Ickes "carried on about how the country would go to hell without leadership"—deliberately in the new President's hearing. Truman did not fire the Old Curmudgeon because, he says, he knew that Ickes would talk himself out of the job sooner or later.[41]

Ickes never became reconciled to Truman as President and took to sending Under Secretary Abe Fortas or Assistant Secretary Chapman to Cabinet meetings rather than attending himself.[42] In June 1945 rumors that he would resign circulated, provoking a flood of sympathetic mail. Late in August Truman announced that Ickes would stay, but the break between the two men could not be postponed much longer. It came about over the Pauley affair.

Truman's nomination of Edwin W. Pauley as Under Secretary of the Navy had intense significance for Harold Ickes. Ickes had thought well of Pauley, whom he credited with persuading Roosevelt to appoint him, Ickes, petroleum administrator, and he had been impressed by Pauley's analyses of the international oil situation during the war. But now a vital question of principle was at stake. From the time he had become oil administrator in the early months of the New Deal, Ickes had emphasized the necessity of curbing overproduction and waste and conserving the nation's diminishing reserves of oil and natural gas. By 1937, with the administration still largely indifferent, he was urging on the industry the need to conserve oil in the interest of national defense, an appeal that he later carried directly to Congress. In this context the question of who was to control the rich oil lands off the coast of California assumed a growing importance, which the crippling demands of war only increased. For many years Ickes had argued that these lands belonged to the whole people, rather than to private oil interests, and that their title was properly vested in the federal government. He had urged Roosevelt to instruct his Attorney General to bring suit against the state of California, which had leased portions of the tidelands to private companies and derived considerable revenue from so doing. This was attempted under Roosevelt, and would be again under Truman, whose Attorney General, Tom Clark, took the case directly to the Supreme Court.

Edwin Pauley owned large amounts of stock in several companies that were obtaining tidelands oil, but Ickes had a more particular reason for objecting to the nomination. As treasurer of the Democratic National Committee, Pauley was the party's chief fund-raiser. As the 1944 election drew near he had suggested to Ickes that if the federal government would drop its plans to assume control of the tidelands oil, he could raise $300,000 from oil men for the campaign. There was no chance that Ickes would agree, and the next year when rumors that Pauley wanted his job began to circulate, Ickes noted menacingly in his diary that if he chose to reveal how Pauley had pressured him over offshore oil, he could end his career.[43] Then Truman nominated Pauley for Under Secretary of the Navy.

It seemed at first that Ickes did not intend to use all his resources to discredit Pauley. He did, however, tell Truman that if he were called before the Senate during the confirmation hearings, he would be obliged to tell the truth; but the President failed to ask what the truth was. Ickes claimed that when he told Truman shortly thereafter that he had been summoned as a witness, the President's reply was that "of course I must tell the truth but he hoped that I would be as gentle with Pauley as possible."[44] Ickes replied that this was his intention.

At the confirmation hearings he was asked by Senator Charles Tobey whether Pauley had ever offered him campaign funds in return for the government's dropping its claims to the tidelands oil deposits in California. Though Ickes claims that as a member of Truman's Cabinet he was embarrassed to have to do so, he answered "yes," Pauley had made such suggestions.[45] Pauley, who came next to the witness stand, testified that he had never accepted "contingent" campaign contributions. He had gone to see Ickes, but only to discuss a $300,000 deficit on the Democratic Committee and to ask his help in raising the money. To Ickes, being called a liar was fighting talk. He discussed Pauley's evidence and the conduct of the hearing with Edwin A. Harris of the *St. Louis Post Dispatch,* who had written a series of articles attacking Pauley's activities during the tidelands oil dispute.[46] Ickes believed that Tobey's original question about campaign funds had been suggested to him by Harris. Now he prompted Harris to prime Tobey further, saying that if Pauley was going to challenge his, Ickes', veracity, he was prepared to take the stand again and reveal everything. Ickes told Tobey that he had kept notes of the incriminating conversation with Pauley and that his summons to the hearings should specify that he bring them. He was duly called and read extracts from this diary into the record.[47]

At his press conference on 7 February, President Truman praised Pauley. When asked whether "this situation" involved any change in his relation with Ickes, he replied: "I don't think so. Mr. Ickes can very well be mistaken the same as the rest of us."[48] Interpreting this as casting doubt on his truthfulness, Ickes seized the opportunity to resign in a blaze of publicity.

When the news of Harold Ickes' resignation broke, the Washington press corps converged on the Interior Building for what they knew would be the Old Curmudgeon's last official press conference. Ickes strode down the aisle of the packed auditorium, his wife at his side, to be greeted when he reached the stage with spontaneous applause. He began to speak. There were two ways of resigning, he told them: a man could leave without comment or he could explain why. He would explain why. He could not remain in an administration where he was required to perjure himself for the sake of the party. As soon as he had heard what President Truman had said at his press conference, his mind had been made up. Truman had known that he objected to Pauley, but had never asked why. Truman had said that he could have been mistaken about Pauley. He was not.

Someone asked what he would do now. He did not know, though there was a possiblity of a newspaper column. How had he responded to the President's request that he treat Pauley gently? He had said that he would, and when the reporters laughed at that, he feigned indignation, protesting that he had not gone into detail about Pauley's misdemeanors. Would he live at Olney? If Jane allowed him to, he said, pointing at her with his thumb. She was its owner.

He spoke of his political philosophy, of the need for public officials to be free of personal ambition or private interest, until eventually one of the newsmen signaled the end of the conference by expressing the assembled reporters' thanks. Amid loud applause, Harold Ickes waved vigorously to the newsmen and shouted "goodbye."[49]

Epilogue

AFTER HIS resignation Harold Ickes assumed the role of watchdog over the nation's affairs in general and the Department of Interior in particular. Almost immediately, he concluded a contract with the *New York Post* syndicate that made him one of the highest paid columnists in the country. He aimed to tell the truth, he announced in his first column, for though he was tired, he and his readers must face courageously the problems of the atom before it destroyed them all. There could be no freedom to stop thinking.[1] He established an office in Georgetown, composed his thrice-weekly column, and maintained an animated and extensive correspondence with those who still worked for the causes that he had always championed.

There was much to do. Delegations of Indians still called upon him to ask his advice, many of them continuing to refer to him as their Mr. Secretary.[2] The Anglo-American Oil Treaty was stalled in the Senate, and the people urgently needed to be made aware of its significance. The tidelands controversy was unresolved. Interior and its new Secretary, Julius Krug, must be kept up to the mark. Neither the battle to conserve the nation's resources nor the struggle to defeat bigotry and discrimination would ever end. There would be plenty to occupy his mind and on which to expend his still considerable energies.

The farm still did not prosper, but as Ickes wrote Reverend R. K. Hanna, who had officiated at his wedding eight years before, the life there was so beneficial to the children that he and Jane were willing to bear the losses. He had always loved the land and Jane now loved it too.[3] In any case, the money from his regular newspaper work, as well as from the large number of lucrative speaking engagements, which were already beginning to mount up, would more than make good any deficiency.

In his early columns Ickes continued to make clear his contempt for the politically innocuous Harry S Truman, and for those who were offering him advice. He was bitterly disillusioned with Truman, he wrote a friend, a man of small stature who turned to even smaller men for assistance. Truman surrounded himself with cronies and had squandered a rich political heritage. He should declare now that he would not be a candidate in 1948.[4] Characteristically, even after making such comments, Ickes could still be surprised that Truman did not turn to him for guidance.

None of Ickes' tenacity had deserted him. He continued to seek justice for his deputy petroleum administrator, Ralph Davies, the only oil executive who, having been drafted for government service during the war, was effectively demoted by his company afterward. The President, Ickes pointed out, had awarded Davies the Medal of Merit; Standard Oil of California had given him "the Double-Cross." In May 1946 Ickes read a statement to a meeting of the company's stockholders charging that John D. Rockefeller had breached antitrust regulations by preventing Davies from becoming president of the company. Ickes later took the case to the Securities and Exchange Commission and, when that failed, to the United States Treasury, where he argued that disguised salary increases paid to H. D. Collier, promoted in Davies' stead, had violated the Salary Stabilization Act.[5]

Ickes remained a formidable opponent. When a report of the House Committee on Un-American Affairs labeled the Southern Conference on Human Welfare a Communist-front organization and named Ickes as having been a member, he hit back in typical fashion, calling Chairman J. Parnell Thomas and his committee cowards and bullies and pointing out that, on the single occasion on which he had addressed a Southern Conference meeting, he had denounced the poll tax, which, since it had never spoken against it, Parnell's committee must favor. It was the poll tax that was un-American, and the committee's practice of condemning without a proper hearing those whom it investigated that threatened the nation's institutions.[6]

It was predictable that Ickes, in the summer of 1947, should have joined the campaign to prevent a proposed raid on the Olympic National Park. Both Secretary Krug and the director of Interior's National Park Service, Newtown Drury, favored a plan permitting 57,000 acres of the park to be logged by lumber interests. Ickes was not impressed to learn that the Forest Service would see to it that only selective lumbering took place. He railed against the would-be exploiters who would butcher these magnificent trees, denounced the plan in his column, tried to enlist the support of Eleanor Roosevelt, and unleashed his friend, columnist Drew Pearson, against the enemy. He would later play a leading part in the struggle to save California's South Calaveras Grove of pines from the lumberman's axe.[7]

Over the last several years of his term as Secretary of the Interior, Ickes had agitated for the adoption of a national oil policy. This goal, too, he was unwillng to abandon. In July 1947 he sent at his own expense an open letter to each member of Congress, urging upon them the need for action. Only two or three acknowledged it. Nor could he generate much support among the public at large, because, he complained, the people refused to believe that they could not continue to obtain what they needed for their comfort and because of highly successful oil industry propaganda.[8]

If his commitment to such farsighted goals was steady and unvarying, Ickes could still be blown about by sudden gusts of passion. When the *Washington Star* dropped his column in November 1947 he dictated (but did not send) a furious protest, using the image which still seemed to him to represent the depths of corruption. The fact that his column would no longer be carried by the *Star* would prevent his having to appear publicly in such questionable company. The newspaper was one of easy morals, granting favors without obtaining physical satisfaction or money in return. Ickes charged that Attorney General Tom Clark had put pressure on the *Star* to drop his column because Ickes had criticized him over the tidelands oil issue. He later wrote Clark, demanding to know why a Justice Department antitrust suit against the Spruce Falls Pulp and Paper Company, in which the *Star* had a 7 percent interest, had been discontinued. When radio station WMAL inadvertently ran an advertisement including his name among a list of *Star* commentators, Ickes lodged a formal complaint with the Federal Communications Commission and demanded redress.[9]

Smouldering jealousies, too, might easily explode into flame. Ickes could never tolerate the suggestion that FDR might seriously have considered Harry Hopkins as his successor, and the recollection that Hopkins had enjoyed a special intimacy with the late President continued to rankle. In May 1948 he noticed a reference to the former idea in a press release announcing a forthcoming *Collier's* article on Hopkins by Robert E. Sherwood. At a private conversation in the White House in 1938, Roosevelt was supposed to have ruled out several presidential possibilities (including Ickes) and assured Hopkins that he would be selected. Ickes wrote immediately to FDR's daughter Anna Boettiger, asking whether she could recall this meeting. Certainly *he* could not. FDR had never mentioned Hopkins' name to him during their several discussions of the matter. Anna replied that she knew nothing about the incident, but Ickes still fretted that the story might come to be considered factual. He scrutinized Sherwoods' book *Roosevelt and Hopkins,* when it appeared some time later, for any additional claims of evidence supposedly bolstering this preposterous idea, and praised Grace Tully, one of FDR's secretaries, for expressing disbelief that the divorced and politically unpopular Hopkins was ever regarded by Roosevelt as a possible successor. Later, congratulating Anna Boettiger on her employment by Stanley Kramer to help write the screenplay for a film about Franklin D. Roosevelt, he declared that Anna had always been closer to her father than any other member of the family— even Harry Hopkins.[10]

Again and again Ickes returned to the question of national leadership. It seemed to him that Truman could never be capable of the kind of vigor and courage the United States so desperately needed. Nor could Henry Wallace, whose presidential ambitions blossomed as the 1948 elections approached. By contrast, Dwight D. Eisenhower possessed the kind of courage and dynamism that Ickes had always admired, and Ickes was involved in a series of maneuvers designed to persuade the war hero to contest the Democratic nomination. Though he did decide to endorse Harry S Truman in 1948 (largely because he believed that Dewey was being put forward by interests anxious to seize the nation's remaining resources), his reservations remained. Truman had always been a small man, Ickes told Raymond Robins, and it was too late for him to grow.[11]

The Ickes family went every year to Southwest Harbor, Maine, for their summer vacation. The young children, Harold Jr. and Elizabeth, enjoyed the hiking and picnics and were instructed in golf and tennis by their mother. Harold Jr. began to learn how to shoot. Raymond, now fully recovered from serious war wounds received at Iwo Jima, was soon to leave, with Miralotte, his wife, for San Francisco, where he would become assistant to Ralph Davies, now president of the American Independent Oil Company. There was much correspondence in the summer of 1949 with Anna Boettiger, Roosevelt's daughter, beset by personal tragedy. Through a long period of crisis involving financial loss, divorce, and illness, Ickes would try to find employment for Anna. He wrote her long supportive letters—letters which recall his kindness to Missy LeHand, FDR's secretary, after a stroke in 1942 had left her without the power of speech, and to the ailing Margaret Robins and her husband, Raymond, whom a grim sequence of physical disasters had made a hopeless invalid. "Jane and I wish we were near enough so that we could put our arms around you and tell you of our entire devotion and love," Ickes wrote to Anna in July 1949. "It would indeed be wonderful if you should be coming east and might be able to come up to Southwest Harbor to relax with us, and bask in each other's friendship."[12]

As Truman's second term progressed, Ickes' attitude toward him began to moderate. He did, however, intemperately attack the President's appointment of Tom Clark to the federal judiciary: "The Supreme Court," he complained, "needs more in a member than a Mona Lisa smile and simpering interest in the Girl Scouts." Clark was a "second-rate political hack," who as Attorney General had failed to carry out the mandate of the Court by assuming federal control of the tidelands oil deposits. Truman clipped the column containing these words from the *New Republic,* for which Ickes had begun to write regularly, and sent it to him with a note saying that Ickes had distorted the facts and that he was ashamed of him. But Ickes, who could never see how insulting he had been, protested that he had not criticized the President personally, just registered disagreement with an official decision. In October 1949 Ickes congratulated Truman for vetoing the Navajo-Hopi Rehabilitation bill, a measure introduced by Secretary Krug, which, while providing extra funds for poverty-stricken Indians, brought the tribes under state law and threatened their culture. And when, in November, the President announced that Oscar L. Chapman would succeed Julius

Krug as Secretary of the Interior, Ickes informed him that he could not have made a better choice. Although Ickes flayed the departing Krug for his "pleasure jaunts," his failure to oppose cuts in the Bureau of Reclamation's budget, and his callous neglect of the Indians, he stopped short of blaming Truman for his subordinate's deficiencies. He would later hail the President's handling of the Korean crisis and enthusiastically endorse his action in dismissing General Douglas MacArthur.[13]

Though Ickes fought in behalf of the Indians literally until the end of his life, he could not prevent the undoing of much of his work. He did believe that a column he wrote for the *New Republic* had helped persuade Truman to kill the offensive Navajo-Hopi bill, since Truman had sent him a copy of his veto mesage. Certainly James E. Curry, attorney for the National Congress of American Indians and the Alaska Native Brotherhood, and a former member of Ickes' department, had no doubts about the effectiveness of his polemical efforts. Although many had helped defeat a recent attempt by Secretary Krug to confiscate lands belonging to the Alaskan Indians, Curry noted in a letter to the *New Republic* that "former Secretary Ickes' characteristically scorching exposure was, in my opinion, what finally turend the tide against it." But when Chapman appointed Dillon Myer the Indian Commissioner in May 1950, the assimilationist policies that the Indian New Deal had attempted to reverse were resumed and many of Ickes' appointees were dismissed. The former Secretary did what he could to stem the tide of reaction. He put pressure on Chapman to reverse Myer's decision to deny Indians the right to select their own legal counsel, a move which would have invalidated contracts that Curry had made with various tribes. Would Chapman, Ickes asked disingenuously, be at all embarrassed if Ickes appeared before him as Curry's counsel when Curry appealed against Myer's ruling? It was only illness that prevented Ickes from carrying out the threat.[14]

Ickes' ability as a political campaigner was still recognized, and there were many requests for assistance. But he wrote Anna Boettiger in March 1950 that he was becoming tired of Democratic leaders' taking him out of the museum at campaign time and returning him there afterward. He had been hard at work on his book on the Roosevelt years, though progress was disappointingly slow. It was snowing at the farm. He could see the robins from his study window, and there was a report that bluebirds were about, though he had rarely managed to see one of those beautiful creatures.[15] In October he turned down a request from Freda Kirchwey, editor of the *Nation,* to contribute an article to that magazine. He had agreed to make a speech against the Ober Law, which threatened the liberties of the people of Maryland; he wished to assist Helen Gahagan Douglas in her senatorial campaign against Richard Nixon; there was his work as chairman of the Board of Trustees of Roosevelt College in Chicago; and always there was the book, about which he was beginning to feel desperate.[16]

During this period he forthrightly and contemptuously denounced McCarthyism and "bumbling, babbling Joe McCarthy," as he called him in the *New Republic* of 7 August 1950. McCarthy had so stripped himself of his last rags of decency that he stood "hideously nude" before the American people. McCarthyism he described as "a putrescent and scabious object that is obnoxious to the senses of sight, smell and hearing—a thing obscene and loathsome, and not to be touched, except with sterilized fire tongs." This scatological or phallophobic imagery is reminiscent of the language he had used against perpetrations of gross physical bullying in earlier years; the invasion of civil liberties seemed comparable to rape.

As Ickes took stock of the world near the end of 1950, the thought that war had broken out again, this time in Korea, oppressed him. He had never approached Christmas with such sadness, he told Stephen Early, but those lucky enough to have young children could at least forget for a short time their apprehensions about the future. The United States seemed to be drifting, its leaders unable to control events, and Harold Ickes was more conscious than he had ever been of his own impotence. As he watched from the sidelines, he wrote Anna Boettiger early in the new year, he wondered over and over where the country was heading. If only there were someone with her father's wisdom and courage to lead. Should America find itself at war with China, all their children would face a fearful future. He did not know who was advising President Truman; nor, it seemed, did anyone else. Big business had made such rapid advances that it would be difficult to preserve the reforms of the Roosevelt years.[17] Even at the end of his life, the moral and psychological imperatives that had driven Harold Ickes for so many years had not weakened.

His health had been poor for some time when the family arrived in Southwest Harbor in the summer of 1951, and Anna Boettiger wrote Jane that she hoped the sea air and restful atmosphere would help him recover. He apologized to his friend, Mrs. William Denman, who had written some time before about the plight of the Navajo and Peyote Indians, for not answering her letter sooner. He was hopelessly behind with his correspondence, had no secretary with him in Maine, and now wrote so poorly that he even had difficulty signing his name. But he responded to her questions courteously and affectionately, as well as complaining wryly about mounting doctors' bills.[18]

Some months later Ickes entered a Washington hospital for treatment of serious complications arising from his arthritic condition. In the following weeks he suffered much pain, made more acute, a medical specialist surmised by the anxiety and frustration that he felt because of the sorry state into which the Department of the Interior had fallen. But he continued to write for the *New Republic,* and his last column was published after his death. In September he had fired a final broadside against Joseph McCarthy, in language that had long been familiar. "Once again," the Old Curmudgeon thundered, "Senator Joseph McCarthy had been guilty of indecent intellectual exposure." Senators had recently been attempting to formulate appropriate standards of ethical behavior, but "while an engraved code of propriety, nicely framed, would decorate the walls of the Senate Chamber, it might be even more helpful if the Senate would provide smelling salts in its budget for visitors to the galleries when McCarthy is befouling that chamber." His condition improved somewhat in mid-January, and he returned to his farm, but on 2 February 1952 the *New York Times* reported that he was back in the hospital, "seriously ill and in a semi-coma." The next day he was dead.[19]

Few of Harold Ickes' contemporaries can have known much of his turbulent inner life, though all who worked with him must often have been made painfully aware of the passions that clouded his motives and the inhibitions that distorted his career. Yet assessments of his public life by the many who admired him display an impressive unanimity. He had restored the reputation of a great department and administered it better than any of his predecessors. He had attempted to protect the weak from their oppressors. He had

fought tenaciously to conserve what remained of the nation's resources. Those judgments of his achievements are amply sustained
by the historical record. But it is out of his first-person records, the
ongoing saga unfolded as he lovingly played Boswell to his own
Johnson, that the three-dimensional Harold Ickes emerges. If he
sometimes created imaginary foes and battered valiantly against the
end of blind alleys, if his insight into the schemes of grasping contractors and power-hungry corporations was matched only by his
inability to understand himself, nevertheless at the center of his
being was a disillusioned yet undefeated commitment to achieving
in material terms and in real time, not in some visionary future, the
liberal goals of America's New Deal.

Notes
Index

Short Titles of Works
by Harold L. Ickes

Autobiography	*Autobiography of a Curmudgeon.* New York: Reynal and Hitchcock, 1943.
Ickes Papers	Library of Congress, Washington, D.C.
Manuscript Diary	Diary 1933–51, Ickes Papers.
"My Twelve Years"	"My Twelve Years with F.D.R.," *Saturday Evening Post,* 5 June 1948–17 July 1948.
"Politics and Public Affairs"	"On My Interest in Politics and Public Affairs," Ickes Papers, Speeches and Writings File 1910–52.
Secret Diary	*The Secret Diary of Harold L. Ickes.* 3 vols. New York: Simon & Schuster, 1953–54.
Unpublished Cabinet Memoirs	Unpublished Cabinet Memoirs, Ickes Papers, Speeches and Writings File 1910–52.
Unpublished Personal Memoirs	Ickes Papers, Speeches and Writings File 1910–52.
Untitled Autobiographical Draft	Ickes Papers, Speeches and Writings File 1910–52.

Notes

Prologue

1. "Throng Honors Marian Anderson in Concert at Lincoln Memorial," *New York Times,* 10 April 1939.

2. Oscar L. Chapman, Memorial Address, 20 April 1952, Ickes Papers, Miscellany 1944–54, Memorials to Ickes, Library of Congress.

3. Ickes Papers, General Correspondence 1946–52, Resignation 1946.

4. Ibid.

5. Ickes to Harry S Truman, 12 February 1946, Ickes Papers, Secretary of Interior File 1933–46.

6. Ickes, Press Conference, 13 January 1946, Ickes Papers, Secretary of Interior File 1933–46, Resignation 1946.

7. Ickes Papers, General Correspondence 1946–52, Resignation 1946.

8. Saul K. Padover, "Ickes: Memoir of a Man without Fear," *Reporter,* 4 March 1952, p. 36.

9. Ickes, "McCarthy Strips Himself," *New Republic,* 7 August 1950, p. 17.

10. J. J. Dillon to Ickes, Ickes Papers, General Correspondence 1946–52, Resignation 1946.

11. "Harold Ickes' Indiscreet Diary of the Roosevelt Years," *Look,* 15 December 1953.

12. *The New Yorker,* 23 January 1954.

13. Ickes, Unpublished Personal Memoirs and Untitled Autobiographical Draft, Ickes Papers, Speeches and Writings File 1910–52.

14. Ickes, Unpublished Personal Memoirs, p. 139.

15. Ickes to H. Luensman, 16 September 1933, Ickes Papers, General Correspondence 1903–52.

16. Merle Miller, *Plain Speaking: An Oral Biography of Harry S Truman* (New York: Berkley Publishing Corporation, 1980), p. 226.

17. Jonathan Daniels, "With a Sense of Rejection," *New York Times,* 5 December 1954.

One. Altoona Boyhood

1. Charles M. Schwab, *Altoona* (Altoona Chamber of Commerce, n.d.); *Altoona Charter Centennial* (Altoona Charter Centennial Committee, n.d.).

2. *Manual of the Second Presbyterian Church of Altoona* (Altoona: Evening Printing House, 1877).

3. Unless otherwise indicated, the account in this chapter of Ickes' early life is drawn from his Unpublished Personal Memoirs. See pp. 20 (quotation), 21–22, 24–25, 26 (quotation), 28, 32, 34, 82, 76–77, 139–141, 142–143 (quotation).

4. Scrapbooks, Personal 1833–1902, Ickes Papers, Miscellany 1884–1954.

5. Harold L. Ickes, *Autobiography of a Curmudgeon* (New York: Reynal and Hitchcock, 1943), p. 4.

6. Harold L. Ickes, *The Secret Diary of Harold L. Ickes,* 3 vols. (New York: Simon & Schuster, 1953–54), I,634.

7. L. Kohlberg, "Development of Moral Character and Moral Ideology," in M. L. Hoffman and L. W. Hoffman, eds., *Review of Child Development Research,* vol. 1 (New York: Russell Sage Foundation, 1964).

8. Rachael M. Henry, "A Theoretical and Empirical Analysis of 'Reasoning' in the Socialization of Young Children," *Human Development* 23 (1980): 105–125; Rachael M. Henry, *The Psychodynamic Foundations of Morality* (Basel: Karger, 1982).

Two. Anna and Chicago Reform

1. Ickes, Unpublished Personal Memoirs, pp. 50–53.

2. *Englewood High School Journal,* 1893, Ickes Papers, Scrapbooks, 1883–1954.

3. J. E. Armstrong to Principal May or Mr. Goodhew, 20 September 1893, Ickes Papers, Scrapbooks, 1883–1954.

4. Ickes, Unpublished Personal Memoirs, College Life and Newspaper Reporter, p. 12; College Years, pp. 5 ff., 35, 26–28.

5. Ibid., pp. 32–33.

6. Ickes, Unpublished Personal Memoirs, College Life and Newspaper Reporter, pp. 15, 18.

7. Harold L. Ickes, "On My Interest in Politics and Public Affairs," Ickes Papers, Speeches and Writings File 1910–52, p. 1.

8. Ickes, *Autobiography,* p. 9.

9. Ickes, "Politics and Public Affairs," p. 12.

10. Ickes, *Autobiography,* pp. 82–85; Carter H. Harrison, *Stormy Years* (Indianapolis: Bobbs Merrill, 1983), p. 104; quoted in Linda Jane Lear, "The Aggressive Progressive: The Political Career of Harold L. Ickes, 1874–1933" (Ph.D. diss., George Washington University, 1974), p. 34.

11. Ickes, "Politics and Public Affairs," p. 28.

12. Ickes, *Autobiography,* p. 35.

13. Ickes, Unpublished Personal Memoirs, College Life and Newspaper Reporter, p. 30.

14. Ickes, "Politics and Public Affairs," pp. 41–42, 40, 43.

15. Ickes to William Allen White, 3 September 1927, William Allen White Papers, Box 121, Library of Congress.

16. Ickes, "Politics and Public Affairs," p. 43.

17. Ibid., pp. 50–51.

18. Ickes, Unpublished Personal Memoirs, Newspaper Reporter, pp. 8–9.

19. Ickes, "Politics and Public Affairs," p. 80.

20. Ickes, *Autobiography,* p. 95.

21. Ickes, "Politics and Public Affairs," p. 103.

22. James Harlan to Ickes, 10 April 1903; Charles T. Hallinan to Ickes, n.d., Ickes Papers, General Correspondence 1903–52.

23. The account of Ickes' private life that follows has, unless otherwise indicated, been taken from his Unpublished Personal Memoirs.

24. Ickes, Unpublished Personal Memoirs, Courtship and Marriage to Anna Wilmarth Thompson, pp. 18–21.

25. Wayne Thompson to Anna Thompson, 19 September 1903, Ickes Papers, Family Papers 1815–1969.

26. Wayne Thompson to Ickes, 24 September 1903, ibid.

27. Anna Thompson to James Thompson, n.d., ibid.

28. Ickes, Unpublished Personal Memoirs, Early Years of Marriage, pp. 14–15.

29. Wilmarth Thompson to Ickes, 2 August 1905, Ickes Papers, Scrapbooks 1883–1954; Ickes to C. L. Breed, 4 February 1908, Ickes Papers, Letterbooks 1905–12.

30. Ickes, Unpublished Personal Memoirs, Courtship and Marriage to Anna Wilmarth Thompson, pp. 23–24.

31. Ickes, *Autobiography,* p. 102.

32. Ickes, "Politics and Public Affairs," pp. 117–118.

33. Ibid., p. 119.

34. Lear, "Aggressive Progressive," p. 120n.

35. Ickes to James S. Harlan, 27 May 1907, Ickes Papers, Letterbooks 1905–12.

36. Ickes, "Politics and Public Affairs," pp. 153–54. Ickes to Jonathan Bourke, 8 September 1910 and 3 October 1910, Ickes Papers, General Correspondence 1903–52.

37. Ickes, *Autobiography,* p. 118.

38. Ickes, "Politics and Public Affairs," p. 170.

39. Ickes, *Autobiography,* p. 127.

40. Ickes, "Politics and Public Affairs," p. 183.

41. Ickes, *Autobiography,* p. 130, Ickes, "Politics and Public Affairs," p. 189; James Hamilton Lewis to Ickes, 1 March 1911, Ickes Papers, General Correspondence 1903–52.

42. For the paragraphs that follow, see Ickes, Unpublished Personal Memoirs, Courtship and Marriage to Anna Wilmarth Thompson, pp. 26, 28, 36, 37, 38, 43.

43. Margaret Dreier Robins to Ickes, 11 September 1909; Ickes to Margaret Dreier Robins, 15 November 1910; Ickes Papers, General Correspondence 1903–52.

44. Ickes to Reporter, Phi Delta Theta Chapter, 31 October 1908, ibid.

45. Ickes, Address at Jane Addams Memorial Dinner, 1949, Ickes Papers, Subject File 1905–52; Ickes, Untitled Autobiographical Draft, pp. 4–15.

46. Ickes, Radio Address, 10 April 1937, Congressional Record 81, 9 (1937): 789.

47. Ickes to Donald R. Richberg, 2 September 1925, Ickes Papers, General Correspondence 1903–52.

48. Ickes, Unpublished Personal Memoirs, Courtship and Marriage to Anna Wilmarth Thompson, p. 44.

49. Ibid., p. 110.

50. Ibid., pp. 116–117.

51. Ickes to Maurice Thompson, 14 June 1909, Ickes Papers, Legal File 1877–1952.

52. Ickes to Mary H. Wilmarth, 24 June 1909, Ickes Papers, Letterbooks 1905–12.

53. Ickes, "Politics and Public Affairs," p. 188.

54. Ickes, *Autobiography,* p. 133.

55. Ibid., pp. 135–136.

56. Ickes, "Politics and Public Affairs," p. 216.

57. Ickes, Unpublished Personal Memoirs, Courtship and Marriage to Anna Wilmarth Thompson, p. 119.

Three. Locust Years

1. Ickes, Unpublished Personal Memoirs, Courtship and Marriage to Anna Wilmarth Thompson, pp. 125–126, 134.

2. Ickes, "Politics and Public Affairs," p. 223.

3. Ickes, Unpublished Cabinet Memoirs, Ickes Papers, Speeches and Writings File 1910–52, p. 17.

4. Ickes, "Politics and Public Affairs," p. 376.

5. Ickes, *Autobiography,* p. 164; Ickes, "Politics and Public Affairs," p. 247.

6. Ibid., p. 176; Ickes to Amos Pinchot, 2 December 1913, Ickes Papers, General Correspondence 1903–52.

7. Raymond Robins to Ickes, 13 January 1915, ibid.

8. Ickes, Unpublished Personal Memoirs, Courtship and Marriage to Anna Wilmarth Thompson, pp. 136, 139–140.

9. Ickes, Unpublished Personal Memoirs, Early Years of Marriage, pp. 1, 4–5.

10. Ickes, Unpublished Personal Memoirs, Wilmarth Thompson as a Young Boy, p. 1.

11. John R. Maze, "The Concept of Attitude," *Inquiry* 16 (1973): 168–205; Sigmund Freud, *Introductory Lectures on Psychoanalysis.* Lecture 10. *Standard Edition of the Complete Psychological Works of Sigmund Freud,* vols. 15, 16 (London: Hogarth Press, 1966).

12. Dwight H. Perkins to Ickes, 12 May 1916; Ickes to Messrs. Perkins, Fellows, and Hamilton, 15 May 1916, Ickes Papers, General Correspondence 1903–52.

13. Ickes to Dwight H. Perkins, 17 May 1916, ibid.

14. For this and the three paragraphs that follow, see Ickes, Unpublished Personal Memoirs, Early Years of Marriage, pp. 1–2, 4, 5.

15. Ickes to Theodore Roosevelt, 17 December 1915, Ickes Papers, General Correspondence 1903–52.

16. Ickes, "Politics and Public Affairs," pp. 290–291, 300.

17. Ickes to Theodore Roosevelt, 24 May 1915, Ickes Papers, General Correspondence 1903–52.

18. Ickes to Theodore Roosevelt, 15 October 1915 and 12 April 1916, ibid.

19. Ickes to Charles Evans Hughes, 12 July 1916, ibid.

20. Ickes, Untitled Autobiographical Draft, pp. 52–53.

21. Ickes to Anna, 3 July 1918, Ickes Papers, Family Papers 1815–1969.

22. See, for example, Ickes to Anna, 9 September 1918, ibid.

23. Ickes, Untitled Autobiographical Draft, pp. 35–36.

24. Ibid., Unpublished Personal Memoirs, Early Years of Marriage, p. 8.

25. For this and the next three paragraphs, see Untitled Autobiographical Draft, pp. 109, 189, 190–191, 193–194.

26. Ickes, "Politics and Public Affairs," pp. 429, 471–473.

27. Ibid., p. 401; James M. Cox Campaign 1920, Ickes Papers, General Correspondence 1903–52.

28. Ickes to Hiram W. Johnson, 11 August 1920 and 25 August 1920, ibid.

29. Ickes to Hiram Johnson, 12 May 1921, 26 May 1921, and 8 July 1921, ibid.

30. For Ickes' scathing opinion of Harding even before the election, see Ickes to William Allen White, 30 June 1920, ibid.; quoted in Lear, "Aggressive Progressive," p. 207.

31. Ickes, "Politics and Public Affairs," p. 482; Ickes to Herbert Croly, 14 September 1921, Ickes Papers, General Correspondence 1903–52.

32. Ickes to Hiram W. Johnson, 17 May 1923, ibid.

33. Ickes to Hiram W. Johnson, 2 July 1923 and 6 October 1923, ibid.

34. Ickes, "Politics and Public Affairs," p. 486; Ickes to Henry J. Allen, 24 November 1923; Ickes to Hiram W. Johnson, 19 October 1923 and 15 July 1924, Ickes Papers, General Correspondence 1903–52.

35. Ickes to Hiram W. Johnson, 11 August 1923, and Hiram W. Johnson to Ickes, 13 August 1923, ibid.

36. Ickes to Hiram W Johnson, 31 August 1923; quoted in Lear, "Aggressive Progressive," p. 254.

37. Ickes to Hiram W. Johnson, 21 January 1924, Ickes Papers, General Correspondence 1903–52.

38. Ickes to Hiram W. Johnson, 9 September 1924, ibid.

39. Ickes to Hiram W. Johnson, 11 November 1924; Ickes to Benjamin F. Proctor, 15 February 1926, ibid.

40. Anna Ickes to Ickes, 14 September 1925; Ickes to Anna Ickes, n.d.; Ickes Papers, Family Papers 1815–1969.

41. Ickes to William E. Dever, 4 March 1927, Ickes to Hiram W. Johnson, 10 June 1927, ibid.; Ickes, "Politics and Public Affairs," p. 454.

42. Ickes to Frank O. Lowden, 1 August 1919; Ickes to Jane Addams, 1 November 1922, Ickes Papers, General Correspondence 1903–52.

43. Lear, "Aggressive Progressive," p. 233; Ickes to Robert W. Bagnall, 6 November 1924, Ickes Papers, General Correspondence 1903–52.

44. Ickes to Hiram W. Johnson, 12 January 1923, ibid.

45. Ickes, Untitled Autobiographical Draft, pp. 359–360.

46. Ickes, Unpublished Cabinet Memoirs, p. 9.

47. Ickes, "Politics and Public Affairs," pp. 454–456; Ickes to Hiram W. Johnson, 9 November, 2 December, 7 December, and 11 December 1931, 29 January 1932; Ickes to Mrs. Hiram W. Johnson, 24 January 1932, Ickes Papers, General Correspondence 1903–52.

48. Ickes to Robert J. Thorne, 3 November 1932, ibid.

49. Ickes, Unpublished Cabinet Memoirs, p. 23.

50. Anna Wilmarth Ickes, *Mesa Land: The History and Romance of the American Southwest* (Boston and New York: Houghton Mifflin, 1933).

51. Ickes, Unpublished Cabinet Memoirs, p. 23.

52. Frances Perkins, Reminiscences, Columbia University Oral History Project, book III, pp. 578–581. Raymond Moley, *After Seven Years,* pp. 126–127; quoted in Arthur M. Schlesinger, Jr., *The Crisis of the Old Order* (Boston: Houghton Mifflin, 1956), p. 472.

53. Ickes, Unpublished Cabinet Memoirs, p. 30.

54. Ickes, *Secret Diary,* II: 663.

55. Ickes to Hiram W. Johnson, 8 May 1924, Ickes Papers, General Correspondence 1903–52.

56. Ickes to Edward D. Loewenthal, 7 July 1930; Ickes to Raymond Robins, 28 July 1930, ibid.

Four. Mr. Ickes Goes to Washington

1. Congressional Record 77, 3 (1933); 3096–98.

2. Ickes to FDR, 12 January 1935, Franklin D. Roosevelt Papers, President's Secretary's File, Ickes, Franklin D. Roosevelt Library, Hyde Park, N.Y.; Ickes, "My Twelve Years With F.D.R.," *Saturday Evening Post,* 12 June 1948, p. 34. (All citations from "My Twelve Years" in this chapter are from the 12 June 1948 issue of the *Saturday Evening Post.*)

3. Freud, "A Special Type of Choice of Object Made by Men," *Standard Edition,* 11: 163–175.

4. Ickes, Unpublished Personal Memoirs, Courtship and Marriage to Anna Wilmarth Thompson, p. 36; Ickes, Untitled Autobiographical Draft, p. 199.

5. Ickes, "My Twelve Years," pp. 35, 107–108; Donald C. Swain, "Harold Ickes, Horace Albright, and the Hundred Days: A Study in Conservation Administration," *Pacific Historical Review* 24 (November 1965): 457; Gifford Pinchot to Ickes, 25 February 1933, Ickes Papers, General Correspondence 1903–52.

6. Ickes, "My Twelve Years," p. 110.

7. William D. Reeves, "PWA and Competitive Administration in the New Deal," *Journal of American History* 60 (1973): 366.

8. Ickes, Untitled Autobiographical Draft, pp. 275, 307–308.

9. Ickes, *Secret Diary,* III: 368.

10. Freud, *Introductory Lectures,* lecture 10.

11. Ickes, "My Twelve Years," p. 111.

12. Ickes, *Back To Work: The Story of PWA* (New York: Macmillan, 1935), pp. 232–233.

13. Ickes, *Secret Diary*, I: 116, 119.

14. Ickes to Heywood Broun, 28 September 1933, Ickes Papers, Secretary of Interior File, Newspaper Criticism.

15. Frank Knox to Ickes, 17 November 1933; Charles E. Merriam to Ickes, 2 August 1933, 2 October 1933; Ickes to Charles E. Merriam, 4 October 1933, ibid.

16. Perkins, Reminiscences, 5: 150–151; Ickes, "My Twelve Years," pp. 111, 113.

17. Raymond Wolters, *Negroes and the Great Depression* (Westport, Conn.: Greenwood, 1970), p. 195.

18. Reeves, "PWA and Competitive Administration," pp. 362–363.

19. Wolters, *Negroes and the Great Depression*, p. 202; Harvard Sitkoff, *A New Deal for Blacks* (New York: Oxford University Press, 1978), I, 66–67.

20. Sitkoff, *New Deal for Blacks*, p. 67.

21. Wolters, *Negroes and the Great Depression*, p. 202; Ickes to Robert Fechner, 26 September 1935, Ickes Papers, Secretary of Interior File.

22. Reeves, "PWA and Competitive Administration," p. 372.

23. Ickes, *Secret Diary*, I: 216–217, 302.

24. Quoted in Reeves, "PWA and Competitive Administration," pp. 371–372.

25. The account which follows of Ickes' life is drawn from his Untitled Autobiographical Draft, pp. 380–404.

26. Ibid., pp. 384–385.

27. Ickes, Diary 1933–51, 4 May 1934, Ickes Papers.

28. Ickes to FDR, 21 March 1934, Franklin D. Roosevelt Papers, President's Secretary's File, Interior.

29. Ickes, Manuscript Diary, 4 May 1934.

30. This and the paragraphs that follow are drawn from Ickes, Untitled Autobiographical Draft, pp. 401–404, 39.

31. Ickes, *Secret Diary*, I: 152.

32. Ickes, Manuscript Diary, 24 December 1939.

33. Ickes, Statement Before Senate Committee on Public Lands, 1938, Ickes Papers, Secretary of Interior File.

34. Ickes, *Secret Diary*, I: 481.

35. Ibid., I; 641; quoted in Clayton R. Koppes, "Oscar L. Chapman: A Liberal at the Interior Department, 1933–1953" (Ph.D. diss., University of Kansas, 1974), pp. 8, 29–30n.

36. Roosevelt Papers, Official File, Interior.

37. L. H. Robins, "Ickes Defines the Task Ahead," *New York Times*, 1 April 1934.

38. See Donald L. Parman, *The Navajos and the New Deal* (New Haven and London: Yale University Press, 1976), chapter 2; Kenneth R. Philip, *John Collier's Crusade for Indian Reform, 1920–1954* (Tucson: University of Arizona Press, 1977) chapters 2, 6; Informal Talk by Hon. Harold Ickes to Blackfeet Indians, 5 August 1934, Ickes Papers, Secretary of Interior File, Indians 1933–35.

39. Ickes, *Secret Diary*, I: 430.

Five. *Extending the Empire: PWA and the Forests*

1. Ickes, Unpublished Personal Memoirs, Early Years of Marriage, pp. 8–9.

2. Material for this and the following three paragraphs is taken from Ickes, Untitled Autobiographical Draft, pp. 223, 224, 226, 368–369, 371.

3. Otto Fenichel, *The Psychoanalytic Theory of Neurosis* (New York: W. W. Norton, 1945), pp. 372–373.

4. Ickes, *Autobiography*, p. 3n.

5. Ickes to Hon. Mabel G. Reinecke, 22 June 1933, Ickes Papers, Secretary of Interior File.

6. Ickes to FDR, 21 March 1934, Roosevelt Papers, President's Secretary's File, Interior.

7. Ickes, *Secret Diary*, I: 121–122.

8. Ibid., p. 204.

9. Ickes, Untitled Autobiographical Draft, pp. 335, 339, 343.

10. Ickes, Manuscript Diary, 2 September 1936.

11. Ickes, Untitled Autobiographical Draft, pp. 344–346.

12. Ickes, Untitled Autobiographical Draft, p. 346, Manuscript Diary, 2 September 1936.

13. Ickes, *Secret Diary*, I: 358, 409 (quotation).

14. Ibid., I: 424, 425, 428.

15. "President Pleads for Conservation as National Policy," *New York Times*, 17 April 1936.

16. Congressional Record 78, 4(1934): 4218.

17. J. R. Maze, "The Concept of Attitude," *Inquiry* 16 (1973), 168–205.

18. John Maze and Graham White, "Harold L. Ickes: A Psychohistorical Perspective," *Journal of Psychohistory* 8 (Spring 1981), 421–444.

19. Ickes to Gifford Pinchot, 20 April 1933, Ickes Papers, Miscellany 1944–1954, Forest Service Transfer 1935; quoted in Eugene Trani, "Conflict or Compromise: Harold L. Ickes and Franklin D. Roosevelt," *North Dakota Quarterly* 36 (1968): 25; Donald C. Swain, "Harold Ickes, Horace Albright, and the Hundred Days: A Study in Conservation Administration," *Pacific Historical Review* 24 (1965): 460–465.

20. Ickes, "After the Oil Deluge, What Price Gasoline?" manuscript submitted to *Saturday Evening Post* for publication 16 February 1935, Ickes Papers, Secretary of Interior File.

21. Ickes, "Saving the Good Earth," manuscript submitted to *Survey Graphic* for publication 2 February 1934, ibid.

22. "Appeals to Youth to Save Wild Life," *New York Times*, 7 February 1936.

23. Donald C. Swain, *Wilderness Defender: Horace Albright and Conservation* (Chicago: University of Chicago Press, 1970), p. 222.

24. Gifford Pinchot to FDR, 17 April 1933; FDR to Gifford Pinchot, 21 April 1933, Ickes Papers, Secretary of Interior File.

25. Gifford Pinchot to Ickes, 19 April 1933; Ickes to Gifford Pinchot, 20 April 1933; Gifford Pinchot to Ickes, 26 April 1933, ibid.

26. Some possible reasons for Ickes' obsession with Forestry are considered in Maze and White, "Harold L. Ickes: A Psychohistorical Perspective."

27. G. H. Collingwood to Gifford Pinchot, 4 June 1934; Gifford Pinchot to G. H. Collingwood, 11 June 1934, Ickes Papers, Secretary of Interior File.

28. Ickes, *Secret Diary,* I: 259.

29. Ickes to FDR, 2 June 1934; quoted in Edgar B. Nixon, ed., *Franklin D. Roosevelt and Conservation, 1911–1945* (Hyde Park, N.Y.: Franklin D. Roosevelt Library, 1957), p. 307.

30. Ickes, *Secret Diary,* I: 343–344.

31. Ibid., pp. 364–365.

32. Foresters Challenge Conservation Claims of Department of the Interior, press release, American Society of Foresters, 24 June 1935; Ickes to H. H. Chapman, 27 June 1935; H. H. Chapman to Ickes, 3 July 1935; Horace Albright to Ickes, 17 July 1935; Ickes Papers, Secretary of Interior File.

33. Ickes, *Secret Diary,* I: 384–385, 417–418.

34. Ickes to Harry Slattery, 30 September 1935, Department of Interior Papers, National Archives, Official File of H. L. Ickes, Conservation.

35. Ickes, *Secret Diary,* I: 604, 605.

36. Harold L. Ickes, Attack on Gifford Pinchot, 27 October 1936; Gifford Pinchot to Warren W. Jones, 4 November 1936, Papers of Gifford Pinchot, Library of Congress.

Six. Harold and the Men around Franklin Roosevelt

1. Ickes, Untitled Autobiographical Draft, Ickes Papers, Speeches and Writings File 1910–52, p. 420, pp. 3–4 of insert following p. 420.

2. Ickes, *Secret Diary,* I: 475.

3. Ickes, Untitled Autobiographical Draft, p. 424.

4. Ickes, Manuscript Diary, 15 May 1938.

5. Ickes, Untitled Autobiographical Draft, p. 422.

6. Ickes, Manuscript Diary, 15 May 1938.

7. Ickes, *Secret Diary,* I: 499.

8. Ickes, Manuscript Diary, 15 May 1938.

9. Material for this and the next thirteen paragraphs comes from Ickes, *Secret Diary,* I: 585, 575, 589, 590, 591–592, 593–597, 609, 620, 639, 646, 655–656, 659, 664, 667, 673.

10. Ickes, *Secret Diary,* II: 139–140.

11. Ibid., p. 247.

12. Ickes, Manuscript Diary, 15 May 1938.

13. Ibid.; Ickes, Untitled Autobiographical Draft, p. 430.

14. Ickes, Manuscript Diary, 15 May 1938.

15. Ickes, *Secret Diary,* II: 137, 149ff., 254, 305 (quotation).

16. Ibid., p. 361.

17. Ickes, *Autobiography,* p. 314. The following account of Ickes' wedding trip is taken from *Autobiography,* chapter 17, and from the Manuscript Diary entry for 17 May 1938.

18. Ickes to FDR, 29 April 1939, Roosevelt Papers, President's Secretary's File, Ickes.

19. Ibid., pp. 666–667, 669.

20. FDR to Ickes, 29 June 1939, Roosevelt Papers, President's Secretary's File, Ickes.

21. Ickes, *Secret Diary,* II: 308, 309.

22. Ibid., II: 114–117.

23. Ickes, "My Twelve Years With F.D.R.," 5 June 1948, p. 92.

24. Ickes, *Secret Diary,* III: 371, 511.

25. Ickes, *Secret Diary,* I: 620.

26. Ickes, *Autobiography,* p. 133.

27. Ickes, *Secret Diary,* III: 131.

28. Ickes to FDR, 8 February 1940, Roosevelt Papers, President's Secretary's File, Ickes.

29. Henry F. Pringle, *The Life and Times of William Howard Taft* (New York: Farrar and Rinehart, 1939), I; 471.

30. Taft and Pinchot quoted in ibid., pp. 492, 508.

31. Ickes, *Secret Diary,* III: 111.

32. Ickes, Manuscript Diary, 19 May 1940.

33. Ickes, *Secret Diary,* III: 117, 124–125.

34. Ibid., III: 127.

35. For this and following paragraphs, see Ickes, Manuscript Diary, 26 November 1939, 23 September 1939, 24 March 1940, 30 March 1940, 7 April 1940, and 8 February 1941.

36. Georgiana X. Preston, "Old Harold in a Lawsuit with His Son over First Wife's Will," *Washington Times-Herald,* 28 March 1942.

37. Ickes to Raymond Robins, 27 March 1944, Ickes Papers, Secretary of Interior File.

Seven. Warfare—Bureaucratic and Foreign

1. Material for the first nine paragraphs of this chapter is based in Ickes, *Secret Diary,* III: 186–187, 191, 218, 207, 193–195, 178, 208, 240, 241.

2. Ickes, "My Twelve Years with F.D.R.," *Saturday Evening Post,* 10 July 1948, pp. 108, 112; Ickes, *Secret Diary,* III: 246.

3. Ickes, *Secret Diary,* III: 252, 249–250, 257, 258.

4. "Ickes Bars Capital Site for 3-Day 'Gentile' Rally," *New York Times,* 30 May 1939.

5. Ickes, Unpublished Cabinet Memoirs, 1940 From the Inside, p. 7.

6. Ickes, *Secret Diary,* III: 259, 263, 289, 290, 361, 368.

7. Ickes, Manuscript Diary, 10 October 1942, 22 November 1942.

8. Ickes, *Secret Diary,* III: 355.

9. Ickes to Editor, *Washington Post,* 18 May 1945, Ickes Papers, Secretary of Interior File, Newspaper Criticism.

10. Ickes, *Secret Diary,* II: 690.

11. Phillip J. Funigiello, "Kilowatts for Defense: The New Deal and the Coming of the Second World War," *Journal of American History* 56 (1969): 605–616.

12. For quotations in this and the next nine paragraphs, see Ickes, *Secret Diary*, III: 399, 400–401, 420–421, 424, 431, 434, 438, 441, 586, 587.

13. Ickes to Ben Cohen, 25 August 1941, Ickes Papers, Secretary of Interior File, Power.

14. Ickes, *Secret Diary*, III: 544–546, 552–557.

15. Ickes to Raymond Robins, 23 June 1941, Ickes Papers, Secretary of Interior File.

16. Material here and in the next ten paragraphs comes from Ickes, *Secret Diary*, III: 547, 511, 557–559, 560, 567, 568, 606, 610–611.

17. Jane Ickes to Margaret Robins, 8 December 1941, Ickes Papers, Family Papers 1815–1969.

18. Ickes, Manuscript Diary, 21 December 1941, 4 January 1942.

19. Ickes to Henry Wallace, 14 January 1942, Ickes Papers, Secretary of Interior File.

20. Ickes, Manuscript Diary, 18 January 1942.

21. Michael B. Stoff, "The New Deal Abroad: Harold Ickes and the Search for Foreign Oil Policy, 1933–1947," Paper presented to Annual Meeting American Historical Association, 30 December 1980; Congressional Record 78, 4 (1934): 4048; "Ickes Threatens Oil Land Seizures," *New York Times*, 15 November 1934; Ickes, "My Twelve Years with F.D.R.," *Saturday Evening Post*, 17 July 1948, p. 102; quoted in M. Judd Harmon, "Some Contributions of Harold L. Ickes," *Western Political Quarterly* 7 (1954): 249.

22. Congressional Record 88, 10 (1942): 3388.

23. Ickes, Manuscript Diary, 1 February 1942, 1 March 1942, 24 May 1942.

24. Ibid., 29 November 1942; Ickes, Unpublished Cabinet Memoirs, chapter 7, p. 24.

25. Ickes to Raymond Robins, 11 December 1942, Ickes Papers, Secretary of Interior File; Ickes, Unpublished Cabinet Memoirs, chapter 7, p. 29.

26. Ickes to Raymond Robins, 18 September 1939, Ickes Papers, General Correspondence 1903–52; Ickes to William Allen White, 4 April 1941, Ickes Papers, Secretary of Interior File; Ickes, Manuscript Diary, 28 September 1940.

27. Jane Ickes to Anna Boettiger, 24 October 1941, Ickes Papers, Family Papers 1815–1969.

28. Ickes, Manuscript Diary, 6 December 1942.

29. Jane Ickes to Margaret Robins, 30 December 1942 and 4 March 1943; Jane Ickes to Eleanor Roosevelt, 9 March 1943, Ickes Papers, Family Papers 1815–1969.

30. Ickes, Manuscript Diary, 1 March 1942, 20 March 1943; Jane Ickes to Margaret Robins, 19 May 1943, Ickes Papers, Family Papers 1815–1969.

31. Ickes to Stacy Mosser, 16 April 1942, Ickes Papers, Secretary of Interior File.

32. Congressional Record 89, 8 (1943), 10682–83.

33. Ibid., 90, 9 (1944): A1403, A1755; Stoff, "New Deal Abroad"; Michael B. Stoff, *Oil, War and American Security: The Search for a National Policy on Foreign Oil, 1941–1947* (New Haven and London: Yale University Press, 1980), pp.

151, 178; Ickes, Column for Release 3 April 1946, Ickes papers, Speeches and Writings File 1910–1952.

34. Ickes, Manuscript Diary, 16 November 1944.

35. FDR to Ickes, 8 November 1944, Ickes to FDR, 11 November 1944, Roosevelt Papers, President's Personal File 3650.

36. Ickes, Manuscript Diary, 16 November 1944.

37. FDR to Ickes, 9 December 1944, Ickes Papers, Secretary of Interior File.

38. Ickes, Manuscript Diary, 24 April 1944.

39. Ickes to FDR, 13 December 1944; FDR to Ickes, 16 December 1944, Roosevelt Papers, President's Secretary's File, Harold Ickes.

40. Frances Perkins, Reminiscences, VIII, 808–809.

41. Miller, *Plain Speaking,* pp. 225–227.

42. Koppes, "Oscar Chapman," p. 21.

43. Ickes, Manuscript Diary, 29 April 1945.

44. Robert J. Donovan, *Conflict and Crisis: The Presidency of Harry S Truman, 1945–1948* (New York: W. W. Norton, 1977), p. 181.

45. Ickes, Manuscript Diary, 3 February 1946.

46. Donovan, *Crisis and Conflict,* p. 181.

47. Ickes, Manuscript Diary, 3 February 1946.

48. Quoted in Donovan, *Conflict and Crisis,* p. 181.

49. Tristram Coffin, Report from Washington, 17 February 1946, Ickes Papers, Secretary of Interior File, Resignation.

Epilogue

1. Ickes, Column for Release 1 April 1946, Ickes Papers, Speeches and Writings File 1910–52.

2. Ruth M. Bronson to Jane Ickes, 7 March 1952, Ickes papers, Miscellany 1844–1854, Memorials to Ickes.

3. Ickes to Rev. Dr. R. K. Hanna, 26 March 1946, Ickes Papers, Secretary of Interior File, Resignation 1946.

4. Ickes, Column for Release 10 April 1946; Ickes to Alice P. Barrows, 18 July 1946; Ickes Column for Release 22 November 1946, Speeches and Writings File 1910–52.

5. Ickes, Column for Release 29 May 1946; Ickes, Statement to Stockholders' Meeting, Standard Oil of California, 2 May 1946, Speeches and Writings File 1910–52; James J. Caffrey to Ickes, 3 April 1947; Ickes to Head, Salary Stabilization Unit, Department of the Treasury, 3 November 1947, General Correspondence 1903–52, Standard Oil 1946–50.

6. Ickes to J. Parnell Thomas, 27 June 1947, Ickes Papers, General Correspondence 1903–52, Un-American Activities Committee.

7. Ickes to Willard G. Van Name, 11 June 1947 and 25 July 1947; Ickes to John B. Elliott, 7 March 1949, Ickes Papers, General Correspondence 1903–52, Parks.

8. Ickes to Hugh Holohan, 18 December 1947, Ickes Papers, General Correspondence 1903–52, Oil 1946–1951.

9. Ickes to B. M. McKelway, 11 November 1947, Ickes to Hon. Tom C. Clark, 8 January 1948, Ickes Papers, General Correspondence 1903–52.

10. Ickes to Anna Boettiger, 19 May 1948 and 26 May 1948; Ickes to Grace Tully, 14 July 1950; Ickes to Anna Boettiger, 8 October 1951, ibid.

11. Ickes to John Boettiger, 2 July 1947; Ickes to Dwight D. Eisenhower, 26 January 1948; Ickes to Raymond Robins, 7 June 1949, ibid.

12. Ickes to Anna Boettiger, 6 July 1950, ibid.

13. *New Republic,* 15 August 1949; Harry S Truman to Ickes, 11 August 1949, Ickes to Truman, 23 August 1949, 21 October 1949, and 14 November 1949, Ickes Papers, General Correspondence 1903–52; Ickes, "Farewell, Secretary Krug," *New Republic,* 28 November 1949; Ickes, Column for Release 11 September 1950, Ickes Papers, Speeches and Writings File 1903–52; Ickes to Truman, 29 August 1950, Ickes Papers, General Correspondence 1903–52.

14. Ickes to John Collier, 25 October 1949; James E. Curry to Editor, *New Republic,* 4 December 1949; Ickes to Oscar L. Chapman, 14 September 1950, Ickes Papers, General Correspondence 1903–52, Indians.

15. Ickes to Anna Boettiger, 20 March 1950, Ickes Papers, General Correspondence 1903–52.

16. Ickes to Freda Kirchwey, 7 October 1950, ibid.

17. Ickes to Stephen Early, 22 December 1950, Ickes to Anna Boettiger, 7 February 1951, ibid.

18. Anna Boettiger to Jane Ickes, 20 June 1951; Ickes to Mrs. William Denman, 20 July 1951, ibid.

19. Francis C. Grant to Jane Ickes, 1 February 1952, Ickes papers, Miscellany 1844–1954; Ickes, "A Fig Leaf for McCarthy," *New Republic,* 17 September 1951, p. 17.

Index